DOCUMENTS IN WORLD HISTORY

Volume II

DOCUMENTS IN WORLD HISTORY

Volume II

The Modern Centuries: From 1500 to the Present

Peter N. Stearns, SENIOR EDITOR
Carnegie Mellon University

Stephen S. Gosch
University of Wisconsin, Eau Claire

Jay Pascal Anglin
University of Southern Mississippi

Erwin P. Grieshaber
Mankato State University

1817

HARPER & ROW, PUBLISHERS, New York
Cambridge, Philadelphia, San Francisco, Washington,
London, Mexico City, São Paulo, Singapore, Sydney

Sponsoring Editor: Robert Miller
Project Coordination: R. David Newcomer Associates
Cover Design: Bob Bull
Text Art: Fineline Illustrations, Inc.
Photo Research: Mira Schachne
Compositor: Auto-Graphics, Inc.
Printer and Binder: R. R. Donnelley & Sons Company
Cover Printer: NEBC

Documents in World History, Volume II,
The Modern Centuries: From 1500 to the Present

Library of Congress Cataloging in Publication Data

Documents in world history.

   Contents: v. 1. The great traditions, from ancient times to 1500–
v. 2. The modern centuries, from 1500 to the present.
   1. World history–Sources.   I. Stearns, Peter N.
D5.D623   1988   909   87-15036
ISBN 0-06-046382-1 (v. 1)
ISBN 0-06-046432-1 (v. 2)

87 88 89 90 9 8 7 6 5 4 3 2 1

Contents

Geographic Contents: The Major Civilizations   xii

Topical Contents   xv

Preface   xviii

Introduction   1

SECTION ONE
The Rise of the West and World Reactions, 1500–1918   **9**

Western Civilization

1   New Tensions in the Western Political Tradition: 11
Absolutism and Parliament
Bishop Bossuet's theory from: J. B. Bossuet, *Politique Tirée des
Propres Paroles de l'Ecriture Sainte,* translated by L. Pearce
Williams, published in Brian Tierney, Donald Kagan, and L. Pearce
Williams, editors, *Great Issues in Western Civilization Vol. I;*
The English Bill of Rights from: E. P. Cheyney, *Readings in English
History;*
French Revolutionary Declaration from: Department of History of the
University of Pennsylvania, editor, *Translations and Reprints from
the Original Sources of European History*

2 The Scientific Revolution and the Enlightenment: 17
New Intellectual Standards in the West

Newton's View of the World from: Sir Isaac Newton, *Optics, or A Treatise of the Reflections, Refractions, Inflections and Colours of Light;*

John Locke on the Power of Reason from: John Locke, *An Essay Concerning Human Understanding;*

Beccaria Applies Rationalism to Punishment from: Cesare Beccaria: *On Crimes and Punishments,* translated by Henry Paolucci;

Locke: Reason and Education from: John Locke, *Some Thoughts Concerning Education;*

Kant Defines the Enlightenment from: Lewis White Beck, editor, *Foundations of the Metaphysics of Morals, What is Enlightenment?*

3 Work and Workers in the Industrial Revolution   25

Child Labor Inquiry from: *British Sessional Papers* 1831–1832, House of Commons;

Rules for Workers from: *The Archives du Haut Rhin,* translated by Peter N. Stearns;

Max Lotz from: Adolf Levenstein, *Aus Der Tief, Arbeiterbriefe,* translated by Gabriela Wettberg

Russian Society

4 Peter the Great Reforms Russia   31

All selections from: Basil Dmytryshyn, *Imperial Russia: A Sourcebook, 1700–1917:*

New Calender from *Polnoe Sobranie Zakonov Russkoi Imperii* (Complete Collection of the Laws of the Russian Empire);

The Duties of the Senate from *Polnoe Sobranie;*

Compulsory Education from *Polnoe Sobranie;*

Instruction to Students from *Pisma I Bumagi Imperatora Petra Velokogo* (Letters and Papers of Emperor Peter the Great);

Right of Factories from *Polnoe Sobranie;*

Founding of the Academy from *Polnoe Sobranie*

5 Russian Peasants: Serfdom and Emancipation   37

Radishchev's Journey from: Alexander Radishchev, *A Journey from St. Petersburg to Moscow;*

Karamazin's Conservative View from: R. Pipes, editor, *Karamazin's Memoir on Ancient and Modern Russia;*

Emancipation Manifesto from: Basil Dmytryshyn, *Imperial Russia: A Sourcebook, 1700–1917*

6 Russian Culture: A Special Brand?   44

Nikolai Danilevsky, *Russia and Europe,* in Hans Kohn, editor, *The Mind of Modern Russia*

China and Japan

7 Matteo Ricci on Ming China   49
Louis J. Gallagher, S. J., translator, *China in the Sixteenth Century:
The Journals of Matthew Ricci: 1583–1610*

**8 China and the West in the Nineteenth Century:
A Dispute over Opium**   54
The Chinese Repository

**9 Japan and the West in the Nineteenth Century:
The Views of a Japanese Educator**   59
Eliichi Kiyooka, translator, *The Autobiography of Yukichi Fukuzawa*

India Under Mughal and British Empires

10 Akbar's India: The View of a Jesuit Missionary   63
Father Monserrate, S. J., *Commentary on his Journey to the Court of
Akbar from 1580 to 1583,* edited by S. N. Banjerjee, translated by
J. S. Hoyland

11 Religion and National Identity in Nineteenth-Century India   68
Rammohun Roy from: Jogendra Chunder Ghose, editor, *The English
Works of Rammohun Roy, Vol. I;*
Maulvi Syed Kutb Shah Sahib from: *Selections from the Records of the
Government of the Punjab and its Dependencies*

The Ottoman Middle East

**12 Suleiman the Lawgiver and Ottoman Military Power:
The Report of a European Diplomat**   73
Edward Seymour Forster, translator, *The Turkish Letters of Ogier
Ghiselin de Busbecq*

**13 Islam and the West in the Nineteenth Century:
The Views of a Muslim Intellectual**   78
Nikki R. Keddie, translator and editor, *An Islamic Response to
Imperialism: Political and Religious Writings of Sayyid Jamel ad-Din
"al-Afghani"*

Latin American Civilization

14 Economy and Society in Iberian America   82
Potosí Mine from: "The Potosí Mine and Indian Forced Labor in Peru,"
in Antonio Vasquez de Espinosa, *Compendium and Description of
the West Indies,* translated by C. U. Clark;
Mexican Textile Factory from: "A Mexican Textile Factory," in
Espinosa, *Compendium;*
Slavery on the Haciendas from: "Slavery on the Haciendas, in
Yucatan," Channing Arnold and Frederick J. Tabor Frost, *American
Egypt: A Record of Travel in Yucatan*

15 **Political Styles in Latin America: Colonial Bureaucracy and National Liberation**   87

Bureaucratic Capitalism from: Don Jorge Juan and Don Antonio De Ulloa, *Discourse and Political Reflections on the Kingdom of Peru,* edited by John J. TePaske, translated by John J. TePaske and Bessie A. Clement;

Bolivar from: Vincente Lecuna and Harold A. Bierck, editors, *Selected Writings of Bolivar*

16 **Baroque Culture in Latin America**   91

Carlos de Siguenza y Góngora, *Glorias de Querétaro en la Nueva Congregación Eclesiastica de Maria Santisima de Guadalupe*

Sub-Saharan Africa

17 **Europe's First Impact on Africa: Outposts and Slave Trade**   95

All selections from: G. S. P. Freeman-Grenville, *The East African Coast;*

Reactions to the Portuguese from: *An Arabic History of Kilwa Kisiwani;*

A Slave Trade Agreement from: M. Morice, *A Slaving Treaty with the Sultan of Kilwa;*

Report of a French Slave-Trader from: J. Crassons de Medeuil, *The French Slave Trade in Kilwa*

18 **The Decades of Imperialism in Africa**   100

An African Account from: "The Uses of Colonial Government," from: Lyndon Harries, editor and translator, *Swahili Prose Texts: A Selection from the Material Collected by Carl Velten from 1893 to 1896;*

African Work in South Africa's Diamond Mines from: John Noble, *Official Handbook: History, Production, and the Resources of the Cape of Good Hope;*

An Imperialist Contract from: Sir Lewis Michell, *The Life of the Right Honourable Cecil John Rhodes,* Vol. I;

The French Arrange Local Government from: John D. Hargreaves, editor, *France and West Africa*

19 **The Interaction between Western and African Cultures: Tradition "Falls Apart"**   104

Chinua Achebe, *Things Fall Apart*

SECTION TWO
The Twentieth Century   **109**

Western Civilization

20 The Twentieth-Century Western State   111
Hitler's Definition from: Adolf Hitler, *Mein Kampf;*
Britain Plans the Welfare State from: "Report by Sir William
   Beveridge," *Social Insurance and Allied Services*

21 The Feminist Revolt   117
Simone de Beauvoir, *The Second Sex*

Soviet Society

22 Lenin and the Russian Revolution   122
V. I. Lenin, *Selected Works;* Robert C. Tucker, editor, *The Lenin
   Anthology;* F. A. Golder, editor, *Documents of Russian History,
   1914–1917*

23 Stalin and the Soviet Union During the 1930s: 127
Progress and Terror
J. V. Stalin, *Works,* Vol. XIII; Yevgeny Yevtushenko, *A Precocious
   Autobiography,* translated by Andrew R. MacAndrew

24 "To Combine Motherhood with Active Participation in Labor":   131
Family and Gender in the Contemporary Soviet Union.
Television series from: *Izvestia; The Current Digest of the Soviet Press;*
Soviet Presidium from: *Pravda; The Current Digest of the Soviet Press*

China and Japan

25 Mao Tse-tung and the Chinese Revolution   136
Mao Tse-tung, *Selected Works;* David Milton, Nancy Milton, and
   Franz Schurmann, editors, *People's China: 1966–1972;*
Jerome Ch'en, *Mao and the Chinese Revolution;* Jerome Ch'en, editor,
   Mao; Stuart Schram, editor, *Chairman Mao Talks to the People:
   Talks and Letters: 1956–1971*

26 A Chinese Peasant Maps His Road to Wealth   142
Wang Xin with Yang Xiaobing, "A Peasant Maps His Road to Wealth,"
   Beijing Review

27 Gender and Age in Contemporary Japan   147
Higuchi Keiko, "Japanese Women in Transition," *Japan Quarterly*

India

28 Gandhi and Modern India   152
The Collected Works of Mahatma Gandhi, Vol. X

29 **Nehru and India during the Second World War**   157
    Jawaharlal Nehru, *The Discovery of India*

30 **Family and Gender in Contemporary India**   161
    Viji Srinivasan, "My Son, My Son," *The Times of India, Sunday
    Review*

The Middle East

31 **The Emergence of Arab Nationalism: Two Views from**   165
    the 1930s
    Sylvia G. Haim, editor, *Arab Nationalism: An Anthology*

32 **Middle Eastern Dreams in Conflict: Two Views**   170
    Nahum Goldman, *The Autiobiography of Nahum Goldman: Sixty Years
    of a Jewish Life;*
    Fawaz Turki, *The Disinherited: Journal of a Palestinian Exile*

33 **The Resurgence of Islam in the Contemporary Middle East**   175
    Hasan Al-Bana from: Kemal Karpat, editor, *Political and Social
    Thought in the Contemporary Middle East;*
    Ayatullah Murtada Mutahhari from: John J. Donohue and John L.
    Esposito, editors, *Islam in Transition: Muslim Perspectives*

Latin America

34 **Twentieth-Century Latin American Politics: The Revolutionary**   180
    Challenge
    Plan of Ayala from: Emiliano Zapata, *The Plan of Ayala;*
    Peronism from: Angel Perelman, *Como Hicimos el 17 de Octobre;*
    translated in Joseph R. Barager, editor, *Why Peron Came to Power.
    The Background to Peronism in Argentine;*
    Castro's Program from: Fidel Castro, *History Will Absolve Me,
    Moncada Trial Defence Speech Santiago de Cuba, October, 16,
    1956*

35 **Searching for the Soul of the Latin American Experience**   187
    Labyrinth of Solitude from: Octavio Paz, *The Labyrinth of Solitude,
    Life, and Thought in Mexico,* translated by Lysander Kemp;
    The Other Mexico from: Octavio Paz, *The Other Mexico: Critique of
    the Pyramid,* translated by Lysander Kemp

36 **Underemployment, The Social Crisis of Latin America in the**   191
    Twentieth Century
    Sven Lindquist, *The Shadow: Latin America Faces the Seventies,*
    translated by Keith Bradfield

Sub-Saharan Africa

37 African Nationalism   194

Marcus Garvey Preaches from: Marcus Garvey, "Redeeming the
African Motherland," in Amy Jacques Garvey, editor, *Philosophy
and Opinions of Marcus Garvey,* Vol. 1.;
Jomo Kenyatta Defines African Nationalism from: Jomo Kenyatta,
Facing Mt. Kenya; Economic Nationalism from: Kwame Nkrumah,
Revolutionary Path

38 Changes in African Society   200

No Long at Ease from: Chinua Achebe, *No Longer At Ease;*
Kenyan Women Speak Out from: Perdita Huston, *Third World Women
Speak Out*

Geographic Contents:
The Major Civilizations

Middle East

12 Suleiman the Lawgiver and Ottoman Military Power: The Report
of a European Diplomat   73

13 Islam and the West in the Nineteenth Century: The Views of a
Muslim Intellectual   78

31 The Emergence of Arab Nationalism: Two Views from the 1930s   165

32 Middle Eastern Dreams in Conflict: Two Views   170

33 The Resurgence of Islam in the Contemporary Middle East   175

East Asia

 7 Matteo Ricci on Ming China   49

 8 China and the West in the Nineteenth Century: A Dispute
over Opium   54

 9 Japan and the West in the Nineteenth Century: The Views of a
Japanese Educator   59

25 Mao Tse-tung and the Chinese Revolution   136

26 A Chinese Peasant Maps His Road to Wealth   142

27 Gender and Age in Contemporary Japan   147

India

10   Akbar's India: The View of a Jesuit Missionary   63

11   Religion and National Identity in Nineteenth Century India   68

28   Gandhi and Modern India   152

29   Nehru and India During the Second World War   157

30   Family and Gender in Contemporary India   161

Eastern Europe

4   Peter the Great Reforms Russia   31

5   Russian Peasants: Serfdom and Emancipation   37

6   Russian Culture: A Special Brand?   44

22   Lenin and the Russian Revolution   122

23   Stalin and the Soviet Union During the 1930s: Progress and Terror   127

24   "To Combine Motherhood with Active Participation in Labor": Family and Gender in the Contemporary Soviet Union   131

The West

1   New Tensions in the Western Political Tradition: Absolutism and Parliament   11

2   The Scientific Revolution of the Enlightenment: New Intellectual Standards in the West   17

3   Work and Workers in the Industrial Revolution   25

20   The Twentieth-Century Western State   111

21   The Feminist Revolt   117

Africa

17   Europe's First Impact on Africa: Outposts and Slave Trade   95

18   The Decades of Imperialism in Africa   100

19   The Interaction between Western and African Culture: Tradition "Falls Apart"   104

37   African Nationalism   194

38   Changes in African Society   200

Latin America

14 Economy and Society in Iberian America   82

15 Political Styles in Latin America: Colonial Bureaucracy and
    National Liberation   87

16 Baroque Culture in Latin America   91

34 Twentieth-Century Latin American Politics: The Revolutionary
    Challenge   180

35 Searching for the Soul of the Latin American Experience   187

36 Underemployment, The Social Crisis of Latin America in the
    Twentieth Century   191

Topical Contents

Religion and Science

2 The Scientific Revolution and the Elightenment: New Intellectual
   Standards in the West   17

11 Religion and National Identity in Nineteenth Century India   68

33 The Resurgence of Islam in the Contemporary Middle East   175

Culture

6 Russian Culture: A Special Brand?   44

9 Japan and the West in the Nineteenth Century: The Views of a
   Japanese Educator   59

16 Baroque Culture in Latin America   91

19 The Interaction between Western and African Culture: Tradition
    "Falls Apart"   104

28 Gandhi and Modern India   152

35 Searching for the Soul of the Latin American Experience   187

38 Changes in African Society   200

Social Structure

3   Work and Workers in the Industrial Revolution   25

5   Russian Peasants: Serfdom and Emancipation   37

17 Europe's First Impact on Africa: Outposts and Slave Trade   95

26 A Chinese Peasant Maps His Road to Wealth   142

38 Changes in African Society   200

The State and Politics

1   New Tensions in the Western Political Tradition: Absolutism and
    Parliament   11

4   Peter the Great Reforms Russia   31

7   Matteo Ricci on Ming China   49

10 Akbar's India: The View of a Jesuit Missionary   63

12 Suleiman the Lawgiver and Ottoman Military Power: The Report
    of a European Diplomat   73

15 Political Styles in Latin America: Colonial Bureaucracy and
    National Liberation   87

20 The Twentieth-Century Western State   111

22 Lenin and the Russian Revolution   122

23 Stalin and the Soviet Union During the 1930s: Progress and
    Terror   127

25 Mao Tse-tung and the Chinese Revolution   136

31 The Emergence of Arab Nationalism: Two Views from the 1930s   165

34 Twentieth-Century Latin American Politics: The Revolutionary
    Challenge   180

Women and the Family

21 The Feminist Revolt   117

24 "To Combine Motherhood with Active Participaton in Labor":
    Family and Gender in the Contemporary Soviet Union   131

27 Gender and Age in Contemporary Japan   147

30 Family and Gender in Contemporary India   161

Trade, Technology, and Cities

 3 Work and Workers in the Industrial Revolution   25

 7 Matteo Ricci on Ming China   49

14 Economy and Society in Iberian America   82

17 Europe's First Impact on Africa: Outposts and Slave Trade   95

36 Underemployment, The Social Crisis of Latin America in the
    Twentieth Century   191

Nationalism and Relations with the West

 6 Russian Culture: A Special Brand?   44

 8 China and the West in the Nineteenth Century: A Dispute Over
    Opium   54

 9 Japan and the West in the Nineteenth Century: The Views of a
    Japanese Educator   59

11 Religion and National Identity in Nineteenth Century India   68

13 Islam and the West in the Nineteenth Century: The Views of a
    Muslim Intellectual   78

15 Political Styles in Latin America: Colonial Bureaucracy and
    National Liberation   87

16 Baroque Culture in Latin America   91

17 Europe's First Impact on Africa: Outposts and Slave Trade   95

18 The Decades of Imperialism in Africa   100

19 The Interaction between Western and African Culture: Tradition
    "Falls Apart"   104

28 Gandhi and Modern India   152

29 Nehru and India During the Second World War   157

31 The Emergence of Arab Nationalism: Two Views from the 1930s   165

32 Middle Eastern Dreams in Conflict: Two Views   170

37 African Nationalism   194

Preface

This volume focuses on key currents in the development of the modern world—not just the American or Western world, but the wider world in which we live today. It deals with the interaction between established civilizations and new forces of change, many of them introduced initially by the West's expanding colonial and commercial network, and with the impact of change on loyalties and beliefs, on social institutions and the conditions of various groups such as workers and women, and on the activities and the organization of the State.

The book examines the formation of the modern world not through an overview or through scholarly interpretation, but by presenting primary sources—that is, documents written at the time. Such an approach is inherently selective, leaving many important developments out; and it is meant to be combined with some kind of textbook coverage. But primary source documents do convey something of the flavor and tensions of history-in-the-making that cannot be captured by a progression of names, dates, and main events or trends. The book presents what people—great and ordinary—expressed in various societies in the modern periods, and it challenges the reader to distill the meaning of those expressions.

The variety of documents offered illustrate characteristic features of key civilizations in the major modern stages of world history from about A.D. 1500 to the present. These documents were not written for posterity; some were not even intended for a wide audience at the time. They are collected here to plumb the depths of history and raise issues of understanding and interpretation that can enliven and enrich the study of world history.

The book covers several facets of the human experience, again in various times and places. It deals with the organization and functions of the state. It treats philosophy and religion and, at points, literature and science. It explores contacts among civilizations, particularly the diverse impacts of Western imperialism and commercial expansion in recent centuries. It also deals with families and women and with issues of social structure.

The book's organization facilitates relating it to a core textbook. Major civilizations are represented with several readings—East Asia, the West, India, the Middle East, Eastern Europe, Africa, and Latin America. Thus a course can trace elements of change and continuity within each civilization. The readings are divided into two modern periods: A.D. 1500–1900, during which the rise of the West and diverse reactions to this rise formed a central thread in world history, and the twentieth century, during which Western influence continued strong but the other major civilizations also began to seek and find their own distinctive modern voices.

The goal of the book is not, however, maximum coverage. Many interesting and significant documents are left out, of necessity. Readings have been chosen that illustrate key features of an area or period, that raise challenging problems of interpretation, and that—at least in many cases—express some charm and human drama. The readings also invite comparisons across cultures and over time. Headnotes not only identify the readings, but they also raise some issues that can be explored.

This book was prepared by four world history teachers at work in several kinds of institutions. It is meant, correspondingly, to serve the needs of different kinds of students. It is motivated by two common purposes: first, a strong belief that some perspective on the world is both desirable and possible as a key element in contemporary American education; and second, that an understanding of world history can be greatly enhanced by exposure not just to an overall factual and interpretive framework, but also to the kinds of challenges and insights raised by primary materials, written not by scholars but by people actually living out the diverse and changing patterns we are grappling to understand.

Dealing with primary sources is not an easy task. Precisely because the materials are not written with American college students in mind, they require some thought: They must be related to other elements we know about the particular society; they must be given meaning; they must be evaluated more carefully than a secondary account or textbook designed deliberately to pinpoint what should be learned. By the same token, however, gaining ease with the meaning of primary sources is a skill that carries well beyond a survey history course, into all sorts of research endeavors. Gaining such skill in the context of the diverse civilizations that compose the world goes some distance toward understanding how our world has become what it is—which is, in essence, the central purpose of history.

Peter N. Stearns

Introduction

The past five centuries have been a busy time in world history. Many Americans, accustomed to a culture that emphasizes change, believe that the modern age has witnessed more fundamental shifts, coming at a more rapid pace, than any other time in the human past. Though the notion of accelerating change may be somewhat exaggerated, it is true that relationships among major areas of the world (including the gradual integration of the Americas into a wider network), basic technologies, belief systems, forms of government, and even fundamental ingredients of daily life such as the relationship between men and women have changed mightily, not only in the United States and Western civilization, but in every major society in the world. This volume, with selected documents on a number of significant areas of change, conveys something of the flavor of the modern world in transition.

The need to study modern world history becomes increasingly apparent. Though the twentieth century has been hailed as "the American century," it is obvious that given the United States' claim to some world leadership, it must interact with various other societies and, in part, on their terms. As a power with worldwide military responsibilities or aspirations, the United States maintains increasingly close diplomatic contacts with all the inhabited continents. Economically, American reliance on exports and imports—once a minor footnote to the nation's industrial vigor—grows greater every year. Cultural influences from abroad are significant. Even though the United States remains a leading exporter of consumer fads and styles, we can see among the American people European cultural standards and popular fashion and musical imports from Britain joined by interest in various offshoots of Buddhism or a fascination with Japan's gifts at social coordination. Even the composition of the United States' population reflects growing worldwide contacts. The United States is now experiencing its highest rates of immigration ever, with new arrivals from Latin America and various parts of Asia joining earlier immigrant groups from Europe and Africa.

Enmeshed in this world, shaping it but also shaped by it, United States citizens need to know something of how that world has been formed and what major historical forces created its diversities and contacts. We need to know, in sum, something about world history. Study of our own past—that is, United States history—or even the larger history of Western civilization from which many American institutions and values spring, risks now being unduly narrow, though worthy and interesting. This is why the study of world history is receiving renewed attention.

The need to know leading themes in world history thus involves the need to understand why, because of earlier tradition, Chinese and Japanese governments are today more effective in regulating personal behaviors such as birth rates than are governments in other parts of Asia, such as India. East Asian traditions never posited the boundary line between state and society that other cultures (including our own in the United States) take for granted, and the contemporary version of this special tradition has produced fascinating results. Tradition combined with more recent changes, including bitter experience with Western intrusions, helps explain why many countries in the Islamic world are demonstrating strong opposition to lifestyles and economic forms that many modern Westerners take for granted. Alliance patterns (such as the Soviet Union and the smaller nations of eastern Europe) and military policies—including key differences among cultures not only in levels of power but also in characteristic interest in aggression and expansion—are other "in the news" issues of vital importance that can be grasped only through an understanding of earlier trends in world history. Our world, obviously, is shaped by the past; we can best understand changes we are experiencing when we compare them to past change. And so, on an interdependent globe, a grasp of world history becomes an intellectual necessity.

A danger exists, however, in stressing the "need" to study world history too piously. It is true that growing global interdependence and communication make knowledge of past world patterns increasingly useful as the basis for interpreting policy options open to the United States or American business—or simply for grasping the daily headlines in more than a superficial manner. But the mission of a world history course does not rest entirely on the desire to create a more informed and mature citizenry. It can also rest on the intrinsic interest and the analytical challenge world history offers.

The modern centuries in particular involve a growing drama of confrontation between deeply rooted, highly valued, and often successful cultural forms and some common forces of change. Over the past 500 years, all the major civilizations have encountered growing pressures from Western ideas and institutions—and often brute force and commercial exploitation from the West as well. During the past century (and in some cases longer) these same civilizations have tried to take into account the new technologies springing from industrialization;

new ways of thinking shaped by modern science and belief systems such as nationalism and socialism; the need to reshape government functions and the contacts between government and citizens; pressures to redefine the family to allow for children's formal education, new roles for women, and often a reduction in traditional birth rates. The modern drama, played out in different specific ways depending on region, has involved combining some of the common, worldwide pressures with retention of key continuities from the past.

The varieties of response have been considerable, because the variety of past cultures is great and because the modern centuries have seen a number of distinctly new experiences through, for example, differences in the timing and form of Western intrusions. Some societies—often after experimenting with other responses—copied Western technologies and organizations sufficiently to industrialize while embellishing key deviations from "Western" standards as well. Other societies have faced greater problems in matching the West's industrial might. Some—such as Latin America—partially merged with cultural styles initially developed in the West; others have tried to remain aloof from Western art or popular culture. Some societies have widely embraced new belief systems, whereas in others—such as the Islamic Middle East—pressures to retain older religious values have maintained great force. The point is clear: No civilization in the modern world has been able to stand pat, and all have responded to challenge in some similar ways—using nationalism, for example, or extending formal systems of education. At the same time, overall responses have been extremely varied, because of continuities from diverse pasts and diverse modern experiences. Defining the tension between common directions of change and the variety that still distinguishes the major civilizations forms one of the key analytical tasks of modern world history.

The examples of both change and variety are endless. Not only general features of key civilizations or periods, but also major events such as the British efforts to import opium into China and the belated ending of the slave trade from Africa, compel attention. Historical events worldwide illustrate ways that different societies interacted and the range of evil and good of which humans have proved capable. Modern world history, in sum, can be interesting, even enjoyable—that is, unless the human panorama offers no appeal. It has grown unfashionable in American education to emphasize joy in learning lest a subject seem frivolous or irrelevant to careers and earning power. But the fact is that world history, like many but not all other academic subjects, offers potential for pleasure as well as support for an informed citizenry.

But if world history is essential, to give an understanding of why our own world is as it is and because of its great intrinsic interest, it is also, without question, challenging. Putting the case mildly, much has happened in the history of the world; and although some developments remain unknown for want of records, the amount that we do know is astounding—and steadily expanding. No person can master the whole; and in presenting a manageable course in world history, selectivity is certainly essential. Fortunately, there is considerable agreement on certain developments that are significant to a study of world history. The student must gain, for example, some sense of the special political characteristics

of Chinese civilization; or of the new world economy that Western Europe organized, to its benefit, after about 1500; or of the ways major technological
changes developed, spread, and impacted leading societies at various points in
time, including the Industrial Revolution and even the more recent innovations in
information technology. The list of history basics, of course, is not uniform, and
it can change with new interests and new data. The conditions of women, for
example, as they varied from one civilization to the next and changed over time
have become a staple of up-to-date world history teaching in ways that could not
have been imagined twenty years ago. Despite changes in the list, though, the
idea of approaching world history in terms of basics—key civilizations, key points
of change, key factors such as technology and family—begins the process of
making the vast menu of data digestible.

   In practice, however, the teaching of world history has sometimes obscured
the focus on basics with a stream-of-narrative textbook approach. The abundance
of facts and their importance and/or interest can produce a way of teaching world
history so bent on leaving nothing out (though in fact much must be omitted even
in the most ponderous tome) that little besides frenzied memorization takes place.
Yet world history, though it must convey knowledge, must also stimulate
thought—about why different patterns developed in various key civilizations,
about what impact new contacts between civilizations had, about how our present
world relates to worlds past.

   One way to stimulate thought—and to give some sense of the spice of
particular currents or episodes in world history—is to provide access to original
sources. This device is often used in American history or the history of Western
civilization. It is less common, however, in world history because the textbook
approach has been so dominant. Readers designed for world history have existed
in the past, but few are currently available. As a result, it has been difficult to
provide readings beyond a core text in world history classes, particularly readings
that cut across individual civilizations. This volume, obviously, is intended to provide a solution to this problem and to facilitate world history teaching that includes
but transcends a purely textbook-survey approach.

   The readings in this volume are designed to illustrate several features of
various civilizations at key points in modern world history through direct evidence.
Thus the readings convey, through direct statements, some sense of how Gandhi
defined Indian nationalism and its relation to the West, or what a number of
twentieth-century social revolutionaries said were their goals. Because the documents were written for specific themes and audiences, they invariably require
some effort of interpretation. The writers, by trying to persuade others of their
beliefs or reporting what they saw at the time, did not focus on distilling the
essence of a religion, a political movement, or a list of government functions for
late twentieth-century students of world history. The reader must provide such
distillation, aided by the brief contexts and questions given in the selection in-
troductions. Analytical thinking is also encouraged and challenged by recurrent
comparisons across space and time. Thus documents dealing with social or family structure in China can be compared to documents on the same subject for
the Middle East, and a picture of China's isolation five hundred years ago begs

for juxtaposition with descriptions of twentieth-century Chinese world contacts to see what changed and what persists.

The documents presented are not randomly chosen; and it will help, in using them, if the principles of organization are made clear—for these principles correspond to some of the selection-for-manageability essential in studying world history. The hope is, of course, that the documents reflect particularly interesting insights; they were selected in part because they are lively, as well as significant. They were *not* selected to maximize factual coverage. This is a difficult goal even in a text, and it becomes almost impossible in a collection of readings. In our choices of materials we wanted to present passages of some substance (rather than snippets) and depth (rather than just a law or two, a real discussion of how government worked). By the same token the materials leave out vastly more possibilities than they embrace, even in the realm of "famous" documents such as treaties and constitutions. The book is thus intended to stimulate, but it is decidedly not intended to pepper the carcass of world history with as much buckshot as possible.

Eschewing coverage as a goal, we follow certain general principles around which an approach to world history can be organized. Quite simply, these principles involve place, time, and topic. By choosing readings—which may or may not be important documents in themselves—that illustrate important societies in distinctive periods of time and in significant facets of the human experience, the book offers a collection of telling insights that usefully complement and challenge the survey approach. Knowing the principles of selection, in turn, facilitates relating the readings to each other and to a more general understanding of world history.

First is the principle of major civilizations in organizing choice of place. The readings focus on seven parts of the world that have produced durable civilizations still in existence, at least in part. They do not simply focus on the West in a world context. East Asia embraces China and a surrounding zone that came under partial Chinese influence—most notably Japan. Indian civilization, which comprises the second case, had considerable influence in other parts of southern Asia, though we do not offer readings on Southeast Asia directly. The Middle East and North Africa, where civilization was first born, forms a third society to be addressed at various points in time, from the glories of the Ottoman Empire that unified much of the region in the fifteenth century, to the obvious troubles and divisions of the late twentieth century. Sub-Saharan Africa, a vast region with great diversity, is the fourth case. Europe—though ultimately sharing some common values through Christianity and a recollection of the glories of Greece and Rome—had developed before the fifteenth century two partially distinct civilizations in the east (centered on Russia) and west. East-west divisions in Europe did not remain constant over the modern centuries, but some demarcation has persisted. Western civilization also spread beyond Europe's borders to the United States, Canada, Australia, and New Zealand. Finally, civilization developed independently in the Americas and then mingled American Indian influences with those of Spain and Portugal to form Latin American civilization, the newest on the world's roster. The seven civilizations represented in the readings are not sacrosanct: They do not embrace all the world's cultures, past or present. They overlap at points, as in the case of East European and Western patterns, and they contain some marked internal divisions, such as between China and Japan in East Asia. But these civilizations do provide some geographical coherence for the study of world history, and they are all represented repeatedly in the selections that follow.

Time is the second organizing principle. World history falls into a number of distinct, if rather general, time periods. Prehistory—before the rise of agriculture and the development of civilization—stretches for hundreds of thousands of years, with divisions according to the evolution of the species and the major stages in early technology. Early civilizations formed around river valleys in Asia and North Africa starting more than 5000 years ago. Then between 1000 B.C. and A.D. 500 larger civilizations took hold—in China and India and around the Mediterranean, establishing some of the modern world's key intellectual and political traditions. A final traditional period took shape after the fall of the classical civilizations. Between 500 and about 1500, major world religions developed further, particularly through the spread of Buddhism, Christianity, and Islam. Essentially new civilizations were launched in Western and Eastern Europe, in sub-Saharan Africa, and in parts of the Americas; and distinct extensions of the older civilizations developed in places like Japan. Again, key traditions were set that continue their influence today.

Many readers of this collection will already have covered the traditional periods of world history. A companion reader, organized in ways similar to this volume, offers source materials on key features of the traditional world and its major civilizations, describing the great religions, durable political patterns, and aspects of social structure and family life. Such features should be compared to developments after A.D. 1500, to obtain a full sense of the interplay between the continuity of civilizations' traditions and the general forces shaping the modern world.

This volume focuses on two basic modern periods that took shape after A.D. 1500. During the first period, that began to form around 1500 and extended to the early twentieth century, the rise of the West and Western sponsorship of a new world economy provided a clear central theme for world history against which other, separate civilizations reacted to produce their own balance between continuity and change. This first modern period of world history was itself divided. Between 1500 and about 1750, the West's challenge was muted in some parts of the world. East Asia, in particular, could opt for a policy of splendid isolation. The West itself was undergoing a fascinating series of changes that produced new political and intellectual forms. Latin America became defined, under heavy Western influence; and Africa, Russia, and India encountered different levels of Western impact. In retrospect, these early modern centuries were a time of transition, with a growing Western role but very diverse reactions, all complicated by the fact that the West itself was changing its geographical shape. After 1750, Western influence intensified, becoming more literally international; and during the nineteenth century, Western controls—through imperialism—extended over new sections of the world. The only societies that remained fully independent were those that struggled frantically to change, notably Russia and Japan. And the West itself underwent the Industrial Revolution, which heightened its economic advantage over the rest of the world while ushering in radically new technological, social, and cultural forms. In the first section of this book, readers can trace patterns in the individual civilizations that apply to the early modern period, before 1750, to compare with the new issues that arose amid nineteenth-century industrialization and imperialism.

The second chronological section of this book is reserved for the twentieth century. In part this simply reflects the fact that twentieth-century developments such as the Russian revolution and feminism are particularly important today because of their proximity. Readings on the twentieth century allow analysis of what has changed and of what persists in the world's major societies. But the twentieth century also serves as the probable beginning of a new period in world history, marked by the relative decline of the West, the development of radically new forms of warfare, and the extensions of at least partial industrialization and urbanization to most portions of the world. Our century is not only, then, close to us by definition; it also seems to harbor an unusual number of fundamental changes in world history. These transitions—and the various efforts to resist them in the name of older values, ranging from Islamic purity to yearnings for Western supremacy—provide some of the overriding themes for the selections in the final group of readings.

Placing stress on the twentieth century is not always characteristic of courses in world history, which often rivet on the fascinating passages of the world in earlier periods of time. And the claim that the twentieth century is ushering in a new period of world history—based on a heightened pace of change in various parts of the world and the decline of at least certain forms of Western predominance—should be tested, not simply accepted on faith. Using the selections dealing with our own century, readers can question the proposition that change is taking new forms in the world at large and compare twentieth-century developments with those that occurred earlier in the modern era. Beginning in the past several decades, are most civilizations becoming comfortable enough with patterns pioneered in the West to produce their own statements of change and not simply react to Western intrusion? However this question is answered (and the answer may vary from case to case), this book's provision of a full section on the twentieth century is meant to encourage making a connection between our time and the past, seeing how older values echo in a modern age, as well as gaining insight into some of the newer issues of world history.

The time factor in this volume can be summarized as follows. By around 1500 several new themes in world history had begun to take shape, including the rise of a more dynamic Western civilization and the development of more intricate economic contacts around the world, now comprised of the Americas as well as the old continents. Soon, the spread of more advanced technologies, population growth in many societies, and challenges to traditional belief systems and governmental forms heightened the complexity of change. However, the modern era divides partially according to an early-modern/industrial-imperialist differentiation, and more fully through a periodization that sees the twentieth century taking on distinctive, though not entirely novel, characteristics of its own within a "modern" framework. Both of the major periods, 1500–1900 and the twentieth century, must be seen through the seven major civilizations, in each of which the central modern drama of change that shapes but also is being shaped by past values takes its own particular form—from China's attempt to develop a political regime suitable for modern economic growth, to Islamic or Soviet attempts to build modern societies free of the trappings of Western consumerism or family instability, to attempts of the West itself to come to terms with its new position in the world.

Finally, in dealing with the major modern periods and the leading civilizations, the readings in this book reflect an attempt to convey four features of any human society. Added to the categories of place (the seven civilizations) and time (the two major modern periods) is a subject categorization that can facilitate any comparisons across place and time. Every society must develop some governmental structure and political values. It must generate a culture, that is, a system of beliefs and artistic expressions that help explain how the world works. Among these, religion is often a linchpin of a society's culture, but science and art play crucial roles as well. Many civilizations have seen tensions among various cultural expressions, which can be a source of creativity. Economic relationships—the nature of agriculture, the level of technology and openness to technological change, the position of merchants—form a third feature of a civilization. And finally, social groupings and hierarchies and family institutions—including gender relations—organize human relationships and provide for the training of children. Until recently, world history focused primarily on the political and cultural side of the major societies, with some bows to technology and trade. More recently, the explosion of social history—with its inquiry into popular as well as elite cultures and into families and social structure—has broadened world history concerns. Readings in this book provide a sense of all four aspects of the leading civilizations—political, economic, cultural, and social—and a feeling for how they changed under the impact of new beliefs, Western conquest, or the growth of industrial cities.

The effort to present lively documents that illuminate several time periods, different cultural traditions, and various features of the way societies function must, again, be evocative. This book is not intended to teach everything one should know about the evolution of Western families, Chinese attempts to change without becoming "Western," or big processess such as the development of the modern world economy. It aims, rather, at providing the flavor of such topics, a sense of how people at the time lived and perceived them, and some understanding of the issues involved in interpreting and comparing diverse documents from the past. The collection is meant to help readers themselves breath life into world history and grasp some of the ways that people, both great and ordinary, have lived, suffered, and created in various parts of the world at various times in the rich human past.

one

THE RISE OF THE WEST AND WORLD REACTIONS, 1500–1918

Spurred by changes in their own civilization—including new political forms, science, and ultimately industrialization—West Europeans gained increasing commercial influence, and to a lesser degree political and cultural influence, among world societies. How to respond to Western intrusions became the central world issue by the nineteenth century. But changes in Russia and new empires in India and the Middle East also formed important chapters in world history in these modern centuries. These developments, plus varying degrees of Western penetration, produced diverse patterns of change, from the emerging amalgam of Latin American civilization to the long-isolated bastions of East Asia.

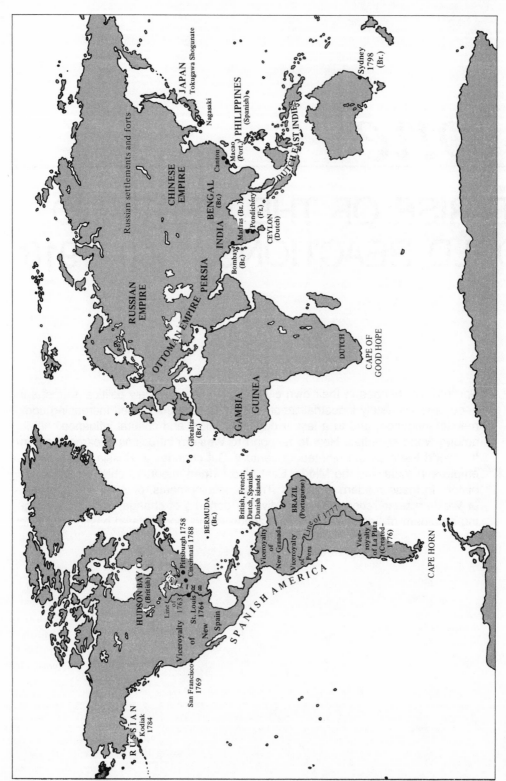

The World After 1763

1

New Tensions in the Western Political Tradition: Absolutism and Parliament

A leading historian-sociologist, Charles Tilly, has recently argued that one of the few great changes in early modern Western history was the strengthening of the state under national monarchs. Without question, many European governments in the seventeenth century completed the tasks of seizing basic political powers from the feudal nobility, developing a strong bureaucracy, and expanding the functions of the central government. New or revived ideals of government power accompanied this shift. In the first selection that follows, Bishop Bossuet expounds the doctrine of a strong king—essential to keep order among unruly subjects, father to his people, owed all respect and obedience. The result, Bossuet argued, would be far from arbitrary rule and would work to the greater benefit of the subjects—but there was no question about who was in command.

Older ideals of limited government did not die, however. They revived in seventeenth-century England at the same time that France was constructing its newly absolute monarchy. Civil war led to the execution of one king; then renewed unrest, in 1688, brought a strong statement of the rights of parliament and of individual liberties. England moved from feudal practices toward parliamentary monarchy. Then in France itself, in the great Revolution of 1789, absolute monarchy was dethroned in favor of a constitutional bill of rights and new powers for

Selection I from J. B. Bossuet, *Politique Tirée des Propres Paroles de l'Ecriture Sainte* (1870), translated by L. Pearce Williams, published in Brian Tierney, Donald Kagan, and L. Pearce Williams, eds., *Great Issues in Western Civilization, Vol. I* (New York: Random House, Inc., 1967), pp. 659–63. Copyright © 1967 by Random House, Inc. Reprinted by permission. Selection II from E. P. Cheyney, *Readings in English History* (New York: Ginn and Company, 1922), pp. 545–47. Selection III from Department of History of the University of Pennsylvania, ed., *Translations and Reprints from the Original Sources of European History* (Philadelphia: 1897), Vol. I, No. 5, pp. 6–8.

an elected parliament. Divided political ideals, in short, led to recurrent upheaval in the West from the seventeenth century through 1848.

The divisions in Western poilitical tradition proved durable. Government functions expanded, though less in England than elsewhere until the twentieth century. Even when kings were toppled, the state continued to wield new powers—as in revolutionary France. But the idea of limiting government through individual rights and controlling it through elected bodies remained an important Western emphasis, later copied in some other parts of the world. Some historians have argued that it was the flexibility of the Western political tradition, in contrast, say, to the purer Russian or Chinese emphasis on the state, that has fostered the development and, at times, the distinctive vigor of Western society.

The selections that follow, then, invite comparison. Were those who sought to limit the state in times of unrest—seventeenth-century England and then eighteenth-century France—talking the same languages, or did goals and methods shift? How did the constitutional parliamentary ideal differ from the absolutist standards of Bossuet? Has the West managed successfully to reconcile its two modern political traditions?

I. ABSOLUTISM: BISHOP BOSSUET'S THEORY OF DIVINE-RIGHT MONARCHY

Justice has no other support than authority and the subordination of powers.

It is this order which restrains license. When everyone does what he wishes and has only his own desires to regulate him, everything ends up in confusion. . . .

By means of government each individual becomes stronger.

The reason is that each is helped. All the forces of the nations concur in one and the sovereign magistrate has the right to reunite them. . . .

Thus the sovereign magistrate has in his hand all the forces of the nation which submits itself to obedience to him. . . .

Thus, an individual is not troubled by oppression and violence because he has an invincible defender in the person of the prince and is stronger by far than all those who attempt to oppress him.

The sovereign magistrate's own interest is to preserve by force all the individuals of a nation because if any other force than his own prevails among the people his authority and his life is in peril. . . .

The law is sacred and inviolable.

In order to understand perfectly the nature of the law it is necessary to note that all those who have spoken well on it have regarded it in its origin as a pact and a solemn treaty by which men agree together under the authority of princes to that which is necessary to form their society.

This is not to say that the authority of the laws depends on the consent and acquiescence of the people; but only that the prince who, moreover by his very station has no other interest than that of the public good, is helped by the sagest heads in the nation and leans upon the experience of centuries gone by. . . .

Everybody thus begins with monarchy and almost everybody has retained it as being the most natural state.

We have also seen that it has its foundation and its model in the rule of the father, that is to say in nature itself.

All men are born subjects: and paternal authority which accustoms them to obey, accustoms them at the same time to have only one chief.

Monarchical government is the best.

If it is the most natural, it is consequently the most durable and from that it follows also the strongest.

It is also the most opposed to divisiveness, which is the worst evil of states, and the most certain cause of their ruin. . . . "Every kingdom divided against itself is brought to desolation; and every city or house divided against itself shall not stand."

We have seen that Our Lord in this sentence has followed the natural progress of government and seems to have wished to show to realms and to cities the same means of uniting themselves that nature has established in families.

Thus, it is natural that when families wish to unite to form a body of State, they will almost automatically coalesce into the government that is proper to them.

When states are formed there is the impulse to union and there is never more union than under a single leader. Also there is never greater strength because everything works in harmony. . . .

Royal authority is paternal and its proper character is goodness.

After what has been said, this truth has no need of proof.

We have seen that kings take the place of God, who is the true father of the human species. We have also seen that the first idea of power which exists among men is that of the paternal power; and that kings are modeled on fathers.

Everybody is also in accord, that the obedience which is owed to the public power can be found in the ten commandments only in the precept which obliges him to honor his parents.

Thus it follows from this that the name of king is a name for father and that goodness is the most natural character of kings. . . .

The prince must provide for the needs of the people.

It is a royal right to provide for the needs of the people. He who undertakes it at the expense of the prince undertakes royalty: this is why it has been established. The obligation to care for the people is the foundation of all the rights that sovereigns have over their subjects.

This is why, in time of great need, the people have the right to have recourse to its prince. . . .

II. THE ENGLISH BILL OF RIGHTS, 1689

Whereas the said late King James II having abdicated the government, and the throne being thereby vacant, his Highness the prince of Orange (whom it hath pleased Almighty God to make the glorious instrument of delivering this kingdom from popery and arbitrary power) did (by the advice of the lords spiritual and temporal, and diverse principal persons of the Commons) caused letters to be written to the lords spiritual and temporal, being Protestants. . . . to meet and sit at Westminster upon the two and twentieth day of January, in this year 1689, in order to such an establishment as that their religion, laws, and liberties might not again be in danger of being subverted; upon which letters elections have been accordingly made.

And thereupon the said lords spiritual and temporal and Commons, pursuant to their respective letters and elections, being now assembled in a full and free representation of this nation, taking into their most serious consideration the best means for attaining the ends aforesaid, do in the first place (as their ancestors in like case have usually done), for the vindication and assertion of their ancient rights and liberties, declare:

1. That the pretended power of suspending laws, or the execution of laws, by regal authority, without consent of parliament is illegal.
2. That the pretended power of dispensing with the laws, or the execution of law by regal authority, as it hath been assumed and exercised of late, is illegal.
3. That the commission for erecting the late court of commissioners for ecclesiastical causes, and all other commissions and courts of like nature, are illegal and pernicious.
4. That levying money for or to the use of the crown by pretense of prerogative, without grant of parliament, for longer time or in other manner than the same is or shall be granted, is illegal.
5. That it is the right of the subjects to petition the king, and all commitments and prosecutions for such petitioning are illegal.
6. That the raising or keeping a standing army within the kingdom in time of peace, unless it be with consent of parliament, is against law.
7. That the subjects which are Protestants may have arms for their defense suitable to their conditions, and as allowed by law.
8. That election of members of parliament ought to be free.
9. That the freedom of speech, and debates or proceedings in parliament, ought not to be impeached or questioned in any court or place out of parliament.
10. That excessive bail ought not to be required, nor excessive fines imposed, nor cruel and unusual punishments inflicted. . . .
13. And that for redress of all grievance and for the amending, strengthening, and preserving of the laws, parliament ought to be held frequently.

And they do claim, demand, and insist upon all and singular the premises, as their undoubted rights and liberties. . . .

III. FRENCH REVOLUTION: DECLARATION OF RIGHTS OF MAN AND THE CITIZEN

I

The representatives of the French people, organized as a National Assembly, believing that the ignorance, neglect or contempt of the rights of man are the sole cause of public calamities and of the corruption of governments, have determined to set forth in a solemn declaration the natural, inalienable and sacred rights of man, in order that this declaration, being constantly before all the members of the social body, shall remind them continually of their rights and duties, in order that the acts of the legislative power, as well as those of the executive power, may be compared at any moment with the ends of all political instititutions and may thus be more respected; and, lastly, in order that the grievances of the citizens, based hereafter upon simple and incontestable principles, shall tend to the maintenance of the constitution and redound to the happiness of all. Therefore the National Assembly recognizes and proclaims, in the presence and under the auspices of the Supreme Being, the following rights of man and of the citizen:—

1. Men are born and remain free and equal in rights. Social distinctions may only be founded upon the general good.
2. The aim of all political association is the preservation of the natural and imprescriptible rights of man. These rights are liberty, property, security and resistance to oppression.
3. The principle of all sovereignty resides essentially in the nation. No body nor individual may exercise any authority which does not proceed directly from the nation.
4. Liberty consists in the freedom to do everything which injures no one else; hence the exercise of the natural rights of each man has no limits except those which assure to the other members of the society the enjoyment of the same rights. These limits can only be determined by law.
5. Law can only prohibit such actions as are hurtful to society. Nothing may be prevented which is not forbidden by law, and no one may be forced to do anything not provided for by law.
6. Law is the expression of the general will. Every citizen has a right to participate personally or through his representative in its formation. It must be the same for all, whether it protects or punishes. All citizens, being equal in the eyes of the law, are equally eligible to all dignities and to all public positions and occupations, according to their abilities, and without distinction except that of their virtues and talents.

II

7. No person shall be accused, arrested or imprisoned except in the cases and according to the forms prescribed by law. Any one soliciting, transmitting, executing or causing to be executed any arbitrary order shall be punished. But any citizen summoned or arrested in virtue of the law shall submit without delay, as resistance constitutes an offence.
8. The law shall provide for such punishments only as are strictly and obviously necessary, and no one shall suffer punishment except it be legally inflicted in virtue of a law passed and promulgated before the commission of the offence.
9. As all persons are held innocent until they shall have been declared guilty, if arrest shall be deemed indispensable, all harshness not essential to the securing of the prisoner's person shall be severely repressed by law.
10. No one shall be disquieted on account of his opinions, including his religious views, provided their manifestation does not disturb the public order established by law.
11. The free communication of ideas and opinions is one of the most precious of the rights of man. Every citizen may, accordingly, speak, write, and print with freedom, but shall be responsible for such abuses of this freedom as shall be defined by law.
12. The security of the rights of man and of the citizen requires public military

force. These forces are, therefore, established for the good of all and not for the personal advantage of those to whom they shall be entrusted.

13. A common contribution is essential for the maintenance of the public forces and for the cost of administration. This should be equitably distributed among all the citizens in proportion to their means.

14. All the citizens have a right to decide, either personally or by their representatives, as to the necessity of the public contribution; to grant this freely; to know to what uses it is put; and to fix the proportion, the mode of assessment, and of collection, and the duration of the taxes.

15. Society has the right to require of every public agent an account of his administration.

16. A society in which the observance of the law is not assured, nor the separation of powers defined, has no constitution at all.

17. Since property is an inviolable and sacred right, no one shall be deprived thereof except where public necessity, legally determined, shall clearly demand it, and then only on condition that the owner shall have been previously and equitably indemnified.

2

The Scientific Revolution and the Enlightenment: New Intellectual Standards in the West

From the fifteenth century through the eighteenth, intellectual life in the West went through a dizzying series of changes, some contradictory. Renaissance thinkers and artists challenged medieval styles and standards, urging a greater focus on humanity and things of this world. The Reformation, shortly on the heels of the Renaissance, argued for a return to religious authority, but it also shattered the unity of Western Christendom. Ultimately—as became clear by the later seventeenth century—the cutting edge of Western intellectual life was redefined away from religion and toward the growing authority of science. By science, in turn, Western intellectuals meant a set of rational operations, including both experiment and deductive reasoning, by which scientists could discover the clearcut laws of nature. (Compare with earlier Greek approach in Volume I, selection 14.) Religious authority was not directly attacked, but it was sidestepped in favor of a belief that humans could know what they needed to know by unaided reason. Knowledge itself could progress, rather than referring constantly to faith or tradition.

Selection I from Sir Isaac Newton, *Optics, or A Treatise of the Reflections, Refractions, Inflections and Colours of Light*, 4th ed. (London: 1730), p.18. Selection II from John Locke, *An Essay Concerning Human Understanding* (Oxford: 1894), pp. 28, 37–38, 121–22, 387, 412–16, 420–21, 425–26. Selection III reprinted with permission of Macmillan Publishing Company. From Cesare Beccaria, *On Crimes and Punishments*, translated by Henry Paolucci, p. 67. Copyright © 1963 by Macmillan Publishing Company. Selection IV from John Locke, *Some Thoughts Concerning Education* (London: 1712), p. 103. Selection V reprinted with permission of Macmillan Publishing Company from Kant, *Foundations of the Metaphysics of Morals, What is Enlightenment?*, p. 14. Translated and Edited by Lewis White Beck. Copyright 1959 by Macmillan Publishing Company.

The following selections, by leading figures in the scientific revolution in the seventeenth century and its aftermath, the eighteenth-century Enlightenment, describe the new intellectual framework. Isaac Newton, whose great discoveries in physics and mathematics brought together more than a century of work on planetary motion and the laws of gravity, shows how science and religion could be combined—but obviously on the terms of science. John Locke, also a seventeenth-century Englishman, sketches new principles of knowledge wherein reason holds the crucial role.

Locke, and Enlightenment figures after him, intended to apply rational principles and the idea of a harmonious, knowable nature to human society. Obviously, education had to change in order to develop the rational spark inherent in each child—and Locke pointed the way. Human institutions, such as criminal punishments, long based on outmoded religion and tradition, could be rethought, again to make the best of the fundamental reason and goodness in each person. An Italian Enlightenment writer, Beccaria, took the lead here. Finally, toward the end of the Enlightenment period, the German philosopher Immanuel Kant summed up the intellectual excitement of his age and its hope for further progress to come through expanding knowledge and rational exercise.

Science and the Enlightenment were not unchallenged in the Western world, but they did reshape previously dominant belief. Western intellectual life came to rest on assumptions radically different from those of a few centuries before. And there was more. The intellectual revolution reverberated in the wider culture of the West, as ordinary people picked up some of the same assumptions and began to challenge many traditions of popular culture. Finally, as the West spread its influence in the wider world, the baggage of the Age of Reason accompanied its journeys, challenging traditional cultures in Asia and Africa. Here, too, the intellectual revolution that started in the West is still working in the world, though with varied results.

I. NEWTON'S VIEW OF THE WORLD (1704)

All these things considered, it seems probable to me, that God in the beginning formed matter in solid, massy, hard, impenetrable, moveable particles [atoms], of such sizes and figures, and with such other properties, and in such proportion to space, as most conduced to the end for which he formed them; and that these primitive particles, being solids, are incomparably harder than any porous bodies compounded of them; even so very hard, as never to wear or break in pieces; no ordinary power being able to divide what God himself made one in the first creation. . . .

Now by the help of these principles, all material things seem to have been composed of the hard and solid particles above-mentioned, variously associated in the first creation by the counsel of an intelligent agent. For it became him who created them to set them in order. And if he did so, it's unphilosophical to seek for any other origin of the world or to pretend that it might arise out of a chaos by the mere laws of nature; though being once formed, it may continue by those laws for many ages.

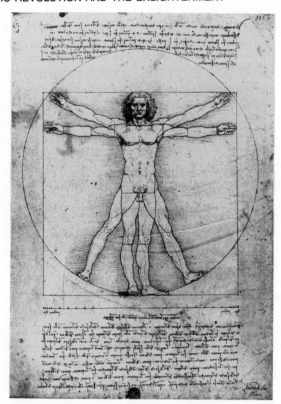

Renaissance art often prefigured the scientific revolution. Anatomical sketches by Leonardo da Vinci. [Alinari/Art Resource, NY]

II. JOHN LOCKE ON THE POWER OF REASON (1690)

I

It is an established opinion amongst some men, that there are in the understanding certain *innate principles;* some primary notions, characters, as it were stamped upon the mind of man; which the soul receives in its very first being, and brings into the world with it. It would be sufficient to convince unprejudiced readers of the falseness of this supposition, if I should only show (as I hope I shall in the following parts of this Discourse) how men, barely by the use of their natural faculties, may attain to all the knowledge they have, without the help of any innate impressions; and may arrive at certainty, without any such original notions or principles.

Of Ideas in General, and Their Origin Every man being conscious to himself that he thinks, and that which his mind is applied about, whilst thinking, being the ideas that are there, it is past doubt, that men have in their minds several ideas, such as those expressed by the words, Whiteness, Hardness, Sweetness, Thinking, Motion, Man,

Elephant, Army, Drunkenness, and others. It is in the first place then to be inquired, how he comes by them. I know it is a received doctrine, that men have native ideas, and original characters, stamped upon their minds, in their very first being. This opinion I have, at large, examined already; and, I suppose, what I have said, in the foregoing book, will be much more easily admitted, when I have shown, whence the understanding may get all the ideas it has, and by what ways and degrees they may come into the mind; for which I shall appeal to every one's own observation and experience.

Let us then suppose the mind to be, as we say, white paper, void of all characters, without any ideas:—How comes it to be furnished? Whence comes it by that vast store which the busy and foundless fancy of man has painted on it with an almost endless variety? Whence has it all the *materials* of reason and knowledge? To this I answer, in one word, from EXPERIENCE. In that all our knowledge is founded; and from that it ultimately derives itself. Our observation employed either about external sensible objects, or about the internal operations of our minds perceived and reflected on by ourselves, is that which supplies our understandings with all the *materials* of thinking. These two are the fountains of knowledge, from whence all the ideas we have, or can naturally have, do spring. . . .

Sense and intuition reach but a very little way. The greatest part of our knowledge depends upon deductions and intermediate ideas: and in those cases where we are fain to substitute assent instead of knowledge, and take propositions for true, without being certain they are so, we have need to find out, examine, and compare the grounds of their probability. In both these cases, the faculty which finds out the means, and rightly applies them, to discover certainty in the one, and probability in the other, is that which we call reason. . . .

II

Assent to supposed innate truths depends on having clear and distinct ideas of what their terms mean, and not on their innateness. A child knows not that three and four are equal to seven, till he comes to be able to count seven, and has got the name and idea of equality; and then, upon explaining those words, he presently assents to, or rather perceives the truth of that proposition. But neither does he then readily assent because it is an innate truth, nor was his assent wanting till then because he wanted the use of reason; but the truth of it appears to him as soon as he has settled in his mind the clear and distinct ideas that these names stand for.

III

Faith and Reason   By what has been before said of reason, we may be able to make some guess at the distinction of things, into those that are according to, above, and contrary to reason. 1. *According to reason* are such propositions whose truth we can discover by examining and tracing those ideas we have from sensation and reflection; and by natural deduction find to be true or probable. 2. *Above reason* are such propositions whose truth or probability we cannot by reason derive from those principles. 3. *Contrary to reason* are such propositions as are inconsistent with or irreconcilable to our clear and distinct ideas. Thus the existence of one God is according to reason; the existence of more than one God, contrary to reason; the resurrection of the dead, above reason. . . .

From these things thus premised, I think we may come to lay down *the measures and boundaries between faith and reason:* the want whereof may possibly have been the cause, if not of great disorders, yet at least of great disputes, and perhaps mistakes in the world. For till it be resolved how far we are to be guided by reason, and how far by faith, we shall in vain dispute, and endeavour to convince one another in matters of religion. . . .

Reason, therefore, here, as contradistinguished to *faith,* I take to be the discovery of the certainty or probability of such propositions or truths, which the mind arrives at by deduction made from such ideas, which it has got by the use of its natural faculties: viz. by sensation or reflection.

Faith, on the other side, is the assent to any proposition, not thus made out by the deductions of reason, but upon the credit of the proposer, as coming from God, in some extraordinary way of communication. This way of discovering truths to men, we call *revelation.* . . .

But yet nothing, I think, can, under that title, [revelation] shake or overrule plain knowledge; or rationally prevail with any man to admit it for true, in a direct contradiction to the clear evidence of his own understanding. . . . And therefore *no proposition can be received for divine revelation . . . if it be contradictory to our clear intuitive knowledge.* Because this would be to subvert the principles and foundations of all knowledge, evidence, and assent whatsoever: and there would be left no difference between truth and falsehood, no measures of credible and incredible in the world, if doubtful propositions shall take place before self-evident; and what we certainly know give way to what we may possibly be mistaken in. In propositions therefore contrary to the clear perception of the agreement or disagreement of any of our ideas, it will be in vain to urge them as matters of faith. They cannot move our assent under that or any other title whatsoever. For faith can never convince us of anything that contradicts our knowledge. . . .

Thus far the dominion of faith reaches, and that without any violence or hindrance to reason; which is not injured or disturbed, but assisted and improved by new discoveries of truth, coming from the eternal fountain of all knowledge. Whatever God hath revealed is certainly true; no doubt can be made of it. This is the proper object of faith: but whether it be a *divine* revelation or no, reason must judge; which can never permit the mind to reject a greater evidence to embrace what is less evident, nor allow it to entertain probability in opposition to knowledge and certainty. There can be no evidence that any traditional revelation is of divine origin, in the words we receive it, and in the sense we understand it, so clear and so certain as that of the principles of reason: and therefore *Nothing that is contrary to, and inconsistent with, the clear and self-evident dictates of reason, has a right to be urged or assented to as a matter of faith, wherein reason hath nothing to do.*

III. BECCARIA APPLIES RATIONALISM TO PUNISHMENT (1764)
A. Crimes and Punishments

To examine and distinguish all the different sorts of crimes and the manner of punishing them would not be our natural task, were it not that their nature, which varies with the different circumstances of times and places, would compel us to enter upon too vast and wearisome a mass of detail. But it will suffice to indicate the most general principles and the most pernicious and common errors, in order to undeceive no less those who, from a mistaken love of liberty, would introduce anarchy, than those who would be glad to reduce their fellow men to the uniform regularity of a convent.

What will be the penalty suitable for such and such crimes?

Is death a penalty really *useful and necessary* for the security and good order of society?

Are torture and torments *just,* and do they attain the *end* which the law aims at?

What is the best way of preventing crimes?

Are the same penalties equally useful in all times?

What influence have they on customs?

These problems deserve to be solved with such geometrical precision as shall suffice to prevail over the clouds of sophistication, over seductive eloquence, or timid doubt. Had I no other merit than that of having been the first to make clearer to Italy that which other nations have dared to write and are beginning to practise, I should deem myself fortunate; but if, in maintaining the rights of men and of invincible truth, I should contribute to rescue from the spasms and agonies of death any unfortunate victim of tyranny or ignorance, both so equally fatal, the blessings and tears of a single innocent man in the transports of his joy would console me for the contempt of mankind. . . .

B. Torture

The torture of a criminal during the course of his trial is a cruelty consecrated by custom in most nations. It is used with an intent either to make him confess his crime, or to explain some contradictions into which he had been led during his examination, or discover his accomplices, or for some kind of metaphysical and incomprehensible purgation of infamy, or, finally, in order to discover other crimes of which he is not accused, but of which he may be guilty.

No man can be judged a criminal until he be found guilty; nor can society take from him the public protection until it has been proved that he has violated the conditions on which it was granted. What right, then, but that of power, can authorize the punishment of a citizen so long as there remains any doubt of his guilt? This dilemma is frequent. Either he is guilty, or not guilty. If guilty, he should only suffer the punishment ordained by the laws, and torture becomes useless, as his confession is unnecessary. If he be innocent his crime has not been proved. Besides, it is confounding all relations to expect that a man should be both the accuser and accused; and that pain should be the test of truth, as if truth resided in the muscles and fibres of a wretch in torture. By this method the robust will escape, and the feeble be condemned.

IV. LOCKE: REASON AND EDUCATION (1693)
I. John Locke (1693)

Keep them [children] from vice and vicious dispositions, and such a kind of behavior in general will come with every degree of their age, as is suitable to that age and the company they ordinarily converse with; and as they grow in years, they will grow in attention and application. But that your words may always carry weight and authority with them, if it shall happen upon any occasion that you bid them leave off the doing of any even childish things, you must be sure to carry the point, and not let him have the mastery. But yet, I say, I would have the father seldom interpose his authority and command in these cases, or in any other, but such as have a tendency to vicious habits. I think there are better ways of prevailing with them: and a gentle persuasion in reasoning when the first point of submission to your will is got, will most times do much better.

It will perhaps be wondered that I mention *reasoning* with children; and yet I cannot but think that the true way of dealing with them. They understand it as early as they do language; and, if I misobserve not, they love to be treated as rational creatures sooner than is imagined. 'Tis pride should be cherished in them, and, as much as can be, made the greatest instrument to turn them by.

But when I talk of reasoning, I do not intend any other but such as is suited to the child's capacity and apprehension. Nobody can think a boy of three or seven years old should be argued with as a grown man. Long discourses and philosophical reasonings, at best, amaze and confound but do not instruct children. When I say, therefore, that they must be *treated as rational creatures,* I mean that you should make them sensible, by the mildness of your carriage, and the composure even in your correction of them, that what you do is reasonable in you, and useful and necessary for them; and that it is not out of *capriccio,* passion, or fancy that you command or forbid them anything. This they are capable of understanding; and there is no virtue they should be excited to nor fault they should be kept from which I do not think they may be convinced of; but it must be by such reasons as their age and understandings are capable of, and those proposed always in very few and plain words.

V. KANT DEFINES THE ENLIGHTENMENT (1784)

Enlightenment is man's release from his self-incurred tutelage. Tutelage is man's inability to make use of his understanding without direction from another. Self-incurred is this tutelage when its cause lies not in lack of reason but in lack of resolution and courage to use it without direction from another. *Sapere aude!* [Dare to know!] "Have courage to use your own reason!"—that is the motto of the enlightenment.

Laziness and cowardice are the reasons why so great a portion of mankind, after nature has long since discharged them from external direction, nevertheless remains under lifelong tutelage, and why it is so easy for others to set themselves up as their guardians. It is so easy not to be of age. If I have a book which understands for me, a pastor who has a conscience for me, a physician who decides my diet, if I can only pay—others will readily undertake the irksome work for me. . . .

For any single individual to work himself out of the life under tutelage which has become almost his nature is very difficult. He has come to be fond of this state, and he is for the present really incapable of making use of his reason, for no one has ever let him try it out. Statutes and formulas, those mechanical tools of the rational employment or rather misemployment of his natural gifts, are the fetters of an everlasting tutelage. Whoever throws them off makes only an uncertain leap over the narrowest ditch because he is not accustomed to that kind of free motion. Therefore, there are only few who have succeeded by their own exercise of mind both in freeing themselves from incompetence and in achieving a steady pace. . . .

If we are asked, "Do we now live in an *enlightened age?*" the answer is "No", but we do live in an *age of enlightenment*. As things now stand, much is lacking which prevents men from being, or easily becoming, capable of correctly using their own reason in religious matters with assurance and free from outside direction. But, on the other hand, we have clear indications that the field has now been opened wherein men may freely deal with these things and that the obstacles to general enlightenment or the release from self-imposed tutelage are gradually being reduced. In this respect, this is the age of enlightenment.

3

Work and Workers in the Industrial Revolution

The Industrial Revolution was one of the great changes in Western and ultimately world history. Taking shape toward the end of the eighteenth century in Britain, industrialization dominated the nineteenth century in Western Europe and North America. Based on radically new technologies, including the use of fossil fuels for power, industrialization revolutionized the production and transportation of goods. It sustained rapid population growth in the West and created growing material abundance as well. This industrialization transformed a social structure once based on the land into divisions based on urban wealth and property. It fostered large organizations and a growing state capable of utilizing new technologies of communication and marshaling large amounts of capital and large numbers of goods and people. It challenged family life by taking work out of the home and redefining the roles of many women and children. It was, in sum, as basic a change in human history as had occurred since the advent of settled agriculture.

One of the many areas altered by industrialization was the nature of work, particularly for those people who labored in the proliferating mines and factories. Some features of industrialization benefited work: machines could lighten labor; factories could provide social stimulation; and some jobs that demanded new technical expertise became unusually interesting. But many workers found industrial working conditions a strain because they challenged a number of tradi-

Selection I from *British Sessional Papers* 1831–1832, House of Commons Vol. XV, pp. 17–19. Selection II from *The Archives du Haut Rhin* 1M123C1, translated by Peter N. Stearns. Selection III from Adolf Levenstein, *Aus Der Tief, Arbeiterbriefe*, translated by Gabriela Wettberg (Berlin: 1905), pp. 48, 57, 60.

tional values and habits. Certainly, changes in work provide one way of measuring the human impact of the vast industrialization process—some would say, of measuring human degradation.

The documents that follow focus on three aspects of industrial work during the nineteenth century. First comes a parliamentary inquiry on child labor, conducted in Britain in the early 1830s and ultimately the source of laws restricting children's work. Child labor was not in fact new, so one question to ask is what aspects of the factory system made it seem newly shocking. A second, related feature of industrial work—and one that persisted far longer than child labor—was the attempt to bring new discipline to the labor force. Shop rules—in this case, from a French factory in the late 1840s—did battle with a number of customary impulses in an effort to make work more predictable, less casual. Finally, new working conditions provoked direct worker comment through protest and individual statements. The comment offered here, by an unusually sensitive German miner around 1900—among other things, an ardent socialist—is not typical, but it does express some widely shared grievances. All three documents suggest the tensions that changes in work could bring. A basic feature of Western life in the nineteenth century, this strain spread with industrialization to other societies later on. How could workers modify or adapt to new work habits? How might changes in work affect other aspects of their lives, in the family, politics, or culture?

I. CHILD LABOR INQUIRY

Mr. Abraham Whitehead

> **431.** What is your business?—A clothier.
> **432.** Where do you reside?—At Scholes, near Holmfirth.
> **433.** Is not that in the centre of very considerable woolen mills? Yes, for a space of three or four miles; I live nearly in the centre of thirty or forty woollen mills. . . .
> **436.** Are the children and young persons of both sexes employed in these mills?—Yes.
> **437.** At how early an age are children employed?—The youngest age at which children are employed is never under five, but some are employed between five and six in woollen mills at piecing.
> **438.** How early have you observed these young children going to their work, speaking for the present in the summer time?—In the summer time I have frequently seen them going to work between five and six in the morning, and I know the general practice is for them to go as early to all the mills. . . .
> **439.** How late in the evening have you seen them at work, or remarked them returning to their homes?—I have seen them at work in the summer season between nine and ten in the evening; they continue to work as long as they can see, and they can see to work in these mills as long as you could see to read. . . .
> **441.** You say that on your own personal knowledge?—I live near to parents who have been sending their children to mills for a great number of years, and I know positively that these children are every morning in the winter seasons

called out of bed between five and six, and in some instances between four and five.

442. Your business as a clothier has often led you into these mills?—Frequently; . . .

. . .

460. What has been the treatment which you have observed that these children received at the mills, to keep them attentive for so many hours at such early ages?—They are generally cruelly treated; so cruelly treated, that they dare not hardly for their lives be too late at their work in a morning. . . . My heart has been ready to bleed for them when I have seen them so fatigued, for they appear in such a state of apathy and insensibility as really not to know whether they are doing their work or not; . . .

461. Do they frequently fall into errors and mistakes in piecing when thus fatigued?—Yes; the errors they make when thus fatigued are, that instead of placing the cording in this way [describing it], they are apt to place them obliquely, and that causes a flying, which makes bad yarn; and when the billy-spinner sees that, he takes his strap or the billy-roller, and says, "Damn thee, close it-little devil, close it," and they smite the child with the strap or the billy-roller. . . .

510. You say that the morals of the children are very bad when confined in these mills; what do you consider to be the situation of children who have nothing to do, and are running about such towns as Leeds, with no employment to keep them out of mischief?—Children that are not employed in mills are generally more moral and better behaved than children who are employed in mills.

511. Those in perfect idleness are better behaved than those that are employed?—That is not a common thing; they either employ them in some kind of business at home, or send them to school.

512. Are there no day-schools to which these factory children go?—They have no opportunity of going to school when they are thus employed at the mill.

II. RULES FOR WORKERS IN THE FACTORY OF BENCK AND CO. IN BÜHL (ALSACE), 1842

Article 1. Every worker who accepts employment in any work-site is obligated to read these rules and to submit to them. No one should be unfamiliar with them. If the rules are violated in any work-site, the offenders must pay fines according to the disorder or damage they have caused.

Art. 2. All workers without exception are obligated, after they have worked in the factory for fourteen days, to give a month's notice when they wish to quit. This provision can be waived only for important reasons.

Art. 3. The work day will consist of twelve hours, without counting rest periods. Children under twelve are excepted; they have to work only eight hours a day.

Art. 4. The bell denotes the hours of entry and departure in the factory when it first rings. At the second ring every worker should be at his work. At quitting time the bell will also be sounded when each worker should clean his workplace and his machine (if he has one). It is forbidden under penalty of fines to abandon the workplace before the bell indicates that the work-site is closed.

Art. 5. It is forbidden to smoke tobacco inside the factory. Whoever violates this prohibition is subjected to a heavy fine and can be dismissed. It is also forbidden under penalty of fines to bring beer or brandy into the factory. Any worker who comes to the factory drunk will be sent away and fined.

Art. 6. The porter, whoever he may be, is forbidden to admit anyone after the workday begins. If someone asks for a worker he will make him wait and have the worker called. All workers are forbidden to bring anyone into the factory and the porter is forbidden to admit anyone. The porter is also forbidden to let any workers in or out without the foreman's permission during the hours of work.

Art. 7. Any worker who misses a day without the Director's permission must pay a fine of two francs. The fine is doubled for a second offense. Any worker who is absent several times is dismissed, and if he is a weaver he is not paid for any piece he may have begun unless he can prove he missed work because of illness and should therefore be paid for work he has already done.

Art. 8. All workers in the factory are obligated to be members of the Sickness Fund, to pay their dues, and conduct themselves according to its statutes.

Art. 9. The foreman and the porter are empowered to retain any worker leaving the factory and to search him, as often as the interests of the Director may require. It is also recommended to the foreman to close the work-site himself, give the key to the porter, and to allow no worker inside during meal periods.

Art. 10. Workers should only go in and out of doors where a porter resides, else they will be fined, brought under suspicion, and dismissed. They cannot refuse to surrender any of their belongings at work, for which they will be reimbursed according to the valuation of the Director and the foreman. Workers are also ordered to be obedient to the foreman, who is fully empowered by the Director. Any disobedience will be punished by fines according to the importance of the case. Any offender is responsible for the consequences of his action. It is also forbidden for any worker to seek work in any of the company's work-sites other than the one in which he is employed; anyone encountered in another work-site will be punished.

Art. 11. Every worker is personally responsible for the objects entrusted to him. Any object that cannot be produced at the first request must be paid for. Weavers are obligated to pay careful attention to their cloth when they dry it. They will be fined and held responsible for any damage.

Art. 12. In return for the protection and care which all workers can expect from the Director, they pledge to him loyalty and attachment. They promise immediately to call to his attention anything that threatens good order or the Director's interests. Workers are also put on notice that any unfortunate who commits a theft, however small it may be, will be taken to court and abandoned to his fate.

III. MAX LOTZ, A GERMAN MINER, DESCRIBES HIS WORK

A trembling of the pupils forms in the eyes of many miners. At first it is not noticeable but it gradually becomes stronger. Where this eye ailment reaches a certain stage the stricken person becomes unable to work in the pit any longer. The stricken man becomes unsure of his grip, he often misses the desired object by one foot. He has particular difficulties in directing his glance upward. If he fixes but barely on an object his eyes begin to tremble immediately. But this calamity only appears in the mine or in artificial light. Above ground and in daylight it is never present. I know a laborer working quite close to me who takes a quart of liquor daily into the shaft. As soon as the trembling begins he takes a sip and the pupil becomes calm for a short while—so he states. Thus one can become a habitual drunk, too.

But this is not all. Almost all miners are anemic. I do not know what causes this pathological diminution of blood corpuscles in miners, whether this results from a general lack of protein in the blood. I suppose that it is caused mainly by the long, daily stay in bad air combined with the absence of sun or day light. I reason that if one places a potted plant in a warm but dark cellar for a long time it will grow significantly more pale and sickly than her beautifully scenting sisters in the rose-colored sunlight. It must be like this for the drudges down there. Anemia renders the miner characteristically pale. . . .

Let's go, shouted Prüfer, who had already picked up a shovel. Four more wagons have to fall. It is almost 12:30 now. [p.m.] All right, I agreed, and we swung the shovels.

Away it goes, commanded Bittner when the wagons were fully loaded. Jump to it, there is plenty of coal. Well, if I were a pickman, mumbled the chief pickman then I'd have myself a drink. And he breathed heavily behind the wagon.

Let's set up the planking until Rheinhold comes back so that things don't look so scruffy, I said to Bittner even though we would rather have stretched out on the pile of coal because we were so tired.

He replied: I don't care, but first I want to wring out my trousers. And standing there naked he started to squeeze the water from the garment. I followed his example. When we had finished, it looked around us as though a bucket full of water had been spilled. I do not exaggerate. In other locations where it was warmer yet, the workers were forced to undergo this procedure several times during their working hours. But let us remain here.

We put our undergarments back on and did not pay attention to the unpleasant feeling which we had doing so. We placed the wooden planks and cleared aside the debris in order to establish good working conditions for the other third which usually did not do the same for us—because they were too fatigued.

The work is becoming increasingly mechanical. No more incentive, no more haste, we muddle along wearily, we are worn out and mindless. There was sufficient coal, Rheinhold could come at any time. My forehead burned like fire. As a consequence of the anemia from which I suffer I occasionally experience a slight dizzy spell. Bittner does not know about it. But in my head it rages and paralyzes me beyond control or without my being able to think. When it becomes unbearable I stop my slow, phlegmatic and energyless working. I then sit on the side wall of the mountain in order to slurp the last remaining coffee. . . .

This is a brief description of one shift in the pit. And this torture, this inhuman haste repeats itself day after day [so] that the various states of exhaustion express themselves mildly or very pronouncedly in the physical state of the individuals. And that is not all; the spirit, too, the conscience of the individual degenerates. And one drudge, grown vacuous through his work, is put beside another one, and another one and finally this "modern" circle has closed in on the entire working force. And he who says that primarily the professional group of the miners is the rudest, least educated and spiritually lowest class of men does not lie. Of course, there are exceptions here, too. But these exceptions are supposed to validate the rule according to a simple type of logic. In any event, it truly takes spiritual magnitude to occupy still oneself with belletristic, scientific and thought-provoking materials after a completed shift. When I come home in that condition I still have to cope with other necessary heavy work around the house. And finally there only remain the evening hours for the writing tasks which I deem noble.

4

Peter the Great Reforms Russia

Peter the Great ruled Russia as tsar from 1682 until 1725. A huge man, Peter pushed his government into many new directions. He brutally repressed protest, executing certain army mutineers personally. He moved vigorously in war, winning new territory in the Baltic region, where he located a new westward-looking capital he modestly called St. Petersburg (now Leningrad). With its military success, Russia was on its way toward becoming a major European power; it was already a growing empire in Central Asia.

Peter was also eager to update Russia's administration and economy, which he saw as essential for military purposes and to establish Russian prestige and position in the wider European arena. His measures were both symbolic and real: he enforced Western-style dress on his boyars (the nobles) and required them to cut off their Mongol-style beards. He developed a major iron industry to serve as a basis for armaments production and to avoid Russian dependence on the West in this crucial sector.

The following selections show a number of Peter's initiatives to reform Russia and bring it in line with key Western patterns. They show why, at that time

All selections from Basil Dmytryshyn, *Imperial Russia: A Sourcebook, 1700–1917* (New York: Holt, Rinehart and Winston, Inc., 1967), pp. 14–16, 18–19, 21–22. Copyright © 1967 by Holt, Rinehart and Winston, Inc. Reprinted by permission. New Calendar from *Polnoe Sobranie Zakonov Russkoi Imperii* (Complete Collection of the Laws of the Russian Empire), 1st series, Vol. 3, No. 1736, pp. 681–82. Duties of the Senate from *Polnoe Sobranie*, Vol. 4, No. 2321, p. 627 and No. 2330, p. 643. Compulsory Education from *Polnoe Sobranie*, Vol. 5, No. 2762, p. 78 and No. 2778, p. 86. Instructions to Students from *Pisma I Bumagi Imperatora Petra Velokogo* (Letters and Papers of Emperor Peter the Great) (St. Petersburg: 1887), Vol. 1, pp. 117–18. Right of Factories from *Polnoe Sobranie*, Vol. 6, No. 3890, pp. 486–93. Founding of the Academy from *Polnoe Sobranie*, Vol. 7, No. 4443.

and since, historians have seen Peter as one of the great "modernizers" in world history, with a Western-inspired vision of what an efficient society should be like and how tradition should yield to its imperatives. In these reforms Peter brings Russia's calender in line with the Julian calendar used elsewhere in Europe (this calendar remained in use until after the revolution in 1918)—a symbolic gesture, but one that affected daily living patterns. Peter also sets up an administrative council to improve the direction of the state bureaucracy and expand its functions. He works to improve education, particularly of the nobility, and to facilitate manufacturing as well. These reforms, in sum, give a good picture of the directions in which the tsar was pushing his vast empire.

Peter's reforms also suggest important links with authoritarian political trends in Russia, including a willingness to regiment ordinary workers and peasants. While other European rulers at this time, such as Louis XIV in France, were claiming new powers in the name of military goals, Peter seemed unusually free to order his nobility about and command their service. He was not interested in aspects of Western politics that stressed restraints on the monarch such as parliaments. Not surprisingly, then, Peter's vision of a Westernized Russia proved selective, as he found certain aspects of the Russian tradition eminently useful. Peter's reforms must be interpreted in terms of how much they changed, but also in terms of their confirmation of distinctive features of the Russian state.

Peter the Great clearly illustrates a reform process from the top down. How do you think Russians at various levels would have reacted? From what you can judge by these documents, was Peter moving Russia in a useful direction?

A DECREE ON A NEW CALENDAR, DECEMBER 20, 1699

The Great Sovereign has ordered it declared: the Great Sovereign knows that many European Christian countries as well as Slavic peoples are in complete accord with our Eastern Orthodox Church, namely: Wallachians, Moldavians, Serbs, Dalmatians, Bulgars, and subjects of our Great Sovereign, the Cherkessy [Ukrainians] and all Greeks from whom we accepted our Orthodox faith—all these peoples number their years from eight days after the birth of Christ, this is from January 1, and not from the creation of the world. There is a great difference in those two calendars. This year is 1699 since the birth of Christ, and on January 1 it will be 1700 as well as a new century. To celebrate this happy and opportune occasion, the Great Sovereign has ordered that henceforth all government administrative departments and fortresses in all their official business use the new calendar beginning January 1, 1700. To commemorate this happy beginning and the new century in the capital city of Moscow, after a solemn prayer in churches and private dwellings, all major streets, homes of important people, and homes of distinguished religious and civil servants should be decorated with trees, pine, and fur branches similar to the decoration of the Merchant Palace or the Pharmacy Building—or as best as one knows how to decorate his place and gates. Poor people should put up at least one tree, or a branch on their gates or on their apartment [doors]. These decorations are to remain from January 1 to January 7, 1700. As a sign of happiness on January 1, friends should greet each other and the New Year and the new century as follows: when the Red Square will be lighted and shooting will begin—followed by that at the homes of boyars, courtiers, and important officials of the tsar, military and merchant classes—everyone who has a musket or any other fire arm should either salute thrice or shoot several rockets or as many as he has. . . .

DECREES ON THE DUTIES OF THE SENATE

This *ukaz* [decree] should be made known. We have decreed that during our absence administration of the country is to be [in the hands of] the Governing Senate [Peter then names its new members.]

. . .

Each *gubernia* [region] is to send two officials to advise the Senate on judicial and legislative matters. . . .

In our absence the Senate is chareged by this *ukaz* with the following:

1. To establish a just court, to deprive unjust judges of their offices and of all their property, and to administer the same treatment to all slanderers.
2. To supervise governmental expenditures throughout the country and cancel unnecessary and, above all, useless things.
3. To collect as much money as possible because money is the artery of war.
4. To recruit young noblemen for officer training, especially those who try to evade it; also to select about 1000 educated boyars for the same purpose.
5. To reform letters of exchange and keep these in one place.
6. To take inventory of goods leased to offices or *gubernias*.
7. To farm out the salt trade in an effort to receive some profit [for the state].
8. To organize a good company and assign to it the China trade.
9. To increase trade with Persia and by all possible means to attract in great numbers Armenians [to that trade]. To organize inspectors and inform them of their responsibilities.

DECREES ON CONPULSORY EDUCATION OF THE RUSSIAN NOBILITY, JANUARY 12, AND FEBRUARY 28, 1714

Send to every *gubernia* [region] some persons from mathematical schools to teach the children of the nobility—except those of freeholders and government clerks—mathematics and geometry; as a penalty [for evasion] establish a rule that no one will be allowed to marry unless he learns these [subjects]. Inform all prelates to issue no marriage certificates to those who are ordered to go to schools. . . .

The Great Sovereign has decreed: in all *gubernias* children between the ages of ten and fifteen of the nobility, of government clerks, and of lesser officials, except those of freeholders, must be taught mathematics and some geometry. Toward that end, students should be sent from mathematical schools [as teachers], several into each *gubernia*, to prelates and to renowned monasteries to establish schools. During their instruction these teachers should be given food and financial remuneration of three *altyns* and two *dengas* per day from *gubernia* revenues set aside for that purpose by personal orders of His Imperial Majesty. No fees should be collected from students. When they have mastered the material, they should then be given certificates written in their own handwriting. When the students are released they ought to pay one ruble each for their training. Without these certificates they should not be allowed to marry nor receive marriage certificates.

AN INSTRUCTION TO RUSSIAN STUDENTS ABROAD STUDYING NAVIGATION

1. Learn [how to draw] plans and charts and how to use the compass and other naval indicators.
2. [Learn] how to navigate a vessel in battle as well as in a simple maneuver, and learn how to use all appropriate tools and instruments; namely, sails, ropes, and oars, and the like matters, on row boats and other vessels.
3. Discover as much as possible how to put ships to sea during a naval battle. Those who cannot succeed in this effort must diligently ascertain what action should be taken by the vessels that do and those that do not put to sea during such a situation [naval battle]. Obtain from [foreign] naval officers written statements, bearing their signatures and seals, of how adequately you [Russian students] are prepared for [naval] duties.
4. If, upon his return, anyone wishes to receive [from the Tsar] greater favors for himself, he should learn, in addition to the above enumerated instructions, how to construct those vessels aboard which he would like to demonstrate his skills.
5. Upon his return to Moscow, every [foreign-trained Russian] should bring with him at his own expense, for which he will later be reimbrused, at least two experienced masters of naval science. They [the returnees] will be assigned soliders, one soldier per returnee, to teach them [what they have learned abroad]. And if they do not wish to accept soldiers they may teach their acquaintances or their own people. The treasury will pay for transportation and maintenance of soldiers. And if anyone other than soldiers learns [the art of navigation] the treasury will pay 100 rubles for the maintenance of every such individual. . . .

A DECREE ON THE RIGHT OF FACTORIES TO BUY VILLAGES, JANUARY 18, 1721

Previous decrees have denied merchants the right to obtain villages. This prohibition was instituted because those people, outside their business, did not have any establishments that could be of any use to the state. Nowadays, thanks to Our decrees, as every one can see, many merchants have companies and many have succeeded in establishing new enterprises for the benefit of the state; namely: silver, copper, iron, coal and the like, as well as silk, linen, and woolen industries, many of which have begun operations. As a result, by this Our *ukaz* aimed at the increase of factories, We permit the nobility as well as merchants to freely purchase villages for these factories, with the sanction of the Mining and Manufacturing College, under one condition: that these villages be always integral parts of these factories. Consequently, neither the nobility nor merchants may sell or mortgage these villages without the factories . . . and should someone decide to sell these villages with the factories because of pressing needs, it must be done with the permission of the Mining and Manufacturing College. And whoever violates this procedure will have his possessions confiscated.

And should someone try to establish a small factory for the sake of appearance in order to purchase a village, such an entrepreneur should not be allowed to purchase anything. The Mining and Manufacturing College should adhere to this rule very strictly. Should such a thing happen, those responsible for it should be deprived of all their movable and immovable property.

A DECREE ON THE FOUNDING OF THE ACADEMY, JANUARY 28, 1724

His Imperial Majesty decreed the establishment of an academy, wherein languages as well as other sciences and important arts could be taught, and where books could be translated. On January 22, [1724], during his stay in the Winter Palace, His Majesty approved the project for the Academy, and with his own hand signed a decree that stipulates that the Academy's budget of 24,912 rubles annually should come from revenues from custom dues and export-import license fees collected in the following cities: Narva, Dorpat, Pernov and Arensburg. . . .

Usually two kinds of institutions are used in organizing arts and sciences. One is known as a University; the other as an Academy or society of arts and sciences.

1. A University is an association of learned individuals who teach the young people the development of such distinguished sciences as theology and jurisprudence (the legal skill), and medicine and philosophy. An Academy, on the other hand, is an association of learned and skilled people who not only know their subjects to the same degree [as their counterparts in the University] but who, in addition, improve and develop them through research and inventions. They have no obligation to teach others.

2. While the Academy consists of the same scientific disciplines and has the same members as the University, these two institutions, in other states, have no connection between themselves in training many other well-qualified people who could organize different societies. This is done to prevent interference into the activity of the Academy, whose sole task is to improve arts and sciences through theoretical research that would benefit professors as well as students of universities. Freed from the pressure of research, universities can concentrate on educating the young people.

3. Now that an institution aimed at the cultivation of arts and sciences is to be chartered in Russia, there is no need to follow the practice that is accepted in other states. It is essential to take into account the existing circumstances of this state [Russia], consider [the quality of Russian] teachers and students, and organize such an institution that would not only immediately increase the glory of this [Russian] state through the development of sciences, but would also, through teaching and dissemination [of knowledge], benefit the people [of Russia] in the future.

4. These two aims will not be realized if the Academy of Sciences alone is chartered, because while the Academy may try to promote and disseminate arts and sciences, these will not spread among the people. The establishment of a university will do even less, simply because there are no elementary schools, gymnasia or seminaries [in Russia] where young people could learn the fundamentals before studying more advanced subjects [at the University] to make themselves useful. It is therefore inconceivable that under these circumstances a university would be of some value [to Russia].

5. Consequently what is needed most [in Russia] is the establishment of an in-

stitution that would consist of the most learned people, who, in turn, would be willing: (a) to promote and perfect the sciences while at the same time, wherever possible, be willing (b) to give public instruction to young people (if they feel the latter are qualified) and (c) instruct some people individually so that they in turn could train young people [of Russia] in the fundamental principles of all sciences.

5

Russian Peasants: Serfdom and Emancipation

More than most Eurasian societies, Russia long remained a land of small cities with limited manufacturing. Not only a majority but a vast majority of her people were peasants well into the nineteenth century. Numbers alone, however, do not account for the omnipresence of peasant issues in Russian history. From a once-held position of substantial freedom and control of village lands, Russian peasants had been subjected to increasingly rigorous serfdom—by the state or by noble landlords—from the fifteenth century onward. Their trend thus reversed that of Western Europe, where serfdom on the whole became lighter over time. The Russian economy relied on agricultural exports forced from peasant labor on the large estates; and Russian politics and society, which traded noble control over their peasants for docility to the Russian Tsar, relied heavily on the subjection of the serfs.

Yet peasant conditions created increasingly visible problems. They violated standards of justice felt keenly by many Russians, including those open to Western ideas during the eighteenth and nineteenth centuries. Serfs rioted frequently, for peasants were quite aware of their own servitude. Furthermore, tight control of peasant labor limited Russia's economic flexibility, making it hard to recruit urban labor and, at least in the eyes of some observers, reducing productivity on the land as well. Finally, prodded by its loss in the Crimean War, the Russian government took the step of emancipation, ending serfdom while trying to preserve the noble-dominated social hierarchy. This move redefined the peasant question, but did not remove it.

The following documents stem from three sources. The first is an account by an early Russian intellectual, Alexander Radishchev (1749–1802), who wrote about peasant conditions in a book, *A Journey from St. Petersburg to Moscow*, repressed by the government until 1905. His account reveals peasant suffering and reactions and also the reformist zeal of a segment of the educated upper class. From the early nineteenth century (1811) comes a second, antireformist tract by a landlord, Nicholas Karamzin, who defends the status quo against hints of change from Tsar Alexander I. His arguments bear attention. Some are obviously simply selfish, or deeply class-biased, but others call attention to wider problems that might result from change. Finally, excerpts from the emancipation decree of 1861 are presented. They reveal how a new tsar, Alexander II, tried to juggle reform interests with noble resistance. The document invites appraisal in terms of how much was changed, and why peasants were so widely disappointed with the results.

I. RADISHCHEV'S JOURNEY

I suppose it is all the same to you whether I traveled in winter or in summer. Maybe both in winter and in summer. It is not unusual for travelers to set out in sleighs and to return in carriages. In summer. The corduroy road tortured my body; I climbed out of the carriage and went on foot. While I had been lying back in the carriage, my thoughts had turned to the immeasurable vastness of the world. By spiritually leaving the earth I thought I might more easily bear the jolting of the carriage. But spiritual exercises do not always distract us from our physical selves; and so, to save my body, I got out and walked. A few steps from the road I saw a peasant ploughing a field. The weather was hot. I looked at my watch. It was twenty minutes before one. I had set out on Saturday. It was now Sunday. The ploughing peasant, of course, belonged to a landed proprietor, who would not let him pay a commutation tax [*obrok*]. The peasant was ploughing very carefully. The field, of course, was not part of his master's land. He turned the plough with astonishing ease.

"God help you," I said, walking up to the ploughman, who, without stopping, was finishing the furrow he had started. "God help you," I repeated.

"Thank you, sir," the ploughman said to me, shaking the earth off the ploughshare and transferring it to a new furrow.

"You must be a Dissenter, since you plough on a Sunday."

"No, sir, I make the true sign of the cross," he said, showing me the three fingers together. "And God is merciful and does not bid us starve to death, so long as we have strength and a family."

"Have you no time to work during the week, then, and can you not have any rest on Sundays, in the hottest part of the day, at that?"

"In a week, sir, there are six days, and we go six times a week to work on the master's fields; in the evening, if the weather is good, we haul to the master's house the hay that is left in the woods; and on holidays the women and girls go walking in the woods, looking for mushrooms and berries. God grant," he continued, making the sign of the cross, "that it rains this evening. If you have peasants of your own, sir, they are praying to God for the same thing."

"My friend, I have no peasants, and so nobody curses me. Do you have a large family?"

"Three sons and three daughters. The eldest is nine years old."

"But how do you manage to get food enough, if you have only the holidays free?"

"Not only the holidays: the nights are ours, too. If a fellow isn't lazy, he won't starve to death. You see, one horse is resting; and when this one gets tired, I'll take the other; so the work gets done."

"Do you work the same way for your master?"

"No, Sir, it would be a sin to work the same way. On his fields there are a hundred hands for one mouth, while I have two for seven mouths: you can figure it out for yourself. No matter how hard you work for the master, no one will thank you for it. The master will not pay our head tax; but, though he doesn't pay it, he doesn't demand one sheep, one hen, or any linen or butter the less. The peasants are much better off where the landlord lets them pay a commutation tax without the interference of the steward. It is true that sometimes even good masters take more than three rubles a man; but even that's better than having to work on the master's fields. Nowadays it's getting to be the custom to let villages to tenants, as they call it. But we call it putting our heads in a noose. A landless tenant skins us peasants alive; even the best ones don't leave us any time for ourselves. In the winter he won't let us do any carting of goods and won't let us go into town to work; all our work has to be for him, because he pays our head tax. It is an invention of the Devil to turn your peasants over to work for a stranger. You can make a complaint against a bad steward, but to whom can you complain against a bad tenant?"

"My friend, you are mistaken; the laws forbid them to torture people."

"Torture? That's true; but all the same, sir, you would not want to be in my hide." Meanwhile the ploughman hitched up the other horse to the plough and bade me goodbye as he began a new furrow.

The words of this peasant awakened in me a multitude of thoughts. I thought especially of the inequality of treatment within the peasant class. I compared the crown peasants with the manorial peasants. They both live in villages; but the former pay a fixed sum, while the latter must be prepared to pay whatever their master demands. The former are judged by their equals; the latter are dead to the law, except, perhaps, in criminal cases. A member of society becomes known to the government protecting him, only when he breaks the social bonds, when he becomes a criminal! This thought made my blood boil.

Tremble, cruelhearted landlord! on the brow of each of your peasants I see your condemnation written.

II. KARAMAZIN'S CONSERVATIVE VIEW

We are told that the present government had the intention of emancipating proprietary serfs. One must know the origins of this bondage. In Russia in the ninth, tenth, and eleventh centuries the only bondmen were the *kholopy,* i.e., either foreigners captured in war or purchased, or criminals deprived by law of citizenship, together with their descendants. But rich men, disposing of a multitude of *kholopy,* populated their lands with them, and in this manner arose the first serf villages in the modern sense of the word. Furthermore, proprietors also admitted into servitude free peasants on terms which more or less constrained the latter's natural and civil liberties; some of these peasants, upon receipt of land from the proprietor, committed themselves and the children to serve him forever. This was the second source of slavery in the countryside. Other peasants— and they constituted the majority—rented land from the owners in return for a payment consisting only of money or a set quantity of cereals, while retaining the right to move on elsewhere after the expiration of a fixed period of time. These free movements, however, had their drawbacks, for great lords and wealthy men lured free peasants away from weak landlords, and the latter, left with deserted fields, were unable to meet their state obligations. Tsar Boris was the first to deprive all peasants of this freedom to move from place to place, that is, he bound them to their masters. Such was the beginning of general bondage. This law was changed, limited, and made subject to exceptions; it was tried in courts for many years; at last it attained to full force, and the ancient distinction between serfs and *kholopy* disappeared entirely. It follows: (1) that the presentday proprietary serfs were never landowners; that is, they never had land of their own, which is the lawful, inalienable property of the gentry; (2) that the serfs who are descended of the *kholopy* are also the lawful property of the gentry and cannot be personally emancipated without the landlords' receiving some special compensation; (3) that only the free peasants who were bound to their masters by Godunov may, in justice, demand their previous freedom; but since (4), we do not know which of them are descended of the *kholopy,* and which of free men, the legislator faces no mean task when he tries to untie this Gordian knot, unless he is bold enough to cut through it by proclaiming all to be equally free: the descendants of war captives, purchased, lawful slaves, as well as the descendants of enserfed peasants, the former being freed by virtue of the law of nature, and the latter by virtue of the power of the autocratic monarch to abrogate the statutes of his predecessors. I do not want to pursue this controversy further, but I should like to point out that as far as the state is concerned, natural law yields to civil law, and that the prudent autocrat abrogates only those laws which have become harmful or inadequate, and which can be replaced by superior ones.

What does the emancipation of serfs in Russia entail? That they be allowed to live where they wish, that their masters be deprived of all authority over them, and that they come exclusively under the authority of the state. Very well. But these emancipated peasants will have no land, which—this is incontrovertible—belongs to the gentry. They will, therefore, either stay on with their present landlords, paying them quitrent, cultivating their fields, delivering bread where necessary—in a word, continuing to serve them as before; or else, dissatisfied with the terms, they move to another, less exacting, landlord. In the first case, is it not likely that the masters, relying on man's natural love for his native soil, will impose on the peasants the most onerous terms? Previously they had spared them, seeing in the serfs their own property, but now the greedy among them will try to exact from the peasants all that is physically possible. The landlords will draw up a contract, the tiller will renege—and there will be lawsuits, eternal lawsuits! In the second case, with the peasant now here, now there, won't the treasury suffer losses in the collection of the soul-tax and other revenues? Will not agriculture suffer as well? Will not many fields lie fallow, and many granaries stay empty? After all, the bread on our markets comes, for the most part, not from the free farmers but from the gentry. And here is one more evil consequence of emancipation: the peasants, no longer subjected to seignorial justice from which there is no appeal and which is free of charge, will take to fighting each other and litigating in the city—what ruin! . . . Freed from the surveillance of the masters who dispose of their own *zemskaia isprava,* or police, which is much more active than all the Land Courts, the peasants will take to drinking and villainy—what a gold mine for taverns and corrupt police officials, but what a blow to morals and to the security of the state! In short, at the present time, the gentry, dispersed throughout the realm, assist the monarch in the preservation of peace and order; by divesting them of this supervisory authority, he would, like Atlas, take all of Russia upon his shoulders. Could he bear it? A collapse would be frightful. The primary obligation of the monarch is to safeguard the internal and external unity of the state; benefiting estates and individuals comes second. Alexander wishes to improve the lot of the peasants by granting them freedom; but what if this freedom should harm the state? And will the peasants be happier, freed from their masters' authority, but handed over to their own vices, to tax farmers, and to unscrupulous judges? There can be no question that the serfs of a sensible landlord, one who contents himself with a moderate quitrent, or with labor on a *desiatina* of plowland for each household, are happier than state peasants, for they have in him a vigilant protector and defender. Is it not better quietly to take measures to bridle cruel landlords? These men are known to the governors. If the latter faithfully fulfill their obligations, such landlords will promptly become a thing of the past; and unless Russia has wise and honest governors, the free peasants will not prosper either. I do not know whether Godunov did well in depriving the peasants of their freedom since the conditions of that time are not fully known. But I do know that this is not the time to return it to them. Then they had the habits of free men—today they have the habits of slaves. It seems to me that from the point of view of political stability it is safer to enslave men than to give them freedom prematurely. Freedom demands preparation through moral improvement—and who would call our system of wine-farming and the dreadful prevalence of drunkenness a sound preparation for freedom? In conclusion, we have this to say to the good monarch: "Sire! history will not reproach you for the evil which you have inherited (assuming that serfdom actually is an unequivocal evil), but you will answer before God, conscience, and posterity for every harmful consequence of your own statutes."

I do not condemn Alexander's law permitting villages to gain their freedom with their masters' permission. But are many of them sufficiently rich to avail themselves of it? Will there be many prepared to surrender all they have in return for freedom?

The serfs of humane landlords are content with their lot; those who serve bad landlords are impoverished—the situation of both categories renders this law ineffectual.

III. THE EMANCIPATION MANIFESTO, 1861

By the Grace of God We, Alexander II, Emperor and Autocrat of All Russia, King of Poland, Grand Duke of Finland, etc., make known to all Our faithful subjects:

Called by Divine Providence and by the sacred right of inheritance to the throne of Our Russian ancestors, We vowed in Our heart to respond to the mission which is entrusted to Us and to surround with Our affection and Our Imperial solicitude all Our faithful subjects of every rank and condition, from the soldier who nobly defends the country to the humble artisan who works in industry; from the career official of the state to the plowman who tills the soil.

Examining the condition of classes and professions comprising the state, We became convinced that the present state legislation favors the upper and middle classes, defines their obligations, rights, and privileges, but does not equally favor the serfs, so designated because in part from old laws and in part from custom they have been hereditarily subjected to the authority of landowners, who in turn were obligated to provide for their well being. Rights of nobles have been hitherto very broad and legally ill defined, because they stem from tradition, custom, and the good will of the noblemen. In most cases this has led to the establishment of good patriarchal relations based on the sincere, just concern and benevolence on the part of the nobles, and on affectionate submission on the part of the peasants. Because of the decline of the simplicity of morals, because of an increase in the diversity of relations, because of the weakening of the direct paternal attitude of nobles toward the peasants, and because noble rights fell sometimes into the hands of people exclusively concerned with their personal interests, good relations weakened. The way was opened for an arbitrariness burdensome for the peasants and detrimental to their welfare, causing them to be indifferent to the improvement of their own existence.

These facts had already attracted the attention of Our predecessors of glorious memory, and they had adopted measures aimed at improving the conditions of the peasants; but these measures were ineffective, partly because they depended on the free, generous action of nobles, and partly because they affected only some localities, by virtue of special circumstances or as an experiment. Thus Alexander I issued a decree on free agriculturists, and the late Emperor Nicholas, Our beloved father, promulgated one dealing with the serfs. In the Western *gubernias,* inventory regulations determine the peasant land allotments and their obligations. But decrees on free agriculturists and serfs have been carried out on a limited scale only.

We thus became convinced that the problem of improving the condition of serfs was a sacred inheritance bequeathed to Us by Our predecessors, a mission which, in the course of events, Divine Providence has called upon Us to fulfill.

We have begun this task by expressing Our confidence toward the Russian nobility, which has proven on so many occasions its devotion to the Throne, and its readiness to make sacrifices for the welfare of the country.

We have left to the nobles themselves, in accordance with their own wishes, the task of preparing proposals for the new organization of peasant life—proposals that would limit their rights over the peasants, and the realization of which would inflict on them [the nobles] some material losses. Our confidence was justified. Through members of the *gubernia* committees, who had the trust of the nobles' associations, the nobility voluntarily renounced its right to own serfs. These committees, after collecting the necessary data, have formulated proposals on a new arrangement for serfs and their relationship with the nobles.

These proposals were diverse, because of the nature of the problem. They have been compared, collated, systematized, rectified and finalized in the main committee instituted for that purpose; and these new arrangements dealing with the peasants and domestics of the nobility have been examined in the Governing Council.

Having invoked Divine assistance, We have resolved to execute this task.

On the basis of the above mentioned new arrangements, the serfs will receive in time the full rights of free rural inhabitants.

The nobles, while retaining their property rights on all the lands belonging to them, grant the peasants perpetual use of their domicile in return for a specified obligation; and, to assure their livelihood as well as to guarantee fulfillment of their obligations toward the government, [the nobles] grant them a portion of arable land fixed by the said arrangements, as well as other property.

While enjoying these land allotments, the peasants are obliged, in return, to fulfill obligations to the noblemen fixed by the same arrangements. In this state, which is temporary, the peasants are temporarily bound.

At the same time, they are granted the right to purchase their domicile, and, with the consent of the nobles, they may acquire in full ownership the arable lands and other properties which are allotted them for permanent use. Following such acquisition of full ownership of land, the peasants will be freed from their obligations to the nobles for the land thus purchased and will become free peasant landowners. . . .

We leave it to the nobles to reach a friendly understanding with the peasants and to reach agreements on the extent of the land allotment and the obligations stemming from it, observing, at the same time, the established rules to guarantee the inviolability of such agreements. . . .

What legally belongs to nobles cannot be taken away from them without adequate compensation, or through their voluntary concession; it would be contrary to all justice to use the land of the nobles without assuming responsibility for it.

And now We confidently expect that the freed serfs, on the eve of a new future which is opening to them, will appreciate and recognize the considerable sacrifices which the nobility has made on their behalf.

6

Russian Culture:
A Special Brand?

Along with the development of the Russian state and the problems of serfdom, attempts to define Russian culture marked the history of the great East European nation during the eighteenth and nineteenth centuries. Like Peter the Great in the area of politics, many Russian intellectuals were attracted to patterns emerging in Western Europe. Thus they sought new science and new art styles. But other Russian thinkers rejected this elite Westernization, entirely or in part. They sought to define a distinctive Russian soul and held the West to be subversive and inferior. Elements of this anti-Western reaction emerged in the aftermath of Peter the Great's reforms. Related elements showed in the conservative attempts to defend serfdom as a valuable Russian institution.

The rise of nationalism, first in Western Europe, ironically added fuel to the Russian anti-Westerners during the nineteenth century. Nationalism offered legitimacy to appeals to special local values in England and France as in Russia; but in the Russian case, the nationalism furthered an older ambivalence about whether Russia should follow or resist the West.

The following selection was authored by an ardent Slavophile, Nikolai Danilevsky, in a multiple-edition book called *Russia and Europe,* first issued in 1869. Danilevsky asserts the special virtues of the Slavic peoples as against other Europeans and the dominance of Russia among the Slavs. Elements of his argument might seem comical: He twists history, he glosses over ongoing problems like peasant discontent after emancipation, and he ludicrously promises stability in a country almost foredoomed to revolution. But Danilevsky's views about Russian distinctiveness and Western evil were widely shared, even by people opposed to the existing tsarist regime. The complexities of his outlook were widely shared also, as he argued on the one hand for Russian superiority and a special, deliberately non-Western definition of freedom while hoping on the other hand for future Russian ability to beat the West at its own game, in science. Complexities of this sort outlived the tsarist regime as well and flourished after the Communist revolution of 1917.

And now let us turn to the Slav world, and chiefly to Russia, its only independent representative, in order to examine the results and the promises of this world, a world still only at the beginning of its cultural-historical life. We must examine it from the viewpoint of the above four foci of reference: religion, culture, politics, and socioeconomic structure, in order to elucidate what we rightfully expect as well as hope from the Slav cultural-historical type.

Religion constituted the most essential element of ancient Russian life, and at the present time, the overwhelming spiritual interest of the ordinary Russian is also involved in it; in truth, one cannot but wonder at the ignorance and the impertinence of these people who could insist (to gratify their fantasies) on the religious indifference of the Russian people.

From an objective, factual viewpoint, the Russian and the majority of Slav peoples became, with the Greeks, the chief guardians of the living tradition of religious truth, Orthodoxy, and in this way they continued the high calling, which was the destiny of Israel and Byzantium: to be the chosen people. . . .

We have already pointed to the special character of the acceptance of Christianity by Russia, not through subjection to a culturally higher Christian nation, nor through political supremacy over a nation, nor by way of an active religious propaganda—but out of an inner discontent, a dissatisfaction with paganism, and out of the unfettered search for truth. . . . The religious aspect of the cultural activity belongs to the Slav cultural type and to Russia in particular; it is its inalienable achievement, founded on the psychology of its people and on its guardianship of religious truth. . . .

Whatever the future may bring we are entitled, on the evidence of the past alone, to consider the Slavs among the most gifted families of the human race in political ability. Here we may turn our attention to the special character of this political ability and show how it manifested itself during the growth of the Russian state. The Russians do not send out colonists to create new political societies, as the Greeks did in antiquity or the English in modern times. Russia does not have colonial possessions, like Rome or like England. The Russian state from early Muscovite times on has been Russia herself, gradually, irresistibly spreading on all sides, settling neighboring nonsettled territories, and assimilating into herself and into her national boundaries foreign populations. This basic character of Russian expansion was misunderstood because of the distortion of the original Russian point of view through Europeanization, the origin of every evil in Russia. . . .

But the expansion of the state, its attainment of stability, strength, and power, constitutes only one aspect of political activity. It has still another one, consisting of the establishment of equal relationships between the citizens themselves and between them and the state, i.e., in the establishment of civil and political freedom. A people not endowed with this freedom cannot be said to possess a healthy political sense. Is the Russian people capable of freedom?

Naturally our "well-wishers" give a negative answer: some regard slavery as a natural element of the Russians, and others are afraid, or pretend to be afraid, that freedom in Russian hands must lead to all sorts of excesses and abuses. But on the basis of Russian history and with knowledge of the views and traits of the Russian people, one can only form an opinion diametrically opposed to this view—namely, that there hardly ever has existed or exists a people so capable of enduring such a large share of freedom as the Russians and so little inclined to abuse it, due to their ability and habit to obey, their respect and trust in the authorities, their lack of love for power, and their loathing of interference in matters where they do not consider themselves competent. If we look into the causes of all political troubles, we shall find their root not in the striving after freedom, but in the love for power and the vain cravings of human beings to interfere in affairs that are beyond their comprehension. . . .

This nature of the Russian people is the true reason why Russia is the only state which never had (and in all probability never will have) a political revolution, i.e., a revolution having as its aim the limitation of the power of the ruler. . . . All the troubles in Russian history were popular rebellions without political character, in the strict meaning of the word; their causes were doubt in the legitimacy of the ruling person, dissatisfaction with the serfdom that was oppressing the people to an ever greater extent than had been foreseen by the laws, and finally high-handedness and violence, which necessarily developed in Russia's borderlands, in the unceasing struggle of the Cossacks with the Tartars and other nomads. . . .

With legality in the succession of the throne secured, with civil order introduced among the Cossacks, and finally with the liberation of the peasants, all the reasons which in former times had agitated the people disappeared; and even an ordinary rebellion, going beyond the limits of a regrettable misunderstanding, has become impossible in Russia so long as the moral character of the Russian people does not change. . . .

To what degree moderation, an easygoing nature, and common sense characterize both the Russian people and Russian society has been clearly demonstrated by the events of the last years. As far as the historical memory of mankind can go back, one can scarcely find faster, more sudden changes, within the general social conditions of popular life than those that took place before our eyes. . . . The change from oppressive servitude to full freedom was sudden. . . . Even when the new authority of the communal organization was not yet established, and the people existed in critical moments without any direct close authority, public order was nowhere disturbed, and no incitements could swerve the population from giving full confidence to the government either then or later. . . . It thus became clear to all, even to those who were ill-disposed to the reform and almost expected it to result in the fall of the hated colossus, that here (as always) Russia could lean on her broad, unshakable foundations.

.   .   .

And so, what do we see? The abuses and the oppression from which Russia suffered before the reforms of the present reign were not smaller, but in many respects they were even more severe than the ones from which France suffered until the Revolution; the transformation was more radical than the one carried out by the French National Assembly. Yet, whereas the broken dam in France released a general flood of harmful antisocial instincts and passions, in Russia it could not disturb the peace, respect, and trust towards the authorities, but even emphasized them and strengthened all the foundations of the state. Are we not then entitled to assert that the Russian people and Russian society, in all social classes, are capable of accepting and enduring any amount of freedom, and that to advise its restriction can only be done by a distorted belief in self-created dangers or (what is even worse) under the influence of certain secret motives, unfair and hostile to Russian aspirations? Thus we may conclude that the Russian people, by their attitude towards the power of the state, by their ability to sacrifice to it their own personal interests, and by their attitude towards the use of political and civil freedom, are gifted with wonderful political sense.

In the socio-economic sphere, Russia is the only large state which has solid ground under its feet, in which there are no landless masses, and in which, consequently, the social edifice does not rest on the misery of the majority of the citizens and on the insecurity of their situation. In Russia only there cannot and does not exist any contradiction between political and economic ideals. This contradiction threatens disaster to European life, a life which has embarked on its historical voyage in the dangerous seas between the Charybdis of Caesarism or military despotism and the Scylla of social revolution. The factors that give such superiority to the Russian social structure over the European, and give it an unshakable stability, are the peasant's land and its common ownership. On this health of Russia's socio-economic structure we found our hope for the great socio-economic significance of the Slav cultural-historical type. This type has been able for the first time to create a just and normal system of human activity, which embraces not only human relations in the moral and political sphere, but also man's mastery of nature, which is a means of satisfying human needs and requirements. Thus it establishes not only formal equality in the relations between citizens, but a real and concrete equality.

However, as regards the prominent place of the Slav cultural-historical type in the field of culture proper, one must admit that so far the Russian and other Slav achievements in the sciences and in the arts are insignificant in comparison with the accomplishments of the two great cultural types, the Greek and the European. . . .

Scientific and artistic activity can thrive only under conditions of leisure, of an overflow of forces that remain free from daily toil. Could much leisure be left over among Russians and Slavs? . . . All these considerations fully answer, it seems to me, the question why until now Russia and the other Slav countries could not occupy a respected position in purely cultural activites. . . . But indications of these aptitudes, of these spiritual forces, which are necessary for brilliant achievements in the fields of science and art are now indisputably present among the Slav peoples in spite of all the unfavorable conditions of their life; and, consequently, we are justified in expecting that with a change in these conditions, these peoples will bring forth remarkable creations. . . .

The Slav cultural type has already produced enough examples of artistic and, to a lesser degree, scientific achievements to allow us to conclude that it has attained a significant degree of development in these fields. The relative youth of the race and the concentration of all its forces upon other, more urgent types of activity have not, until now, given the Slavs the opportunity of acquiring cultural significance, in the exact meaning of the phrase. This should not embarrass us; rather, it points to the right path in our development. As long as there is no strong foundation, we cannot and we must not think of the erection of a durable edifice; we can only set up temporary buildings, which cannot be expected to display the talents of the builder in every respect. The political independence of the race is the indispensable foundation of culture, and consequently all the Slav forces must be directed towards this goal. Independence is indispensable . . . [for] without the consciousness of Slav racial unity, as distinct from other races, an independent culture is impossible. . . .

The requisite preliminary achievement of political independence has still another importance in the cultural as well as in all other spheres: the struggle against the Germano-Roman world (without which Slav independence is impossible) will help to eradicate the cancer of imitativeness and the servile attitude towards the West, which through unfavorable conditions has eaten its way into the Slav body and soul. Only now has the historical moment for this cultural development arrived: only with the emancipation of the peasantry can the period of Russian cultural life begin, and her purely state period of life (which consisted in leading the people from tribal will to civil liberty) end. But first, as a *sine qua non* condition of success, strong and powerful Russia has to face the difficult task of liberating her racial brothers; for this struggle, she must steel them and herself in the spirit of independence and Pan-Slav consciousness.

7

Matteo Ricci on Ming China

In an earlier selection (in Volume I) we saw that when Marco Polo traveled in China during the thirteenth century, he saw considerable evidence of economic vitality; this was also true for Matteo Ricci (1552–1610), the Jesuit missionary who was assigned to China three centuries later. As in the time of the Sung (960–1279), the period of 1500 to 1800 in Chinese history—the second half of the Ming dynasty (1368–1644) and the first half of Ching rule (1644–1911)—was a time of vigorous population growth and rapid commercial expansion. Crop yields increased and new land was brought under cultivation. Urbanization proceeded rapidly. The trade in bulk commodities such as salt, grain, cotton, timber, and iron flourished. In addition, this was a time of growth in China's maritime commerce with Southeast Asia and more distant regions.

Matteo Ricci was well suited to observe many of these trends in Chinese life; he lived and traveled in the country from 1583 until his death in 1610. An extraordinarily learned scholar, Ricci became fluent in Chinese in order to advance the cause of his faith. Ultimately his great learning so impressed the emperor that Ricci was made a court mathematician and astronomer.

Ricci's journals, excerpts from which follow, were published in Rome in 1615. They were the first detailed report on China by a European since Marco Polo. What did the priest find significant about China? In what ways does he compare China to Europe? How does his account compare with Marco Polo's (see Volume I, selection 23)? Compare Ricci's observations on China with those

From Louis J. Gallagher, S.J., trans., *China in the Sixteenth Century: The Journals of Matthew Ricci: 1583–1610* (New York: Random House, 1953), pp. 10–18, 20–21, 23, 268–70. Copyright © 1953 by Random House. Reprinted by permission.

of Monserrate on India (selection 10) and Busbecq on the Ottoman Turks (selection 12).

Due to the great extent of this country north and south as well as east and west, it can be safely asserted that nowhere else in the world is found such a variety of plant and animal life within the confines of a single kingdom. The wide range of climatic conditions in China gives rise to great diversity of vegetable products, some of which are most readily grown in tropical countries, others in arctic, and others again in the temperate zones. The Chinese themselves, in their geographies, give us detailed accounts of the fertility of the various provinces and of the variety of their products. . . . Generally speaking, it may be said with truth that all of these writers are correct when they say that everything which the people used for their well-being and sustenance, whether it be for food or clothing or even delicacies and superfluities, is abundantly produced within the borders of the kingdom and not imported from foreign climes. I would even venture to say that practically everything which is grown in Europe is likewise found in China. If not, then what is missing here is abundantly supplied by various other products unknown to Europeans. To begin with, the soil of China supplies its people with every species of grain—barley, millet, winter wheat, and similar grains.

Rice, which is the staple article of Chinese diet, is produced here in far greater abundance than in Europe. Vegetables, especially beans, and the like, all of which are used not only as food for the people but also as fodder for cattle and beasts of burden, are grown in unlimited variety. The Chinese harvest two and sometimes three crops of such plants every year, owing not only to the fertility of the soil and the mildness of the climate but in great measure to the industry of the people. With the exception of olives and almonds, all the principal fruits known in Europe grow also in China. . . .

Much the same can be said of the variety and quality of table vegetables and the cultivation of garden herbs, all of which the Chinese use in far greater quantities than is common among the people of Europe. In fact, there are many among the common folk who live entirely upon a vegetable diet through the whole course of their lives, either because they are forced to do so by reason of poverty or because they embrace this course of life for some religious motive. . . .

This country is so thoroughly covered by an intersecting network of rivers and canals that it is possible to travel almost anywhere by water. Hence, an almost incredible number of boats of every variety pass hither and thither. Indeed there are so many of them that one of the writers of our day does not hesitate to affirm that there are as many people living on the water as there are dwellers on land. This may sound like an exaggeration and yet it all but expresses the truth, as it would seem, if one were to travel here only by water. In my opinion it might be said with greater truth and without fear of exaggeration, that there are as many boats in this kingdom as can be counted up in all the rest of the world.

This statement is true if we restrict our count to the number of boats sailing on fresh water. As to their ships that pass out into the sea, they are very few and not to be compared with ours either in number or in structure. . . .

All of the known metals without exception are to be found in China. Besides brass and ordinary copper alloys, the Chinese manufacture another metal which is an imitation silver but which costs no more than yellow brass. From molten iron they fashion many more articles than we do, for example, cauldrons, pots, bells, gongs, mortars, gratings, furnaces, martial weapons, instruments of torture, and a great number of other things, all but equal in workmanship to our own metalcraft. . . . The ordinary tableware of the Chinese is clay pottery. It is not quite clear to me why it is called porcelain in the West. There is nothing like it in European pottery either from the standpoint of the material itself or its thin and fragile construction. The finest specimens of porcelain are made from clay found in the province of Kiam, and these are shipped not only to every part of China but even to the remotest corners of Europe where they are highly prized by those who appreciate elegance at their banquets rather than pompous display. This porcelain, too, will bear the heat of hot foods without cracking and, what is more to be wondered at, if it is broken and sewed with a brass wire it will hold liquids without any leakage. . . .

Two or three things are entirely unknown to Europeans of which I must give a brief account. First, there is a certain bush from the leaves of which is decocted that celebrated drink, known to the Chinese, the Japanese, and to their neighbors as tea. Its use cannot be of long duration among the Chinese, as no ideography in their old books designates this particular drink and their writing characters are all ancient. Indeed it might be that this same plant can be found in our own fields. Here they gather its leaves in the springtime and place them in a shady place to dry, and from the dried leaves they brew a drink which they use at meals and which is served to friends when they come to visit. On such occasions it is served continually as long as they remain together engaged in conversation. This beverage is sipped rather than drunk and it is always taken hot. It is not unpleasant to the taste, being somewhat bitter, and it is usually considered to be wholesome even if taken frequently. . . .

Finally we should say something about the saltpeter, which is quite plentiful but which is not used extensively in the preparation of gunpowder, because the Chinese are not expert in the use of guns and artillery and make but little use of these in warfare. Saltpeter, however, is used in lavish quantities in making fireworks for display at public games and on festival days. The Chinese take great pleasure in such exhibitions and make them the chief attraction of all their festivities. Their skill in the manufacture of fireworks is really extraordinary, and there is scarcely anything which they cannot cleverly imitate with them. They are especially adept in reproducing battles and in making rotating spheres of fire, fiery trees, fruit, and the like, and they seem to have no regard for expense where fireworks are concerned. When I was in Nankin I witnessed a pyrotechnic display for the celebration of the first month of the year, which is their great festival, and on this occasion I calculated that they consumed enough powder to carry on a sizable war for a number of years.

. . .

The art of printing was practiced in China at a date somewhat earlier than that assigned to the beginning of printing in Europe, which was about 1405. It is quite certain that the Chinese knew the art of printing at least five centuries ago, and some of them assert that printing was known to their people before the beginning of the Christian era, about 50 B.C. . . .

Their method of making printed books is quite ingenious. The text is written in ink, with a brush made of very fine hair, on a sheet of paper which is inverted and pasted on a wooden tablet. When the paper has become thoroughly dry, its surface is scraped off quickly and with great skill, until nothing but a fine tissue bearing the characters remains on the wooden tablet. Then, with a steel graver, the workman cuts away the surface following the outlines of the characters until these alone stand out in low relief. From such a block a skilled printer can make copies with incredible speed, turning out as many as fifteen hundred copies in a single day. Chinese printers are so skilled in engraving these blocks, that no more time is consumed in making one of them than would be required by one of our printers in setting up a form of type and making the necessary corrections. . . .

The simplicity of Chinese printing is what accounts for the exceedingly large number of books in circulation here and the ridiculously low prices at which they are sold. Such facts as these would scarcely be believed by one who had not witnessed them. . . .

This land possesses few instruments for measuring time and in those instruments which they have, it is measured either by water or by fire. The instruments run by water are fashioned like huge waterpots. In those which are operated by fire, time is measured by an odoriferous ash, somewhat in imitation of our reversible grates through which ashes are filtered. A few instruments are made with wheels and are operated by a kind of bucket wheel in which sand is employed instead of water, but all of them fall short of the perfection of our instruments, are subject to many errors, and are inaccurate in the measurement of time. Concerning sundials, they know that these take their name from the equator but they have not learned how to set them up with relation to the variations of latitude.

. . .

This metropolitan city is called Nankin, but the Portuguese who know this wonderful city by reputation from the inhabitants of the Province of Fuquian, call the city Lankin, because in that province the letter N is generally replaced by an L. Being the residential seat of a district Governor, it has another name and is commonly called Intiensu. In the judgment of the Chinese this city surpasses all other cities in the world in beauty and in grandeur, and in this respect there are probably very few others superior or equal to it. It is literally filled with palaces and temples and towers and bridges, and these are scarcely surpassed by similar structures in Europe. In some respects, it surpasses our European cities. The climate is mild and the soil is fertile. There is a gaiety of spirit among the people, who are well mannered and nicely spoken, and the dense population is made up of all classes; of hoi-polloi, of the lettered aristocracy and the Magistrates. These latter are equal in number and in dignity to those of Pekin, but due to the fact that the king does not reside here, the local Magistrates are not rated as equal with those of the Capital City. Yet in the whole kingdom of China and in all bordering countries, Nankin is rated as the first city. It is surrounded by three circles of walls. The first and innermost of these, and also the most decorative, contains the palace of the king. The palace, in turn, is surrounded by a triple wall of arches, and of circling moats, filled with circulating water. This palace wall is about four or five Italian miles in length. Considering the whole structure, rather than any particular feature of it, there is probably no king in the world with a palace surpassing this one. The second wall, encircling the inner one, which contains the king's palace, encloses the greater and the more important part of the city. It has twelve gates, which are covered with iron plates and fortified by cannon from within. This high wall is almost eighteen Italian miles in circumference. The third and exterior wall is not continuous. At places that were judged to be danger spots, they scientifically added to natural fortifications. It is difficult to determine the full length of the circuit of this particular wall. The natives here tell a story of two men who started from opposite sides of the city, riding on horses toward each other, and it took a whole day before they came together.

This will afford some idea of the prodigious expanse of this city, and being circular in form, it contains more space within it than if it were of any other design. Inside of this wall there are expansive parks, mountains and forests interspersed with lakes, and yet the inhabited section of the city is by far the largest part of it. One would scarcely believe it, had he not seen it, but the military guard of the city alone is forty thousand soldiers. This place is situated about thirty-two degrees longitude and figuring its latitude mathematically, it stands almost in the center of the kingdom. The river mentioned flows along the west side of the city. One might doubt whether its commercial value is more of an asset to the city than its beauty is an ornament. It washes the city bank and at certain places flows into the town, forming canals on which large boats may enter. These canals were dug by the ancestors of the present inhabitants, in hard and long enduring labor.

This city was once the capital of the entire realm and the ancient abode of kings through many centuries, and though the king changed his residence to Pekin, in the north, . . . Nankin lost none of its splendor or of its reputation. Or if perchance it did, that fact would only prove that it was formerly more wonderful than it is at present. . . .

8

China and the West in the Nineteenth Century: A Dispute over Opium

Although European merchants and missionaries had been active in China since the time of Matteo Ricci, the West had little impact on China until the nineteenth century. The key event in opening China to Western influences was the 1839–42 conflict between the British and the Chinese known as the Opium War.

The Chinese had used opium medicinally since Tang times. However, the widespread smoking of the drug—leading to addiction—only developed at the end of the eighteenth century. This was due largely to the actions of the British East India Company, which sent huge quantities of opium to China in exchange for tea. Despite the opposition of the Chinese government, the opium trade greatly accelerated during the 1820s and 1830s.

In 1839 the Emperor sent Lin Tse-hsu, a highly regarded official, to Canton with instructions to end the trade in opium. It was in these circumstances that Lin addressed the letter below to Queen Victoria. He also had a large quantity of the drug seized and publicly destroyed. The British responded by attacking Canton and several other ports. Completely overwhelmed, the Chinese were compelled to surrender in 1842. Under the subsequent Treaty of Nanking, the Chinese withdrew their objection to the opium trade and made other concessions to the British. For the West, the door to China was now open.

What reasons does Commissioner Lin give for opposing the sale of opium? What does his letter reveal about the thinking of the Chinese elite? How does he see China in relation to Great Britain? Compare his response to the West

From *The Chinese Repository*, Vol. VIII (February 1840), pp. 497–503.

with those of the intellectuals in India, Japan, and the Middle East found later in this volume.

Lin, high imperial commissioner, a president of the Board of War, viceroy of the two Kiang provinces, &c., Tang, a president of the Board of War, viceroy of the two Kwang provinces, &c., and E, a vice-president of the Board of War, lieut.-governor of Kwang-tung, &c., hereby conjointly address this public dispatch to the queen of England for the purpose of giving her clear and distinct information (on the state of affairs) &c.

It is only our high and mighty emperor, who alike supports and cherishes those of the Inner Land, and those from beyond the seas—who looks upon all mankind with equal benevolence—who, if a source of profit exists anywhere, diffuses it over the whole world—who, if the tree of evil takes root anywhere, plucks it up for the benefit of all nations:—who, in a word, hath implanted in his breast that heart (by which beneficent nature herself) governs the heavens and the earth! You, the queen of your honorable nation, sit upon a throne occupied through successive generations by pre-decessors, all of whom have been styled respectful and obedient. Looking over the public documents accompanying the tribute sent (by your predecessors) on various oc-casions, we find the following:—"All the people of my (i.e., the king of England's) country, arriving at the Central Land for purposes of trade, have to feel grateful to the great emperor for the most perfect justice, for the kindest treatment," and other words to that effect. Delighted did we feel that the kings of your honorable nation so clearly understood the great principles of propriety, and were so deeply grateful for the heavenly goodness (of our emperor):—therefore, it was that we of the heavenly dynasty nourished and cherished your people from afar, and bestowed upon them redoubled proofs of our urbanity and kindness. It is merely from these circumstances, that your country—de-riving immense advantage from its commercial intercourse with us, which has endured now two hundred years—has become the rich and flourishing kingdom that it is said to be!

But, during the commercial intercourse which has existed so long, among the numerous foreign merchants resorting hither, are wheat and tares, good and bad; and of these latter are some, who, by means of introducing opium by stealth, have seduced our Chinese people, and caused every province of the land to overflow with that poison. These then know merely to advantage themselves, they care not about injuring others! This is a principle which heaven's Providence repugnates; and which mankind conjointly look upon with abhorrence! Moreover, the great emperor hearing of it, actually quivered with indignation, and especially dispatched me, the commissioner, to Canton, that in conjunction with the viceroy and lieut.-governor of the province, means might be taken for its suppression! . . .

We find that your country is distant from us about sixty or seventy thousand [Chinese] miles, that your foreign ships come hither striving the one with the other for our trade, and for the simple reason of their strong desire to reap a profit. Now, out of the wealth of our Inner Land, if we take a part to bestow upon foreigners from afar, it follows, that the immense wealth which the said foreigners amass, ought properly speaking to be portion of our own native Chinese people. By what principle of reason then, should these foreigners send in return a poisonous drug, which involves in destruction those very natives of China? Without meaning to say that the foreigners harbor such destructive intentions in their hearts, we yet positively assert that from their inordinate thirst after gain, they are perfectly careless about the injuries they inflict upon us! And such being the case, we should like to ask what has become of that conscience which heaven has implanted in the breasts of all men?

We have heard that in your own country opium is prohibited with the utmost strictness and severity:—this is a strong proof that you know full well how hurtful it is to mankind. Since then you do not permit it to injure your own country, you ought not to have the injurious drug transferred to another country, and above all others, how much less to the Inner Land! Of the products which China exports to your foreign countries, there is not one which is not beneficial to mankind in some shape or other. There are those which serve for food, those which are useful, and those which are calculated for re-sale;—but all are beneficial. Has China (we should like to ask) ever yet sent forth a noxious article from its soil? Not to speak of our tea and rhubarb, things which your foreign countries could not exist a single day without, if we of the Central Land were to grudge you what is beneficial, and not to compassionate [*sic*] your wants, then wherewithal could you foreigners manage to exist? And further, as regards your woolens, camlets, and longells, were it not that you get supplied with our native raw silk, you could not get these manufactured! If China were to grudge you those things which yield a profit, how could you foreigners scheme after any profit at all? Our other articles of food, such as sugar, ginger, cinnamon, &c., and our other articles for use, such as silk piece-goods, chinaware, &c., are all so many necessaries of life to you; how can we reckon up their number! On the other hand, the things that come from your foreign countries are only calculated to make presents of, or serve for mere amusement. It is quite the same to us if we have them, or if we have them not. If then these are of no material consequence to us of the Inner Land, what difficulty would there be in prohibiting and shutting our market against them? It is only that our heavenly dynasty most freely permits you to take off her tea, silk, and other commodities, and convey them for consumption everywhere, without the slightest stint or grudge, for no other reason, but that where a profit exists, we wish that it be diffused abroad for the benefit of all the earth!

Your honorable nation takes away the products of our central land, and not only do you thereby obtain food and support for yourselves, but moreover, by re-selling these products to other countries you reap a threefold profit. Now if you would only not sell opium, this threefold profit would be secured to you: how can you possibly consent to forgo it for a drug that is hurtful to men, and an unbridled craving after gain that seems to know no bounds! Let us suppose that foreigners came from another country, and brought opium into England, and seduced the people of your country to smoke it, would not you, the sovereign of the said country, look upon such a procedure with anger, and in your just indignation endeavor to get rid of it? Now we have always heard that your highness possesses a most kind and benevolent heart, surely then you are incapable of doing or causing to be done unto another, that which you should not wish another to do unto you! We have at the same time heard that your ships which come to Canton do each and every of them carry a document granted by your highness' self, on which are written these words "you shall not be permitted to carry contraband goods;" (the ship's register?) this shows that the laws of your highness are in their origin both distinct and severe, and we can only suppose that because the ships coming here have been very numerous, due attention has not been given to search and examine; and for this reason it is that we now address you this public document, that you may clearly know how stern and severe are the laws of the central dynasty, and most certainly you will cause that they be not again rashly violated!

Moreover, we have heard that in London the metropolis where you dwell, as also in Scotland, Ireland, and other such places, no opium whatever is produced. It is only in sundry parts of your colonial kingdom of Hindostan, such as Bengal, Madras, Bombay, Patna, Malwa, Benares, Malacca, and other places where the very hills are covered with the opium plant, where tanks are made for the preparing of the drug; month by month, and year by year, the volume of the poison increases, its unclean stench ascends upwards, until heaven itself grows angry, and the very gods thereat get indignant! You, the queen of the said honorable nation, ought immediately to have the plant in those parts plucked up by the very root! Cause the land there to be hoed up afresh, sow in its stead the five grains, and if any man dare again to plant in these grounds a single poppy, visit his crime with the most severe punishment. By a truly benevolent system of government such as this, will you indeed reap advantage, and do away with a source of evil. Heaven must support you, and the gods will crown you with felicity! This will get for yourself the blessing of long life, and from this will proceed the security and stability of your descendants! . . .

Suppose the subject of another country were to come to England to trade, he would certainly be required to comply with the laws of England, then how much more does this apply to us of the celestial empire! Now it is a fixed statute of this empire, that any native Chinese who sells opium is punishable with death, and even he who merely smokes it, must not less die. Pause and reflect for a moment: if you foreigners did not bring the opium hither, where should our Chinese people get it to re-sell? It is you foreigners who involve our simple natives in the pit of death, and are they alone to be permitted to escape alive? If so much as one of those deprive one of our people of his life, he must forfeit his life in requital for that which he has taken:—how much more does this apply to him who by means of opium destroys his fellow-men? Does the havoc which he commits stop with a single life? Therefore it is that those foreigners who now import opium into the Central Land are condemned to be beheaded and strangled by the new statute, and this explains what we said at the beginning about plucking up the tree of evil, wherever it takes root, for the benefit of all nations. . . .

Our celestial empire rules over ten thousand kingdoms! Most surely do we possess a measure of godlike majesty which ye cannot fathom! Still we cannot bear to slay or exterminate without previous warning, and it is for this reason that we now clearly make known to you the fixed laws of our land. If the foreign merchants of your said honorable nation desire to continue their commercial intercourse, they then must tremblingly obey our recorded statutes, they must cut off for ever the source from which the opium flows, and on no account make an experiment of our laws in their own persons! Let then your highness punish those of your subjects who may be criminal, do not endeavor to screen or conceal them, and thus you will secure peace and quietness to your possessions, thus will you more than ever display a proper sense of respect and obedience, and thus may we unitedly enjoy the common blessings of peace and happiness. What greater joy! What more complete felicity than this!

Let your highness immediately, upon the receipt of this communication, inform us promptly of the state of matters, and of the measure you are pursuing utterly to put a stop to the opium evil. Please let your reply be speedy. Do not on any account make excuses or procrastinate. A most important communication.

9

Japan and the West in the Nineteenth Century: The Views of a Japanese Educator

From the seventeenth century to the middle of the nineteenth century the regime of the Tokugawa shoguns kept Japan in near total isolation from the rest of the world. In 1854, however, the policy of a "closed country" collapsed under the threat of attack by ships from the U.S. Navy. Acceding to the demands of Commodore Matthew Perry, the Japanese opened relations with the United States. Similar agreements with the European great powers soon followed. Like China, Japan was now open to massive Western influence.

The treaties of the 1850s triggered far-reaching changes in Japanese life. Widespread protest against the new "open country" policy of the shoguns culminated in the overthrow of the Tokugawa regime in 1868, an event known as the Meiji Restoration. Then, in an amazing turn of events, the samurai who had led in founding the new Meiji regime immediately embarked on a course that would transform Japan into a modern country, one able to meet the Western powers on equal terms.

The great changes that reshaped nineteenth-century Japan are vividly illustrated in the writings of Yukichi Fukuzawa (1834–1901), the famous educator and advocate of Western learning. Beginning in 1860, he made several trips to the United States and Europe. His many books and newspaper articles about life in the West had a wide audience in Japan.

In the following excerpts from his *Autobiography,* published in 1899, Fukuzawa recalls his first visits to the West and sums up his ideas on education.

From Eiichi Kiyooka, trans., *The Autobiography of Yukichi Fukuzawa* (New York: Columbia University Press, 1966), pp. 110–17, 134–35, 214–17. Copyright © 1966 by Columbia University Press. Reprinted by permission.

What impressed him about the West? Note his attitude toward China and the rest of Asia. How does his response to the West compare to that of Commissioner Lin (selection 8)? How do you explain in the differences?

． ． ．

I am willing to admit my pride in this accomplishment for Japan. The facts are these: It was not until the sixth year of Kaei (1853) that a steamship was seen for the first time; it was only in the second year of Ansei (1855) that we began to study navigation from the Dutch in Nagasaki; by 1860, the science was sufficiently understood to enable us to sail a ship across the Pacific. This means that about seven years after the first sight of a steamship, after only about five years of practice, the Japanese people made a trans-Pacific crossing without help from foreign experts. I think we can without undue pride boast before the world of this courage and skill. . . .

As I consider all the other peoples of the Orient as they exist today, I feel convinced that there is no other nation which has the ability or the courage to navigate a steamship across the Pacific after a period of five years of experience in navigation and engineering. Not only in the Orient would this feat stand as an act of unprecedented skill and daring. Even Peter the Great of Russia, who went to Holland to study navigation, with all his attainments could not have equalled this feat of the Japanese. Without doubt, the famous emperor was a man of genius, but his people did not respond to his leadership in the practice of science as did our Japanese in this great adventure.

As soon as our ship came into the port of San Francisco, we were greeted by many important personages who came on board from all over the country. Along the shores thousands of people were lined up to see the strange newcomers.

． ． ．

Our hosts in San Francisco were very considerate in showing us examples of modern industry. There was as yet no railway laid to the city, nor was there any electric light in use. But the telegraph system and also Galvani's electroplating were already in use. Then we were taken to a sugar refinery and had the principle of the operation explained to us quite minutely. I am sure that our hosts thought they were showing us something entirely new, naturally looking for our surprise at each new device of modern engineering. But on the contrary, there was really nothing new, at least to me. I knew the principle of the telegraphy even if I had not seen the actual machine before; I knew that sugar was bleached by straining the solution with bone-black, and that in boiling down the solution, the vacuum was used to better effect than heat. I had been studying nothing else but such scientific principles ever since I had entered Ogata's school.

Rather, I was surprised by entirely different things in American life. First of all, there seemed to be an enormous waste of iron everywhere. In garbage piles, on the seashores—everywhere—I found lying old oil tins, empty cans, and broken tools. This was remarkable to us, for in Yedo, after a fire, there would appear a swarm of people looking for nails in the ashes.

Then too, I was surprised at the high cost of daily commodities in California. We had to pay a half-dollar for a bottle of oysters, and there were only twenty or thirty in the bottle at that. In Japan the price of so many would be only a cent or two.

Things social, political, and economic proved most inexplicable. One day, on a sudden thought, I asked a gentleman where the descendants of George Washington might be. He replied, "I think there is a woman who is directly descended from Washington. I don't know where she is now, but I think I have heard she is married." His answer was so very casual that it shocked me.

Of course, I knew that America was a republic with a new president every four years, but I could not help feeling that the family of Washington would be revered above all other families. My reasoning was based on the reverence in Japan for the founders of the great lines of rulers—like that for Ieyasu of the Tokugawa family of Shōguns, really deified in the popular mind. So I remember the astonishment I felt at receiving this indifferent answer about the Washington family. As for scientific inventions and industrial machinery, there was no great novelty in them for me. It was rather in matters of life and social custom and ways of thinking that I found myself at a loss in America. . . .

Before we sailed, the interpreter, Nakahama, and I each bought a copy of Webster's dictionary. This, I know, was the very first importation of Webster's into Japan. Once I had secured this valuable work, I felt no disappointment on leaving the new world and returning home again.

. . .

When I asked a gentleman [in England] what the "election law" was and what kind of a bureau the Parliament really was, he simply replied with a smile, meaning I suppose that no intelligent person was expected to ask such a question. But these were the things most difficult of all for me to understand. In this connection, I learned that there were bands of men called political parties—the Liberals and the Conservatives—who were always fighting against each other in the government.

For some time it was beyond my comprehension to understand what they were fighting for, and what was meant, anyway, by "fighting" in peace time. "This man and that man are enemies in the House," they would tell me. But these "enemies" were to be seen at the same table, eating and drinking with each other. I felt as if I could not make much out of this. It took me a long time, with some tedious thinking, before I could gather a general notion of these separate mysterious facts. In some of the more complicated matters, I might achieve an understanding five or ten days after they were explained to me. But all in all, I learned much from this initial tour of Europe.

. . .

In my interpretation of education, I try to be guided by the laws of nature and I try to co-ordinate all the physical actions of human beings by the very simple laws of "number and reason." In spiritual or moral training, I regard the human being as the most sacred and responsible of all orders, unable in reason to do anything base. Therefore, in self-respect, a man cannot change his sense of humanity, his justice, his loyalty or anything belonging to his manhood even when driven by circumstances to do so. In short, my creed is that a man should find his faith in independence and self-respect.

From my own observations in both Occidental and Oriental civilizations, I find that each has certain strong points and weak points bound up in its moral teachings and scientific theories. But when I compare the two in a general way as to wealth, armament, and the greatest happiness for the greatest number, I have to put the Orient below the

Occident. Granted that a nation's destiny depends upon the education of its people, there must be some fundamental differences in the education of Western and Eastern peoples.

In the education of the East, so often saturated with Confucian teaching, I find two things lacking; that is to say, a lack of studies in number and reason in material culture, and a lack of the idea of independence in spiritual culture. But in the West I think I see why their statesmen are successful in managing their national affairs, and the businessmen in theirs, and the people generally ardent in their patriotism and happy in their family circles.

I regret that in our country I have to acknowledge that people are not formed on these two principles, though I believe no one can escape the laws of number and reason, nor can anyone depend on anything but the doctrine of independence as long as nations are to exist and mankind is to thrive. Japan could not assert herself among the great nations of the world without full recognition and practice of these two principles. And I reasoned that Chinese philosophy as the root of education was responsible for our obvious shortcomings.

With this as the fundamental theory of education, I began and, though it was impossible to institute specialized courses because of lack of funds, I did what I could in organizing the instructions on the principles of number and reason. And I took every opportunity in public speech, in writing, and in casual conversations, to advocate my doctrine of independence. Also I tried in many ways to demonstrate the theory in my actual life. During my endeavor I came to believe less than ever in the old Chinese teachings. . . .

The true reason of my opposing the Chinese teaching with such vigor is my belief that in this age of transition, if this retrogressive doctrine remains at all in our young men's minds, the new civilization cannot give its full benefit to this country. In my determination to save our coming generation, I was prepared even to face single-handed the Chinese scholars of the country as a whole.

Gradually the new education was showing its results among the younger generation; yet men of middle age or past, who held responsible positions, were for the most part uninformed as to the true spirit of Western culture, and whenever they had to make decisions, they turned invariably to their Chinese sources for guidance. And so, again and again I had to rise up and denounce the all-important Chinese influence before this weighty opposition. It was not altogether a safe road for my reckless spirit to follow.

10

Akbar's India: The View of a Jesuit Missionary

In 1526 Babur the Tiger (1483–1530), heir to a long line of Turkish and Mongol warriors, overthrew the last of the Delhi sultans and founded a new Muslim state in north India, the Mughal Empire. The new dynasty reached its high point under Babur's grandson, Akbar (r. 1556–1605), who controlled most of the northern subcontinent. Akbar's empire was probably the strongest in the history of India. Indeed, he may have been the most powerful ruler in the world at the end of the sixteenth century.

Akbar's accomplishments were many. He conquered huge stretches of territory and governed them effectively, ending centuries of political fragmentation and instability. His government's efficiency contributed to economic growth and the expansion of trade, and this seems to have benefited many of the peasants. Born a Muslim, Akbar attempted to bring about a reconciliation between the adherents of his faith and the Hindu majority. In addition, the Mughal ruler was a great patron of architecture and painting, both of which flourished during his reign.

Ever curious about religious ideas, Akbar enjoyed the company of Sufi mystics, Hindu and Jain holy men, Parsis, Sikhs, and Christian missionaries. From 1580 to 1582 one of his visitors at court was the Portuguese Jesuit, Father Monserrate. Below are passages from the priest's account of the Mughal ruler and his empire. Although written during the 1580s, it was only published in this century.

From Father Monserrate, S. J., *Commentary on his Journey to the Court of Akbar from 1580 to 1583*, edited by S. N. Banjerjee, translated by J. S. Hoyland (London: Oxford University Press, 1922), pp. 196–202, 207, 213–14, 219.

What do we learn about Akbar and his policies from Monserrate? Note the priest's observations about taxation, banking, agriculture, and urban life. Does Monserrate reveal any prejudice? How does Monserrate's description of India compare with those of Busbecq on the Ottoman Turks and Ricci on Ming China (selections 12 and 7, respectively)?

This Prince [Akbar] is of a stature and of a type of countenance well-fitted to his royal dignity, so that one could easily recognise, even at the first glance, that he is the King. He has broad shoulders, somewhat bandy legs well-suited for horsemanship, and a light-brown complexion. He carries his head bent towards the right shoulder. His forehead is broad and open, his eyes so bright and flashing that they seem like a sea shimmering in the sunlight. His eyelashes are very long, as also are those of the . . . [Scythians, Chinese, Japanese,] and most other north-Asiatic races. His eyebrows are not strongly marked. His nose is straight and small, though not insignificant. His nostrils are widely opened, as though in derision. Between the left nostril and the upper lip there is a mole. He shaves his beard, but wears a moustache like that of a Turkish youth who has not yet attained to manhood (for on reaching manhood they begin to affect a beard). Contrary to the custom of his race he does not cut his hair; nor does he wear a hat, but a turban, into which he gathers up his hair. He does this, they say, as a concession to Indian usages, and to please his Indian subjects. He limps in his left leg, though indeed he has never received any injury there. His body is exceedingly well-built and is neither too thin nor too stout. He is sturdy, hearty and robust. When he laughs, his face becomes almost distorted. His expression is tranquil, serene and open, full also of dignity, and when he is angry, of awful majesty. When the priests first saw him he was thirty-eight years of age. It is hard to exaggerate how accessible he makes himself to all who wish audience of him. For he creates an opportunity almost every day for any of the common people or of the nobles to see him and converse with him; and he endeavours to show himself pleasant-spoken and affable rather than severe toward all who come to speak with him. It is very remarkable how great an effect this courtesy and affability has in attaching to him the minds of his subjects. For in spite of his very heterodox attitude towards the religion of Muhammad, and in spite also of the fact that Musalmans regard such an attitude as an unforgivable offence, . . . Akbar . . . has not yet been assassinated. He has an acute insight, and shows much wise foresight both in avoiding dangers and in seizing favourable opportunities for carrying out his designs. Yet all these fine qualities both of body and mind lose the greater part of their splendour because the lustre of the True Faith is lacking.

[Akbar] . . . is greatly devoted to hunting, though not equally so to hawking. As he is of a somewhat morose disposition, he amuses himself with various games. These games afford also a public spectacle to the nobility and the common people, who indeed are very fond of such spectacles. They are the following:—Polo, elephant-fighting, buffalo-fighting, stag-fighting and cock-fighting, boxing contests, battles of gladiators, and the flying of tumbler-pigeons. He is also very fond of strange birds, and indeed of any novel object. He amuses himself with singing, concerts, dances, conjurer's tricks, and the jokes of his jesters, of whom he makes much. However, although he may seem at such times to be at leisure and to have laid aside public affairs, he does not cease to revolve in his mind the heavy cares of state. He is especially remarkable for his love of keeping great crowds of people around him and in his sight; and thus it comes about that his court is always thronged with multitudes of men of every type, though especially with the nobles, whom he commands to come from their provinces and reside at court for a certain period each year. When he goes outside the palace, he is surrounded and followed by these nobles and a strong body-guard. They have to go on foot until he gives them a nod to indicate that they may mount. All this adds greatly to the wonderful majesty and greatness of the royal court. . . .

The splendour of his palaces approaches closely to that of the royal dwellings of Europe. They are magnificently built, from foundation to cornice, of hewn stone, and are decorated both with painting and carving. Unlike the palaces built by other Indian kings, they are lofty; for an Indian palace is generally as low and humble as an idol-temple. Their total circuit is so large that it easily embraces four great royal dwellings, of which the King's own palace is the largest and the finest. The second palace belongs to the queens, and the third to the royal princes, whilst the fourth is used as a store house and magazine. The roofs of these palaces are not tiled, but are dome-shaped, being protected from the weather on the outside by solid plaster covering the stone slabs. This forms a roof absolutely impervious to moisture. The palaces are decorated also with many pinnacles, supported on four columns, each of which forms a small covered portico. Not a little is added to the beauty of the palaces by charming pigeon-cotes, partly covered with rough-cast, and partly showing walls built of small blue and white bricks. The pigeons are cared for by eunuchs and servant-maids. Their evolutions are controlled at will, when they are flying, by means of certain signals, just as those of well-trained soldiery are controlled by a competent general by means of bugles and drums. It will seem little short of miraculous when I affirm that when sent out, they dance, turn somersaults all together in the air, fly in orderly rhythm, and return to their starting point, all at the sound of a whistle. They are bidden to perch on the roof, to conceal themselves within their nesting-places, or to dart out of them again; and they do everything just as they are told. . . .

He is a great patron of learning, and always keeps around him erudite men, who are directed to discuss before him philosophy, theology, and religion, and to recount to him the history of great kings and glorious deeds of the past. He has an excellent judgment and a good memory, and has attained to a considerable knowledge of many subjects by means of constant and patient listening to such discussions. Thus he not only makes up for his ignorance of letters (for he is entirely unable either to read or write), but he has also become able clearly and lucidly to expound difficult matters. He can give his opinion on any question so shrewdly and keenly, that no one who did not know that he is illiterate would suppose him to be anything but very learned and erudite. And so indeed he is, for in addition to his keen intellect, of which I have already spoken, he excels many of his most learned subjects in eloquence, as well as in that authority and dignity which befits a King. The wise men are wont every day to hold disputations on literary subjects before him. He listens with delight, not to actors, but to mimics and jesters, thinking their style of speaking to have a literary flavour. . . .

[Akbar] . . . has more than 300 wives, dwelling in separate suites of rooms in a very large palace. Yet when the priests were at the court he had only three sons and two daughters. . . .

The King exacts enormous sums in tribute from the provinces of his empire, which is wonderfully rich and fertile both for cultivation and pasture, and has a great trade both in exports and imports. He also derives much revenue from the hoarded fortunes of the great nobles, which by law and custom all come to the King on their owners' death. In addition, there are the spoils of conquered kings and chieftains, whose treasure is seized, and the great levies exacted, and gifts received, from the inhabitants of newly-subdued districts in every part of his dominions. These gifts and levies are apt to be so large as to ruin outright many of his new subjects. He also engages in trading on his own account, and thus increases his wealth to no small degree; for he eagerly exploits every possible source of profit.

Moreover, he allows no bankers or money-changers in his empire except the superintendents and tellers of the royal treasuries. This enormous banking-business brings the King great profit; for at these royal treasuries alone may gold coin be changed for silver or copper, and vice versa. The government officers are paid in gold, silver or copper according to their rank. Thus it comes about that those who are paid in one type of coin need to change some of it into another type. . . .

This empire is very beautiful and healthy, although in many places not well provided with fruit trees. On account of the diversity of the climate in different parts it produces many and various types of crops. Thus in the southern area or zone (as geographers would call it), the same crops are found as in the maritime district (near Goa). But the farther one goes towards the north the more similar does one find the staple products to those of Europe, though indeed the following are the only representatives of the long list of European fruits and trees which grow in India with real exuberance (and these only on the Himalaya range), viz. the grape, the peach, the mulberry, the fig (in a few places), and the pine tree. The whole country bears pomegranates in abundance. The Cotonian apple, the pear and similar fruits are imported from Persia. Rice, wheat, millet and pulse are produced in great quantities. Amongst a great number of non-fruit-bearing trees, I recognised as European only the plane, though there are willows in Indoscythia. In many places in the neighbourhood of the Indus flax and hemp are sown. The plant which is commonly called 'bangue,' [Indian hemp] and which when used as a drink produces intoxication and stupefaction of the mind and senses, has leaves very similar to those of the hemp-plant. It does not however grow on one stalk only, but has a low stem, from which spring a number of other branches, like a bush. Indigo and opium are largely grown in the south, and bring no small profit to the royal revenues. Indigo is a plant from which a juice is extracted yielding a blue dye when it hardens. . . .

To say something about Indian towns:—they appear very pleasant from afar; for they are adorned with many towers and high buildings, in a very beautiful manner. But when one enters them, one finds that the narrowness, aimless crookedness, and ill-planning of the streets deprive these cities of all beauty. Moreover the houses are purposely built without windows on account of the filth of the streets. None the less the rich adorn the roofs and arched ceilings of their houses with carvings and paintings: plant ornamental gardens in their courtyards: make tanks and fish-ponds, which are lined with tiles of various colours: construct artificial springs and fountains, which fling showers of water far into the air: and lay down promenades paved with brickwork or marble. Yet such houses will show nothing in their facades or entrances by which the eye of the passer-by might be attracted, and nothing by which it might be known that inside is anything out of the ordinary.

The common people live in lowly huts and tiny cottages: and hence if a traveller has seen one of these cities, he has seen them all.

11

Religion and National Identity in Nineteenth-Century India

India was the one great Asian civilization to come under direct colonial rule by Europeans. As Mughal authority disintegrated after 1700, the British East India Company took control over key areas of the subcontinent. By 1800 the British were dominant (though Mughal emperors continued to reign symbolically until 1858) and remained so until the establishment of an independent India and Pakistan in 1947.

The coming of the British triggered massive changes on the subcontinent, some of which are illustrated in the two readings below. Rammohun Roy (1772–1833), the author of the first selection, has often been referred to as the father of modern India. Fluent in several languages, Roy's numerous writings had a major impact on Indian intellectuals in the nineteenth century. He was the central figure in the rejuvenation of Hinduism, a development that profoundly shaped the subsequent course of Indian nationalism.

The second selection, by the Indian Muslim leader Maulvi Syed Kutb Shah Sahib, takes us into the heart of the pivotal event in nineteenth-century India, the Sepoy Mutiny of 1857–58. Actually a massive popular uprising against British rule, the "mutiny" was triggered by the revolt of Hindu and Muslim soldiers (the sepoys) against their British officers. Fourteen months of bitter fighting ensued before the uprising was crushed.

As you read the sources below, entertain the following questions: What is

Selection I from Jogendra Chunder Ghose, ed., *The English Works of Rammohun Roy*, Vol. I (Calcutta: Oriental Press, 1885), pp. 169–71. Selection II from *Selections from the Records of the Government of the Punjab and its Dependencies*, New Series, No. VII (Lahore: Punjab Printing Company, Ltd., 1870), pp. 173–75.

it about British rule that most disturbed Roy and Maulvi Syed Shah? What do these writers reveal about relations between Hindus and Muslims? How do these readings illustrate the relationship between religion and national identity in nineteenth-century India?

I. RAMMOHUN ROY (1821)

For a period of upwards of fifty years, this country (Bengal) has been in exclusive possession of the English nation; during the first thirty years of which from their word and deed it was universally believed that they would not interfere with the religion of their subjects, and that they truly wished every man to act in such matters according to the dictates of his own conscience. Their possessions in Hindoostan and their political strength have, through the grace of God, gradually increased. But during the last twenty years, a body of English Gentlemen who are called missionaries, have been publicly endeavouring, in several ways, to convert Hindoos and Mussalmans of this country into Christianity. The first way is, that of publishing and distributing among the natives various books, large and small, reviling both religions, and abusing and ridiculing the gods and saints of the former: the second way is, that of standing in front of the doors of the natives or in the public roads to preach the excellency of their own religion and the debasedness of that of others: the third way is, that if any natives of low origin become Christians from the desire of gain or from any other motives, these Gentlemen employ and maintain them, as a necessary encouragement to others to follow their example.

It is true that the apostles of Jesus Christ used to preach the superiority of the Christian religion to the natives of different countries. But we must recollect that they were not of the rulers of those countries where they preached. Were the missionaries likewise to preach the Gospel and distribute books in countries not conquered by the English, such as Turkey, Persia, etc. which are much nearer England, they would be esteemed a body of men truly zealous in propagating religion and in following the example of the founders of Christianity. In Bengal, where the English are the sole rulers, and where the mere name of Englishman is sufficient to frighten people, an encroachment upon the rights of her poor timid and humble inhabitants and upon their religion, cannot be viewed in the eyes of God or the Public as a justifiable act. For wise and good men always feel disinclined to hurt those that are of much less strength than themselves, and if such weak creatures be dependent on them and subject to their authority, they can never attempt, even in thought to mortify their feelings.

We have been subjected to such insults for about nine centuries, and the cause of such degradation has been, our excess in civilization and abstinence from the slaughter even of animals; as well as our division into castes which has been the source of want of unity among us.

It seems almost natural that when one nation succeeds in conquering another, the former, though their religion may be quite ridiculous, laugh at and despise the religion and manners of those that are fallen into their power. For example, Mussalmans, upon their conquest of India, proved highly inimical to the religious exercises of Hindoos. When the generals of . . . [Genghis Khan], who denied God and were like wild beasts in their manners, invaded the western part of Hindoostan, they universally mocked at the profession of God and of futurity expressed to them by the natives of India. The savages of Arracan [the upper coast of Burma] on their invasion of the eastern part of Bengal, always attempted to degrade the religion of Hindoos. In ancient days, the Greeks and Romans, who were gross idolaters and immoral in their lives, used to laugh at the religion and conduct of their Jewish subjects, a sect who were devoted to the belief of one God. It is therefore not uncommon if the English missionaries, who are of the conquerors of this country, revile and mock at the religion of its natives. But as the English are celebrated for the manifestation of humanity and for administering justice, and as a great many Gentlemen among them are noticed to have had an aversion to violate equity, it would tend to destroy their acknowledged character, if they follow the example of the former savage conquerors in disturbing the established religion of the country; because to introduce a religion by means of abuse and insult, or by affording the hope of wordly gain, is inconsistent with reason and justice. If by the force of argument they can prove the truth of their own religion and the falsity of that of Hindoos, many would of course embrace their doctrines, and in case they fail to prove this, they should not undergo such useless trouble, nor tease Hindoos any longer by their attempts at conversion. In consideration of the small huts in which Brahmins of learning generally reside, and the simple food, such as vegetables etc. which they are accustomed to eat, and the poverty which obliges them to live upon charity, the missionary Gentlemen may not, I hope, abstain from controversy from contempt of them, for truth and true religion do not always belong to wealth and power, high names, or lofty palaces.

II. MAULVI SYED KUTB SHAH SAHIB

. . . The English are people who overthrow all religions. You should understand well the object of destroying the religions of Hindustan; they have for a long time been causing books to be written and circulated throughout the country by the hands of their priests, and, exercising their authority, have brought out numbers of preachers to spread their own tenets: this has been learned from one of their own trusted agents. Consider, then, what systematic contrivances they have adopted to destroy our religions. For instance, first, when a woman became a widow they ordered her to make a second marriage. Secondly, the self-immolation of wives on the funeral pyres of their deceased husbands was an ancient religious custom; the English had it discontinued, and enacted their own regulations prohibiting it. Thirdly, they told people it was their wish that they (the people) should adopt their faith, promising that if they did so they would be respected by Government; and further required them to attend churches, and hear the tenets preached there. Moreover, they decided and told the rajahs [princes] that such only as were born of their wives would inherit the government and property, and that adopted heirs would not be allowed to succeed, although, according to your Scriptures, ten different sorts of heirs are allowed shares in the inheritance. By this contrivance they will rob you of your governments and possessions, as they have already done with Nagpur and Lucknow. Consider now another of their designing plans: they resolved on compelling prisoners, with the forcible exercise of their authority, to eat their bread. Numbers died of starvation, but did not eat it, others ate it, and sacrificed their faith. They now perceived that this expedient did not succeed well, and accordingly determined on having bones ground and mixed with flour and sugar, so that people might unsuspectingly eat them in this way. They had, moreover, bones and flesh broken small and mixed with rice, which they caused to be placed in the markets for sale, and tried, besides, every other possible plan to destroy our religions. At last some Bengali, after due reflection, said that if the troops would accede to the wishes of the English in this matter all the Bengalis would also conform to them. The English, hearing this approved of it, and said, "Certainly this is an excellent idea," never imagining they would be themselves exterminated. They accordingly now ordered the Brahmans and others of their army to bite cartridges, in the making up of which fat had been used. The Mussulman soldiers perceived that by this expedient the religion of the Brahmans and Hindus only was in danger, but nevertheless they also refused to bite them. On this the English now resolved on ruining the faith of both, and blew away from guns [by tying them to the mouths of cannons which were then fired] all those soldiers who persisted in their refusal. Seeing this excessive tyranny, the soldiery now, in self-preservation, began killing the English, and slew them wherever they were found, and are now considering means for slaying the few still alive here and there. It is now my firm conviction that if these English continue in Hindustan they will kill every one in the country, and will utterly overthrow our religions; but there are some of my countrymen who have joined the English, and are now fighting on their side. I have reflected well on their case also, and have come to the conclusion that the English will not leave your religion to both you and them. You should understand this well. Under these circumstances, I would ask, what course have you decided on to protect your lives and faith? Were your views and mine the same, we might destroy them entirely with a very little trouble; and if we do so, we shall protect our religions and save the country. And as these ideas have been cherished and considered merely from a concern for the protection of the religions and lives of all you Hindus and Mussulmans of this country, this letter is printed for your information. All you Hindus are hereby solemnly adjured, by your faith in Ganges, Tulsi, and Saligram; and all you Mussulmans, by your belief in God and the Koran, as these English are the common enemy of both, to unite in considering their slaughter extremely expedient, for by this alone will the lives and faith of both be saved. It is expedient, then, that you should coalesce and slay them. The slaughter of kine [cows] is regarded by the Hindus as a great insult to their religion. To prevent this a solemn compact and agreement has been entered into by all the Mahomedan chiefs of Hindustan, binding themselves, that if the Hindus will come forward to slay the English, the Mahomedans will from that very day put a stop to the slaughter of cows, and those of them who will not do so will be considered to have abjured the Koran, and such of them as will eat beef will be regarded as though they had eaten pork; but if the Hindus will not gird their loins to kill the English, but will try to save them, they will be as guilty in the sight of God as though they had committed the sins of killing cows and eating flesh. Perhaps the English may, for their own ends, try to assure the Hindus that as the Mussulmans have consented to give up killing cows from respect for the Hindu religion, they will solemnly engage to do the same, and will ask the Hindus to join them against the Mussulmans; but no sensible man will be gulled by such deceit, for the solemn promises and professions of the English are always deceitful and interested. Once their ends are gained they will infringe their engagements, for deception has ever been habitual with them, and the treachery they have always practised on the people of Hindustan is known to rich and poor. Do not therefore give heed to what they may say. Be well assured you will never have such an opportunity again. We all know that writing a letter is equivalent to an advance half way towards fellowship. I trust you will all write answers approving of what has been proposed herein. This letter has been printed under the direction of Moulavy Syad Kutb Shah Sahib, at the Bahaduri press, in the city of Bareilly.

12

Suleiman the Lawgiver and Ottoman Military Power: The Report of a European Diplomat

The Ottoman Empire was one of the most powerful states in the world during the sixteenth century, particularly during the reign of Suleiman the Lawgiver (r. 1520–1566), the greatest of the Turkish sultans. As a result of a stunning series of military victories early in Suleiman's reign, the boundries of the Ottoman state reached from Baghdad to Morocco and from Mecca almost to the gates of Vienna. Constantinople, the Ottoman capital, was the center of a remarkably effective governmental system. The Turks not only conquered new lands under Suleiman's lead, they also ruled their new possessions with a high degree of efficiency.

One of the most valuable reports on Suleiman's state comes from the letters written by Ogier Ghiselin de Busbecq, the Austrian ambassador in Constantinople from 1554 to 1562. While it is true that by the time Busbecq reached the Ottoman capital the military power of the Turks had began to weaken, it is also the case that the memory of the 1529 seige of Vienna, when Suleiman's forces had surrounded the city for two weeks, was still fresh in the minds of many Austrians. Indeed, Busbecq's mission was to use his considerable diplomatic skills to impede or delay a second Turkish assault on the Hapsburg capital.

In the following passages from Busbecq's letters, what do we learn about Suleiman and the Turkish army? What seems to account for Ottoman military success? Are there hints of exaggeration in Busbecq's account? Why might he overplay Turkish military strength? Compare Busbecq's report with those of Mon-

From Edward Seymour Froster, trans., *The Turkish Letters of Ogier Ghiselin de Busbecq* (Oxford: Oxford University Press, 1968), pp. 58–59, 65–66, 109–14, 145–47. Copyright © 1968 by Oxford University Press. Reprinted by permission.

serrate on India and Ricci on China (selections 10 and 7, respectively). Were the Ottomans devising a distinctive form of government during the early modern centuries?

The Sultan was seated on a rather low sofa, not more than a foot from the ground and spread with many costly coverlets and cushions embroidered with exquisite work. Near him were his bow and arrows. His expression, as I have said, is anything but smiling, and has a sternness which, though sad, is full of majesty. On our arrival we were introduced into his presence by his chamberlains, who held our arms—a practice which has always been observed since a Croatian sought an interview and murdered the Sultan . . . [Murad I, 1360–89] in revenge for the slaughter of his master, Marcus the Despot of Serbia. After going through the pretence of kissing his hand, we were led to the wall facing him backwards, so as not to turn our backs or any part of them towards him. He then listened to the recital of my message, but, as it did not correspond with his expectations (for the demands of my imperial master were full of dignity and independence, and, therefore, far from acceptable to one who thought that his slightest wishes ought to be obeyed), he assumed an expression of disdain, and merely answered 'Giusel, Giusel', that is, 'Well, Well'. We were then dismissed to our lodging.

· · ·

You will probably wish me to describe the impression which . . . [Suleiman] made upon me. He is beginning to feel the weight of years, but his dignity of demeanour and his general physical appearance are worthy of the ruler of so vast an empire. He has always been frugal and temperate, and was so even in his youth, when he might have erred without incurring blame in the eyes of the Turks. Even in his earlier years he did not indulge in wine or in those unnatural vices to which the Turks are often addicted. . . . He is a strict guardian of his religion and its ceremonies, being not less desirous of upholding his faith than of extending his dominions. For his age—he has almost reached his sixtieth year—he enjoys quite good health, though his bad complexion may be due to some hidden malady; and indeed it is generally believed that he has an incurable ulcer or gangrene on his leg. This defect of complexion he remedies by painting his face with a coating of red powder, when he wishes departing ambassadors to take with them a strong impression of his good health; for he fancies that it contributes to inspire greater fear in foreign potentates if they think that he is well and strong. I noticed a clear indication of this practice on the present occasion; for his appearance when he received me in the final audience was very different from that which he presented when he gave me an interview on my arrival.

· · ·

The Sultan, when he sets out on a campaign, takes as many as 40,000 camels with him, and almost as many baggage-mules, most of whom, if his destination is Persia, are loaded with cereals of every kind, especially rice. Mules and camels are also employed to carry tents and arms and warlike machines and implements of every kind. The territories called Persia which are ruled by the Sophi, as we call him (the Turkish name being Kizilbash), are much less fertile than our country; and, further, it is the custom of the inhabitants, when their land is invaded, to lay waste and burn everything, and so force the enemy to retire through lack of food. The latter, therefore, are faced with serious peril, unless they bring an abundance of food with them. They are careful, however, to avoid touching the supplies which they carry with them as long as they are marching against their foes, but reserve them, as far as possible, for their return journey, when the moment for retirement comes and they are forced to retrace their steps through regions which the enemy has laid waste, or which the immense multitude of men and baggage animals has, as it were, scraped bare, like a swarm of locusts. It is only then that the Sultan's store of provisions is opened, and just enough food to sustain life is weighed out each day to the Janissaries and the other troops in attendance upon him. The other soldiers are badly off, if they have not provided food for their own use; most of them, having often experienced such difficulties during their campaigns—and this is particularly true of the cavalry—take a horse on a leading-rein loaded with many of the necessities of life. These include a small piece of canvas to use as a tent, which may protect them from the sun or a shower of rain, also some clothing and bedding and a private store of provisions, consisting of a leather sack or two of the finest flour, a small jar of butter, and some spices and salt; on these they support life when they are reduced to the extremes of hunger. They take a few spoonfuls of flour and place them in water, adding a little butter, and then flavour the mixture with salt and spices. This, when it is put on the fire, boils and swells up so as to fill a large bowl. They eat of it once or twice a day, according to the quantity, without any bread, unless they have with them some toasted bread or biscuit. They thus contrive to live on short rations for a month or even longer, if necessary. Some soldiers take with them a little sack full of beef dried and reduced to a powder, which they employ in the same manner as the flour, and which is of great benefit as a more solid form of nourishment. Sometimes, too, they have recourse to horseflesh; for in a great army a large number of horses necessarily dies, and any that die in good condition furnish a welcome meal to men who are starving. I may add that men whose horses have died, when the Sultan moves his camp, stand in a long row on the road by which he is to pass with their harness or saddles on their heads, as a sign that they have lost their horses, and implore his help to purchase others. The Sultan then assists them with whatever gift he thinks fit.

·   ·   ·

But to return to the point from which I digressed. I mentioned that baggage animals are employed on campaign to carry the arms and tents, which mainly belong to the Janissaries. The Turks take the utmost care to keep their soldiers in good health and protected from the inclemency of the weather; against the foe they must protect themselves, but their health is a matter for which the State must provide. Hence one sees the Turk better clothed than armed. He is particularly afraid of the cold, against which, even in the summer, he guards himself by wearing three garments, of which the innermost—call it shirt or what you will—is woven of coarse thread and provides much warmth. As a further protection against cold and rain tents are always carried, in which each man is given just enough space to lie down, so that one tent holds twenty-five or thirty Janissaries. The material for the garments to which I have referred is provided at the public expense. To prevent any disputes or suspicion of favour, it is distributed in the following manner. The soldiers are summoned by companies in the darkness to a place chosen for the purpose—the balloting station or whatever name you like to give it—where are laid out ready as many portions of cloth as there are soldiers in the company; they enter and take whatever chance offers them in the darkness, and they can only ascribe it to chance whether they get a good or a bad piece of cloth. For the same reason their pay is not counted out to them but weighed, so that no one can complain that he has received light or chipped coins. Also their pay is given them not on the day on which it falls due but on the day previous.

The armour which is carried is chiefly for the use of the household cavalry, for the Janissaries are lightly armed and do not usually fight at close quarters, but use muskets. When the enemy is at hand and a battle is expected, the armour is brought out, but it consists mostly of old pieces picked up in various battlefields, the spoil of former victories. These are distributed to the household cavalry, who are otherwise protected by only a light shield. You can imagine how badly the armour, thus hurriedly given out, fits its wearers. One man's breastplate is too small, another's helmet is too large, another's coat of mail is too heavy for him to bear. There is something wrong everywhere; but they bear it with equanimity and think that only a coward finds fault with his arms, and vow to distinguish themselves in the fight, whatever their equipment may be; such is the confidence inspired by repeated victories and constant experience of warfare. Hence also they do not hesitate to re-enlist a veteran infantryman in the cavalry, though he has never fought on horseback, since they are convinced that one who has warlike experience and long service will acquit himself well in any kind of fighting.

·   ·   ·

A window was allotted to me at the back of the house, looking out upon the street by which the Sultan was to leave the city. I was delighted with the view of the departure of this splendid army. The Ghourebas and Ouloufedjis rode in pairs, the Silihdars and Spahis in single file. These are the names given to the household cavalry, each forming a separate body and having its own quarters. Their total number is said to be about 6,000 men. There was also a vast number of the household slaves of the Sultan himself and of the Pashas and the other high officials.

The Turkish horseman presents a very elegant spectacle, mounted on a horse of Cappadocian or Syrian or some other good breed, with trappings and horsecloths of silver spangled with gold and precious stones. He is resplendent in raiment of cloth of gold and silver, or else of silk or satin, or at any rate of the finest scarlet, or violet, or dark green cloth. At either side is a fine sheath, one to hold the bow, the other full of bright-coloured arrows, both of wonderful Babylonian workmanship, as also is the ornamented shield which is attached to the left arm and which is only suited to ward off arrows and the blows dealt by a club or sword. His right hand is encumbered by a light spear, usually painted green, unless he prefers to keep that hand free; and he is girt with a scimitar studded with gems, while a steel club hangs from his horsecloth or saddle. "Why so many weapons?" you will ask. My answer is that he is practised in the use of all of them. "But how," you ask, "can any one use both a bow and a spear? Will he seize his bow only when he has thrown or broken his spear?" No: he keeps his spear in his possession as long as possible, and, when circumstances demand the use of the bow in its turn, he puts the spear, which is light and therefore easily handled, between the saddle and his thigh, in such a position that the point projects a long way behind and the pressure of the knee holds it firm as long as he thinks fit. When circumstances make it necessary for him to fight with the spear, he puts the bow into the quiver or else fixes it across the shield on his left arm. I do not propose, however, to spend more words in explaining the skill in arms which they have acquired by long practice in warfare and continual exercise. On their heads they wear turbans made of the whitest and finest cotton stuff, in the middle of which rises a fluted peak of purple silk. This head-dress is often adorned with black feathers.

After the cavalry had passed, there followed a long column of Janissaries, scarcely any of whom carried any other arms except their muskets. Almost all wore uniforms of the same shape and colour, so that you could recognize them as the slaves or house-hold of the same master. There was nothing very striking in their attire, which had no slits or eyelet-holes; for they declare that their clothes wear out quite enough without their making cuts in them themselves. The only ornaments in which they indulge are plumes and crests and the like, and here they let their fancy run riot, particularly the veterans who brought up the rear. The plumes which they insert in their frontlets give the appearance of a moving forest. Behind them followed their captains and colonels, each with their distinguishing marks of rank. Last came their commander-in-chief, riding by himself. Next followed the chief officials, including the Pashas; then the infantry forming the royal bodyguard in their special uniform and equipment, and carrying their bows, for they are all archers. Next came the Sultan's own chargers, remarkable for their fine appearance and trappings, led by grooms. The Sultan himself was mounted on a splendid horse. His expression was severe and frowning, and he was obviously in an angry mood. Behind him were three young pages, one carrying a flask of water, another a cloak, and the third a casket. They were followed by several eunuchs of the bedchamber. The rear of the procession was formed by a squadron of about two hundred horsemen.

13

Islam and the West in the Nineteenth Century: The Views of a Muslim Intellectual

In the nineteenth century the relationship between the Islamic Middle East and Europe was radically different from what it had been two or three centuries earlier. As we have seen, sixteenth-century European travelers like Busbecq rightly regarded the Turkish army as a formidable force. But Ottoman military power declined rapidly after 1700. In the eighteenth century the Russians drove the Turks out of the Crimea, and the Austrians did the same in Hungary. By the end of the nineteenth century the once-great Ottoman Empire was called "the sick man of Europe" and had also lost control of the Balkans and North Africa.

The drastic change in the relationship between Europe and the Middle East deeply affected the thinking of Muslim intellectuals; many of them responded to the Western challenge by reaffirming their identification with traditional Islamic theology. Others, such as Sayyid Jamal ad-Din "al-Afghani" (1838–1897), began to rethink their faith. Born and raised in Persia (present-day Iran), Jamal ad-Din, also known as Afghani, traveled widely in the Islamic world and Europe from the 1850s until his death. A tireless propagandist, he had a major impact on Muslim thinkers in Iran and Egypt, and he is regarded as a hero by many of today's Middle Eastern intellectuals.

In the following excerpts from Jamal ad-Din's writings, dating from the 1880s, what is the importance of science? What changes does Jamal ad-Din see in the relationship between Islam and science? Is he hostile to Islam? How

From Nikki R. Keddie, trans. and ed., *An Islamic Response to Imperialism: Political and Religious Writings of Sayyid Jamel ad-Din "al-Afghani"* (Berkeley, Calif.: University of California Press, 1968), pp. 56, 87, 102–105, 107. Copyright © 1968 by University of California Press. Reprinted by permission.

do the ideas of Jamal ad-Din compare with those of the nineteenth-century Asian intellectuals you have read in previous selections?

In the human world the bonds that have been extensive . . . have been two. One is this same unity of language of which nationality and national unity consist, and the other is religion. There is no doubt that the unity of language is more durable for survival and permanence in this world than unity of religion since it does not change in a short time in contrast to the latter. We see that a single people with one language in the course of a thousand years changes its religion two or three times without its nationality, which consists of unity of language, being destroyed. One may say that the ties and the unity that arise from the unity of language have more influence than religious ties in most affairs of the world.

. . .

All religions are intolerant, each one in its way. The Christian religion, I mean the society that follows its inspirations and its teachings and is formed in its image, has emerged from the first period to which I have just alluded; thenceforth free and independent, it seems to advance rapidly on the road of progress and science, whereas Muslim society has not yet freed itself from the tutelage of religion. Realizing, however, that the Christian religion preceded the Muslim religion in the world by many centuries, I cannot keep from hoping that Muhammadan society will succeed someday in breaking its bonds and marching resolutely in the path of civilization after the manner of Western society. . . .

In truth, the Muslim religion has tried to stifle science and stop its progress.

. . .

Now I would like to speak of science, teaching, and learning. How difficult it is to speak about science. There is no end or limit to science. The benefits of science are immeasurable; and these finite thoughts cannot encompass what is infinite. Besides, thousands of eloquent speakers and sages have already expressed their thoughts to explain science and its nobility. Despite this, nature does not permit me not to explain its virtues.

Thus I say: If someone looks deeply into the question, he will see that science rules the world. There was, is, and will be no ruler in the world but science. If we look at the Chaldean conquerors, like Semiramis, who reached the borders of Tatary and India, the true conquerors were not the Chaldeans but science and knowledge.

The Egyptians who increased their realm. . . . it was not the Egyptians but Science that did it. The Phoenicians who, with their ships, gradually made colonies of the British Isles, Spain, Portugal, and Greece—in reality it was science, not the Phoenicians, which so expanded their power. Alexander never came to India or conquered the Indians; rather what conquered the Indians was science.

The Europeans have now put their hands on every part of the world. The English have reached Afghanistan; the French have seized Tunisia. In reality this usurpation, aggression, and conquest has not come from the French or the English. Rather it is science that everywhere manifests its greatness and power. Ignorance had no alternative to prostrating itself humbly before science and acknowledging its submission.

In reality, sovereignty has never left the abode of science. However, this true ruler, which is science, is continually changing capitals. Sometimes it has moved from East to West, and other times from West to East. More than this, if we study the riches of the world we learn that wealth is the result of commerce, industry, and agriculture. Agriculture is achieved only with agricultural science, botanical chemistry, and geometry. Industry is produced only with physics, chemistry, mechanics, geometry, and mathematics; and commerce is based on agriculture and industry.

Thus it is evident that all wealth and riches are the result of science. There are no riches in the world without science, and there is no wealth in the world other than science. In sum, the whole world of humanity is an industrial world, meaning that the world is a world of science. If science were removed from the human sphere, no man would continue to remain in the world.

Since it is thus, science makes one man have the strength of ten, one hundred, one thousand, and ten thousand persons. The acquisitions of men for themselves and their governments are proportional to their science. Thus, every government for its own benefit must strive to lay the foundation of the sciences and to disseminate knowledge. Just as an individual who has an orchard must, for his own profit, work to level the ground and improve its trees and plants according to the laws of agronomy, just so rulers, for their own benefit, must strive for the dissemination of the sciences. Just as, if the owner of an orchard neglects to tend it according to the laws of agronomy, the loss will revert to him, so, if a ruler neglects the dissemination of the sciences among his subjects, the harm will revert to that government. . . .

. . .

The science that has the position of a comprehensive soul and the rank of a preserving force is the science of *falsafa* or philosophy, because its subject is universal. It is philosophy that shows man human prerequisites. It shows the sciences what is necessary. It employs each of the sciences in its proper place.

If a community did not have philosophy, and all the individuals of that community were learned in the sciences with particular subjects, those sciences could not last in that community for a century, that is, a hundred years. That community without the spirit of philosophy could not deduce conclusions from these sciences.

The Ottoman Government and the Khedivate of Egypt have been opening schools for the teaching of the new sciences for a period of sixty years, and until now they have not received any benefit from those sciences. The reason is that teaching the philosophical sciences was impossible in those schools, and because of the nonexistence of philosophy, no fruit was obtained from those sciences that are like limbs. Undoubtedly, if the spirit of philosophy had been in those schools, during this period of sixty years they themselves, independent of the European countries, would have striven to reform their kingdoms in accord with science. Also, they would not send their sons each year to European countries for education, and they would not invite teachers from there to their schools. I may say that if the spirit of philosophy were found in a community, even if that community did not have one of those sciences whose subject is particular, undoubtedly their philosophic spirit would call for the acquisition of all the sciences.

The first Muslims had no science, but, thanks to the Islamic religion, a philosophic spirit arose among them, and owing to that philosophic spirit they began to discuss the general affairs of the world and human necessities. This was why they acquired in a short time all the sciences with particular subjects that they translated from the Syriac, Persian, and Greek into the Arabic language. . . .

It is philosophy that makes man understandable to man, explains human nobility, and shows man the proper road. The first defect appearing in any nation that is headed toward decline is in the philosophic spirit. After that deficiencies spread into the other sciences, arts, and associations.

As the relationship between the preeminence of philosophy and the sciences has been explained, we now wish to say something about the quality of teaching and learning among the Muslims. Thus, I say that the Muslims these days do not see any benefit from their education. For example, they study grammar, and the purpose of grammar is that someone who has acquired the Arabic language be capable of speaking and writing. The Muslims now make grammar a goal in itself. For long years they expend philosophic thought on grammar to no avail, and after finishing they are unable to speak, write, or understand Arabic.

.   .   .

The strangest thing of all is that our ulama these days have divided science into two parts. One they call Muslim science, and one European science. Because of this they forbid others to teach some of the useful sciences. They have not understood that science is that noble thing that has no connection with any nation, and is not distinguished by anything but itself. Rather, everything that is known is known by science, and every nation that becomes renowned becomes renowned through science. Men must be related to science, not science to men.

How very strange it is that the Muslims study those sciences that are ascribed to Aristotle with the greatest delight, as if Aristotle were one of the pillars of the Muslims. However, if the discussion relates to Galileo, Newton, and Kepler, they consider them infidels. The father and mother of science is proof, and proof is neither Aristotle nor Galileo. The truth is where there is proof, and those who forbid science and knowledge in the belief that they are safeguarding the Islamic religion are really the enemies of that religion. The Islamic religion is the closest of religions to science and knowledge, and there is no incompatibility between science and knowledge and the foundation of the Islamic faith.

14

Economy and Society in Iberian America

Upon settling in the Americas, Spanish and Portuguese colonists created new economic systems that tied the New World to European capitalism. By the middle of the sixteenth century, Spaniards discovered large veins of silver north of Mexico City at Zacatecas and in the southern Andes at Potosí. As the great wealth of these discoveries became apparent, Spaniards shaped the other sectors of the American economy to support silver. Colonists formed large landed estates (*haciendas*) and textile mills (*obrajes*) to supply animals, food, and clothing to mining centers and to growing cities that served as administrative centers as well as commercial and transportation hubs. Although most of the silver was exported to Europe, either going into the king's treasury or paying for luxury goods, enough minted money stayed in the New World to monetize the economy. In this process money exchange replaced tribute as the means by which producers transferred goods to consumers. In Portuguese America a similar process took place except the product was sugar, not silver. Sugar plantations, particularly in northeastern Brazil, forged a direct economic link to Europe, spurred the development of ranches and farms, and monetized the economy. Despite boom and bust periods, the economic ties between Europe and America became stronger, and the monetary economy spread ever more widely.

Selection I from "The Potosí Mine and Indian Forced Labor in Peru," in Antonio Vasquez de Espinosa, *Compendium and Description of the West Indies,* translated by C. U. Clark (Washington, D.C.: The Smithsonian Institution, 1942), pp. 623–25. Selection II from "A Mexican Textile Factory," in Espinosa, *Compendium,* pp. 133–34. Selection III from "Slavery on the Haciendas, in Yucatan," *American Egypt: A Record of Travel in Yucatan* by Channing Arnold and Frederick J. Tabor Frost (London: Hutchinson and Co., 1909), pp. 324–25, 361, 365–67.

The formation of haciendas, plantations, mills, and mines had dramatic social consequences. To solve their labor needs, Spaniards and Portuguese recruited Native Americans and African Blacks. The unequal exploitive relationship between European owner and colored worker, whether Indian, Black, or mixed, became the chief characteristic of society. The first two passages, describing work in the silver mine at Potosí and in a textile mill in Puebla, Mexico, were written by a Carmelite monk who traveled throughout Spanish America between 1612 and 1620. The last description of hacienda labor in Yucatan (the home of the Mayan Indians) was written by two Englishmen in 1909.

From one angle, the descriptions are similar, showing how deeply ingrained forced labor systems became in Latin-American society from the sixteenth to the twentieth centuries. All three passages describe labor coercion for the benefit of the masters. Even paternalistic concern for the workers appears absent. In times of dire need, workers became a commodity to be used up just as any other expendable resource. Yet the tone of the passages differs greatly. For the seventeenth-century Carmelite, abuse of Indian workers seemed to be a normal activity of sinful men. In contrast the twentieth-century Englishmen burned with righteous indignation. They wanted the system abolished. Many contemporary descriptions of inequities in Latin American society exhibit the same moral outrage as that of these two Englishmen. Consider the potential political outcome of condemning an entire system as opposed to exposing abusive individuals only.

I. THE POTOSÍ MINE AND INDIAN FORCED LABOR IN PERU

Continuing to Describe the Magnificence of the Potosí Range; and of the Indians There under Forced Labor (Mita) in Its Operations.

1652. According to His Majesty's warrant, the mine owners on this massive range have a right to the mita of 13,300 Indians in the working and exploitation of the mines, both those which have been discovered, those now discovered, and those which shall be discovered. It is the duty of the Corregidor of Potosí to have them rounded up and to see that they come in from all the provinces between Cuzco over the whole of El Collao and as far as the frontiers of Tarija and Tomina; this Potosí Corregidor has power and authority over all the Corregidors in those provinces mentioned; for if they do not fill the Indian mita allotment assigned each one of them in accordance with the capacity of their provinces as indicated to them, he can send them, and does, salaried inspectors to report upon it, and when the remissness is great or remarkable, he can suspend them, notifying the Viceroy of the fact.

These Indians are sent out every year under a captain whom they choose in each village or tribe, for him to take them and oversee them for the year each has to serve; every year they have a new election, for as some go out, others come in. This works out very badly, with great losses and gaps in the quotas of Indians, the villages being depopulated; and this gives rise to great extortions and abuses on the part of the inspectors toward the poor Indians, ruining them and thus depriving the caciques and chief Indians of their property and carrying them off in chains because they do not fill out the mita assignment, which they cannot do, for the reasons given and for others which I do not bring forward.

1653. These 13,300 are divided up every 4 months into 3 mitas, each consisting of 4,433 Indians, to work in the mines on the range and in the 120 smelters in the Potosí and Tarapaya areas; it is a good league between the two. These mita Indians earn each day, or there is paid each one for his labor, 4 reals. Besides these there are others not under obligation, who are mingados or hire themselves out voluntarily: these each get from 12 to 16 reals, and some up to 24, according to their reputation of wielding the pick and knowing how to get the ore out. These mingados will be over 4,000 in number. They and the mita Indians go up every Monday morning to the locality of Guayna Potosí which is at the foot of the range; the Corregidor arrives with all the provincial captains or chiefs who have charge of the Indians assigned them, and he there checks off and reports to each mine and smelter owner the number of Indians assigned him for his mine or smelter; that keeps him busy till 1 p.m., by which time the Indians are already turned over to these mine and smelter owners.

After each has eaten his ration, they climb up the hill, each to his mine, and go in, staying there from that hour until Saturday evening without coming out of the mine; their wives bring them food, but they stay constantly underground, excavating and carrying out the ore from which they get the silver. They all have tallow candles, lighted day and night; that is the light they work with, for as they are underground, they have need of it all the time. The mere cost of these candles used in the mines on this range will amount every year to more than 300,000 pesos, even though tallow is cheap in that country, being abundant; but this is a very great expense, and it is almost incredible, how much is spent for candles in the operation of breaking down and getting out the ore.

These Indians have different functions in the handling of the silver ore; some break it up with bar or pick, and dig down in, following the vein in the mine; others bring it up; others up above keep separating the good and the poor in piles; others are occupied in taking it down from the range to the mills on herds of llamas; every day they bring up more than 8,000 of these native beasts of burden for this task. These teamsters who carry the metal do not belong to the mita, but are mingados—hired.

II. A MEXICAN TEXTILE FACTORY

Continuing the Description of the Features of This City and Diocese, and of Other Cities.

There are in this city [Puebla] large woolen mills in which they weave quantities of fine cloth, serge, and grogram, from which they make handsome (gentiles) profits, this being an important business in this country; and those who run these mills are still heathen (gentiles) in their Christianity. To keep their mills supplied with labor for the production of cloth and grograms, they maintain individuals who are engaged and hired to ensnare poor innocents; seeing some Indian who is a stranger to the town, with some trickery or pretext, such as hiring him to carry something, like a porter, and paying him cash, they get him into the mill; once inside, they drop the deception, and the poor fellow never again gets outside that prison until he dies and they carry him out for burial. In this way they have gathered in and duped many married Indians with families, who have passed into oblivion here for 20 years, or longer, or their whole lives, without their wives and children knowing anything about them; for even if they want to get out, they cannot, thanks to the great watchfulness with which the doormen guard the exits. These Indians are occupied in carding, spinning, weaving, and the other operations of making cloth and grograms; and thus the owners make their profits by these unjust and unlawful means.

And although the Royal Council of the Indies, with the holy zeal which animates it for the service of God our Lord, of His Majesty, and of the Indians' welfare, has tried to remedy this evil with warrants and ordinances, which it constantly has sent and keeps sending, for the proper administration and the amelioration of this great hardship and enslavement of the Indians, and the Viceroy of New Spain appoints mill inspectors to visit them and remedy such matters, nevertheless, since most of those who set out on such commissions, aim rather at their own enrichment, however much it may weigh upon their consciences, than at the relief of the Indians, and since the mill owners pay them well, they leave the wretched Indians in the same slavery; and even if some of them are fired with holy zeal to remedy such abuses when they visit the mills, the mill owners keep places provided in the mills in which they hide the wretched Indians against their will, so that they do not see or find them, and the poor fellows cannot complain about their wrongs. This is the usual state of affairs in all the mills of this city and jurisdiction, and that of Mexico City; the mill owners and those who have the mills under their supervision, do this without scruple, as if it were not a most serious mortal sin.

III. SLAVERY ON THE HACIENDAS, IN YUCATAN

The Yucatecans have a cruel proverb, *"Los Indios no oigan sino por las nalgas"* ("The Indians can hear only with their backs"). The Spanish half-breeds have taken a race once noble enough and broken them on the wheel of a tyranny so brutal that the heart of them is dead. The relations between the two peoples is ostensibly that of master and servant; but Yucatan is rotten with a foul slavery—the fouler and blacker because of its hypocrisy and pretence.

The peonage system of Spanish America, as specious and treacherous a plan as was ever devised for race-degradation, is that by which a farm labourer is legally bound to work for the land-owner, if in debt to him, until that debt is paid. Nothing could sound fairer: nothing could lend itself better to the blackest abuse. In Yucatan every Indian peon is in debt to his Yucatecan master. Why? Because every Indian is a spend-thrift? Not at all; but because the master's interest is to get him and keep him in debt. This is done in two ways. The plantation-slave must buy the necessaries of his humble life at the plantation store, where care is taken to charge such prices as are beyond his humble earnings of sixpence a day. Thus he is always in debt to the farm; and if an Indian is discovered to be scraping together the few dollars he owes, the books of the hacienda are "cooked,"—yes, deliberately "cooked,"—and when he presents himself before the magistrate to pay his debt, say, of twenty dollars (£2) the haciendado can show scored against him a debt of fifty dollars. The Indian pleads that he does not owe it. The haciendado-court smiles. The word of an Indian cannot prevail against the Se-ñor's books, it murmurs sweetly, and back to his slave-work the miserable peon must go, first to be cruelly flogged to teach him that freedom is not for such as he, and that struggle as he may he will never escape the cruel master who under law as at present administered in Yucatan has as complete a disposal of his body as of one of the pigs which root around in the hacienda yard.

Henequen (Spanish *jeniquen* or *geniquen*) is a fibre commercially known as Sisal hemp, from the fact that it is obtained from a species of cactus, the *Agave Sisalensis*, first cultivated around the tiny port of Sisal in Yucatan. The older Indian name for the plant is *Agave Ixtli*. From its fleshy leaves is crushed out a fine fibre which, from the fact that it resists damp better than ordinary hemp, is valuable for making ships' cables, but the real wealth-producing use of which is so bizarre that no one in a hundred guesses would hit on it. It is used in the myriad corn-binding machines of America and Canada. They cannot use wire, and cheap string is too easily broken. Henequen is at once strong enough and cheap enough. Hence the piles of money heaping up to the credit of Yucatecans in the banks of Merida. . . .

[At the mill] three or four Indians set to work to arrange the leaves so that their black-pointed ends are all in one direction. Next these thorny points are severed by a machete and in small bundles of six or eight the leaves are handed to men who are feeding a sliding belt-like platform about a yard wide, and on this they are conveyed to the machine. Before they enter its great blunt-toothed, gaping jaws, they are finally arranged, as the sliding belt goes its unending round, so that they do not enter more than one at a time. Woe betide the Indian who has the misfortune to get his fingers in these revolving jaws of the gigantic crusher, and many indeed are there fingerless, handless, and armless from this cause. . . .

For there is money for every one who touches the magic fibre except the miserable Indian, by whose never-ending labours the purse-proud monopolists of the Peninsula are enabled to be ever adding to their ill-gotten gold. There are in Yucatan to-day some 400 henequen plantations of from 25 to 20,000 acres, making the total acreage under cultivation some 140,000 acres. The cost of production, including shipping expenses, export duties, etc., is now about 7 pesos (14*s.*) per 100 kilogrammes. The average market price of henequen is 28 pesos per 100 kilogrammes, so the planter gets a return of 400 per cent. All this is obviously only possible as long as he can get slave-labour and the hideous truth about the exploitation of the Mayans is kept dark. The Indian gets a wage of 50 centavos for cutting a thousand leaves, and if he is to earn this in a day he must work ten hours. Near the big towns, 75 centavos are paid, but practically, on many haciendas, it is so managed that the labour is paid for by his bare keep.

15

Political Styles
in Latin America:
Colonial Bureaucracy
and National Liberation

The first governments in Latin American history, after the overthrow of Indian states, were colonial administrations set up by Spain and Portugal. The initial selection in this section deals with important aspects of their political style.

In theory, Spanish and Portuguese governmental systems concentrated power in the hands of their monarchs. Once a decision was made, it was supposedly executed by a hierarchy of officials descending from the king and his advisors in Europe to a vice-king, or viceroy, in the New World to local officials, or *corregidores*. Since local officials often lived far from centers of administration, they had the opportunity to exercise much freedom in the application of the law. But more than distance, the social and economic positions of local officials influenced the execution of their duties. Being often poor relatives of high churchmen or top governmental officials, they came to the New World to gain wealth and elevate their status. Furthermore, since the few lucrative jobs in mining and merchant activity were long ago occupied, and since manual labor, whether agricultural or artisan, was performed by the colored majority, Spanish newcomers sought government positions as a way of entering the economy in a favorable capacity. Few alternatives for upward mobility existed, a condition that remained endemic and persists today. Local officeholding became a means of enrichment.

Selection I from Don Jorge Juan and Don Antonio De Ulloa, *Discourse and Political Reflections on the Kingdom of Peru*, edited by John J. TePaske, translated by John J. TePaske and Bessie A. Clement (Norman, Okla.: University of Oklahoma Press, 1978), pp. 70–72. Copyright © 1978 by University of Oklahoma Press. Reprinted by permission. Selection II from Vincente Lecuna and Harold A. Bierck, eds., *Selected Writings of Bolivar* (New York: Colonial Press, 1951), Vol. I, pp. 31–32. Copyright © 1951 by Bank of Venezuela. Reprinted by permission.

Just as the owners of haciendas and mines exploited the labor of Indians and Blacks, so the *corregidores* extorted money from Indian communities. They manipulated the tribute tax, which since 1650 was a head tax on adult male Indians paid in money. The first selection describes the activities of a *corregidor* in the viceroyalty of Peru in the 1740s. The account was written by two agents of the king sent specifically to find corruption. Potential exaggeration on the part of the king's "spies" is lessened by the structure of the system. Since the *corregidores* had to pay a "surety bond" before collecting the money, they were forced to make up what they already had pledged. The system invited extortion.

Many historians argue that the nature of colonial administration helped shape later political values and institutions in Latin America—even when colonial controls themselves were thrown off. What kind of political heritage is suggested by this report on Peru—for later Latin American rulers and also for the ruled?

The second selection comes from the nationalist wars of independence against Spain. After a first, unsuccessful battle against Spanish troops in 1812, Latin American nationalists regrouped. Led by Simon Bolívar, they declared a war to the death against Spain and appealed to local populations—in this case, people in the Venezuelan city of Trujillo—for support. The proclamation, issued in June 1813, shows Bolívar's goals and the nature of his nationalism. Where did he learn ideals of this sort? What relation do they bear to the principles of the French revolution? How do they relate to the principles of Spanish administration described in the first selection? Finally, what kind of government would these ideals suggest once the Spaniards had been expelled?

I. BUREAUCRATIC CAPITALISM: PROFITING FROM OFFICE

Corregidores use many methods to enrich themselves at the expense of the Indians, and we shall start with the collection of tribute. In this matter they institute severe treatment, ignore justice, forget charity, and totally disregard the fear of God. Tribute is one revenue that corregidores count as profit or personal gain from their corregimiento. Clearly if they made collections honestly, they would not profit personally from the tribute, would do no harm to the Indians, and would not defraud the king; but all three result from their corrupt conduct. Their insatiable greed seeks nothing but its own satisfaction; overwhelmed by avarice, corregidores satisfy it by any means possible. They keep accounts in such a way that when they have completed their term in office and the accounts are examined as part of their *residencia* [judicial review after completion of office], they are absolved of all guilt simply by payment of a bribe to the judge making the investigation.

Tribute paid by the Indians to Your Majesty is a perquisite of the corregimientos. If corregidores initially find some reason for not assuming the obligation to collect tribute, they discover their own revenues are so small that they are obliged to do so in order to enjoy their full salaries and enrich themselves. Royal treasury officials of the corregimiento confer the right to collect tribute on corregidores after requiring payment of a surety bond as security for the money collected. Since bonds must be paid to these royal officials, they appoint functionaries satisfactory to them. While they have no obligation to name the corregidor, this is usually the case in order to avoid conflicts that might arise if someone else were named.

In the province of Quito [Ecuador] collections are made in two ways—one for the king's account and another for the corregidores'. Using the first method, the corregidor submits to the royal treasury officials an account of the total amount collected, checked against a census of the Indians in the corregimiento based on the baptismal and death records for each parish. Using the second method, royal officials auction off the right to collect tribute to the highest bidder. In this case the corregidor gets preference, if he wishes to take this privilege for the highest amount bid. Although an official account is drawn up, the Indians are told only whom they should pay. The corregidor is obligated to send to the royal treasury only the total amount of tribute bid. He is not required to give detailed accounts. In the province of Quito they began to use the first method at the order of the Viceroy of Peru, the Marqués de Villagarcía, as a result of our visit with him. This occurred because of the great amount of fraud perpetrated by the corregidores to the detriment of the royal treasury. Corregidores included in their accounts only the number of Indians they wished to mention, a group much smaller than those from whom they actually collected tribute. The remainder were listed as absent, disabled, or unable to pay. Another reason for the change in method was delay in payments to the royal treasury. Corregidores used tribute monies for their own trade and personal profit. Thus, besides the losses, the royal treasury suffered greatly from delays, so long in some instances that eight to ten years passed without closing the accounts. Ultimately, the new method was a way of protecting corregidores from the extortions of royal treasury officials, which often resulted in complete loss of the tribute.

II. BOLÍVAR

Venezuelans: An army of your brothers, sent by the Sovereign Congress of New Granada [present-day Colombia] has come to liberate you. Having expelled the oppressors from the provinces of Mérida and Trujillo, it is now among you.

We are sent to destroy the Spaniards, to protect the Americans, and to reëstablish the republican governments that once formed the Confederation of Venezuela. The states defended by our arms are again governed by their former constitutions and tribunals, in full enjoyment of their liberty and independence, for our mission is designed only to break the chains of servitude which still shackle some of our towns, and not to impose laws or exercise acts of dominion to which the rules of war might entitle us.

Moved by your misfortunes, we have been unable to observe with indifference the afflictions you were forced to experience by the barbarous Spaniards, who have ravished you, plundered you, and brought you death and destruction. They have violated the sacred rights of nations. They have broken the most solemn agreements and treaties. In fact, they have committed every manner of crime, reducing the Republic of Venezuela to the most frightful desolation. Justice therefore demands vengeance, and necessity compels us to exact it. Let the monsters who infest Colombian soil, who have drenched it in blood, be cast out forever; may their punishment be equal to the enormity of their perfidy, so that we may eradicate the stain of our ignominy and demonstrate to the nations of the world that the sons of America cannot be offended with impunity.

Despite our just resentment toward the iniquitous Spaniards, our magnanimous heart still commands us to open to them for the last time a path to reconciliation and friendship; they are invited to live peacefully among us, if they will abjure their crimes, honestly change their ways, and coöperate with us in destroying the intruding Spanish government and in the reëstablishment of the Republic of Venezuela.

Any Spaniard who does not, by every active and effective means, work against tyranny in behalf of this just cause, will be considered an enemy and punished; as a traitor to the nation, he will inevitably be shot by a firing squad. On the other hand, a general and absolute amnesty is granted to those who come over to our army with or without their arms, as well as those who render aid to the good citizens who are endeavoring to throw off the yoke of tyranny. Army officers and civil magistrates who proclaim the government of Venezuela and join with us shall retain their posts and positions; in a word, those Spaniards who render outstanding service to the State shall be regarded and treated as Americans.

And you Americans who, by error or treachery, have been lured from the paths of justice, are informed that your brothers, deeply regretting the error of your ways, have pardoned you as we are profoundly convinced that you cannot be truly to blame, for only the blindness and ignorance in which you have been kept up to now by those responsible for your crimes could have induced you to commit them. Fear not the sword that comes to avenge you and to sever the ignoble ties with which your executioners have bound you to their own fate. You are hereby assured, with absolute impunity, of your honor, lives, and property. The single title, "Americans," shall be your safeguard and guarantee. Our arms have come to protect you, and they shall never be raised against a single one of you, our brothers.

This amnesty is extended even to the very traitors who most recently have committed felonious acts, and it shall be so religiously applied that no reason, cause, or pretext will be sufficient to oblige us to violate our offer, however extraordinary and extreme the occasion you may give to provoke our wrath.

Spaniards and Canary Islanders, you will die, though you be neutral, unless you actively espouse the cause of America's liberation. Americans, you will live, even if you have trespassed.

16

Baroque Culture in Latin America

The intellectual, cultural, and religious life of Latin America during its formative period was largely Iberian but contained important indigenous and African elements as well. Peninsular Iberians living in the New World, as well as their American-born descendants (creoles), copied forms from the Old World, whether in architecture, poetry, or Catholic ritual. The varieties of Old World regional practices gave way in the New World to one broadly adopted style that spread throughout the region. The best example of this is the grid plan for city planning. By the late seventeenth century Spanish-American intellectuals focused their copying efforts on a baroque style coming from Spain. Since these literary creoles could not hope to match Spanish masters, such as Cervantes, they paraded their talents briefly during ceremonial occasions. At the numerous religious or civic celebrations during the year, patrons provided prizes for the best poems. Since content was determined ahead of time, only verbal dexterity and ornate form counted.

Although European practices established the outward forms of culture, Spaniards in the New World accepted patterns from other traditions. For example the complex intricacies of baroque style even penetrated the life of the ordinary people. Commoners could not write, but they could dress up. To make their contributions to religious celebrations, the Indians organized costume parades,

From Carlos de Siguenza y Góngora, *Glorias de Querétaro en la Nueva Congregación Eclesiastica de Maria Santisima de Guadalupe* (Mexico City, 1680, repr. 1945); translated by Irving A. Leonard, in *Baroque Times in Old Mexico* (Ann Arbor, Mich.: the University of Michigan Press, 1959), pp. 125–28. Copyright © 1959 by the University of Michigan Press. Reprinted by permission of the University of Michigan Press.

or *máscaras*. As described by Carlos de Sigüenza y Góngara in 1680, the natives of Querétaro, a grain-producing area north of Mexico City, dedicated their *máscara* to the Virgin of Guadalupe, for whom they had recently built a new church that was officially opened on the day of the parade. The description of the *máscara* shows that the Indians remembered their separate cultural inheritance. It also shows that by encouraging cultural mixture, the Spaniards provided a place for the Indians within society. For cynical commentators, the inclusion of Indians in Spanish ceremonial life was deliberate policy. It enabled the Spaniards to better control society. How might that be the case? Are there political dimensions to cultural practices? In what ways did the result contribute to shaping a culture different from both Indian tradition and European models?

If I could present this *máscara* to the ears as it delighted the eyes, I doubt not that I could achieve with my words what the Indians accomplished in it with their adornments. I shall do all that I can, though I know that I shall expose myself to the censure of incredulity. . . .

At three o'clock in the afternoon the masquerade in four sections started to make its appearance on the city streets. The first part was not especially noteworthy as it

The Portuguese Baroque style of architecture was used frequently in South America: San Francisco church in Salvador de Bahia, Brazil. [AP/Wide World Photos]

consisted of a disorganized band of wild Chichimeca Indians who swarmed about the thoroughfares garbed in the very minimum that decency allows. They had daubed their bodies with clay paints of many hues, and their disheveled hair was made even more unsightly by filthy feathers thrust into it in no particular pattern. Like imaginary satyrs and demoniacal furies they whooped, yelled, and howled, waved clubs, and flourished bows and arrows in such a realistic imitation of their warlike practices, that spectators were quite startled and terrified.

More enthusiastic applause greeted the second section, a company of infantrymen formed by one hundred and eight youths marching six abreast, each one bedecked in finest Spanish regalia, with bright-colored plumes fluttering from the crest of helmets and multihued ribbons streaming in the breeze from their shoulders. They presented a noble and inspiring appearance, but nothing amazed me quite as much as the superb precision and perfect rhythm with which they marched, with no other practice or training than that acquired in festive parades and on like occasions. Veterans could not have kept their ranks more evenly, or shown greater dexterity in firing and reloading, or manoeuvered their squads more expertly. . . . This indicates very clearly . . . that these American-born youths are not incapable of discipline should it be necessary to make professional soldiers of them. The rapidity and skill with which the company leader flourished his pike astonished everyone.

Next came four buglers, mounted on well-trained horses barely visible under scarlet trappings and silver trimmings. The clear, shrill notes of their instruments heralded the approach of the most important section of this brilliant *máscara*. This was the part representing the nobility and lords of the aboriginal aristocracy which, even though it was pagan and heathenish, must be reckoned as majestic and august inasmuch as it held sway over a vast northern empire in the New World. In taking part in these festivities it is quite unthinkable that these Indians should put on tableaux borrowed from an alien culture when they have such an abundance of themes and subjects for pageantry in the lives of their kings and emperors and in the annals of their history. So it was that, on this occasion, they appeared in the ancient garbs of their people as portrayed in their hieroglyphic paintings and as still preserved in tribal memory. All were dressed alike with an amazing array of adornments. . . .

Bringing up the rear of this colorful section was a figure representing the august person of the most valiant Emperor Charles V of Spain and the Holy Roman Empire, whose dominions extended from Germany in the north to the western hemisphere of America. He was arrayed in full armor, burnished black and engraved in gold. Like the Indian monarchs preceding him in the procession, he rode behind airy steeds that pranced with grace and stately rhythm as if fully aware of the sublime majesty of the ruler who held the reins. Indeed, these gallant horses, with the rhythmic swaying of plumes and the even gait of their hooves and the carriage gliding like Apollo's chariot across the heavens, made them seem so like Pegasus that onlookers burst into enthusiastic applause. In short, the elegance and splendor of the trappings harmonized completely with the august majesty of the figure represented.

Then came the triumphal float, lovelier than the starry firmament and its twinkling constellations. The base, supported by wheels, was six yards long, about half that width, and from the ground it was raised about a yard and a half. On this ample space rested the form of a large ship plowing through imitation waves of silver and bluish white gauze. The sides covering the underparts of the float bore complex designs of involuted spirals, ornate capitals, and decorative emblems, imbuing the whole with an aura of brilliance and splendor. From a large figurehead at the bow of the ship ribbons of scarlet taffeta fell away, intertwined so intricately with the harness traces that they actually seemed to be drawing the conveyance. Above the stern of the simulated vessel rose two exceedingly graceful arches, forming a throne, in the middle of which reposed a large, curved shell, supported from behind by a pair of Persian caryatids. Within it was an image of the Virgin of Guadalupe, and from her canopied throne descended a staircase with silken mats. Further embellishing this lovely ensemble were varicolored taffeta streamers, and a plethora of bouquets of many hues. Like an ambulant springtime, it appeared, dedicated to the immortal Queen of the heavenly paradise, and far exceeding in beauty the Hanging Gardens of Babylon which, in their time, were dedicated to Semiramis. At appropriate intervals stood six graceful angels, symbolizing some of the attributes of the most Holy Virgin. Kneeling on the first step of the throne was a lovely child garbed in the native raiment of the Indians, who thus represented the whole of America, particularly this northern part which, in pagan days, was known as Anahuac. One hand held a heart while the other supported an incensor diffusing perfumes and delicate aromas. All about this triumphal float the Indians were dancing one of the famous, royal *toncontines* of the ancient Mexicans. If their costumes in such ceremonial festivities were lavishly colorful in the days of their monarchs, how much more they would be on so auspicious an occasion as this one!

17

Europe's First Impact on Africa: Outposts and Slave Trade

Many developments took place in sub-Saharan Africa from the fifteenth through the eighteenth centuries. Major regional kingdoms were established in several sectors. Bantu immigration to the south persisted, spreading agriculture. Conversions to Islam increased in the area below the Sahara, particularly in the eighteenth century, and European adventurers and traders made their first contacts with the vast African subcontinent.

Because many African societies lacked writing and instead expressed their values and history through art and oral traditions, many key political and cultural developments were not recorded during this period using conventional historical records. Documentation focuses on the European impact, which was not the only major current of the period; and it focuses on European, not African, perceptions. This poses unusual dangers for the student of premodern African history in terms of incompleteness and distortion.

The European arrival, however, was a major new ingredient in African history. Because most Europeans worked through local traders and set up only small outposts of their own, their cultural impact before 1800 was limited. Even their political impact was highly localized, except in a few regions such as the Dutch-held Cape region in the south. African rulers used European funds and armaments in their own political rivalries, and while Westerners were often on the

All selections from G. S. P. Freeman-Grenville, *The East African Coast* (Oxford: Clarendon Press, 1962), pp. 47–48, 191, 196–97. Copyright © 1962 by Oxford University Press. Reprinted by permission. Selection I from *An Arabic History of Kilwa Kisiwani* (1520). Selection II from M. Morice, *A Slaving Treaty with the Sultan of Kilwa* (1776). Selection III from J. Crassons de Medeuil, *The French Slave Trade in Kilwa* (1784–1785).

stage, they did not yet write the script. Direct penetration into the interior was rare. But Europe's vast appetite for slaves, intended for use in the Americas, did have huge consequences for many regions, reducing population and economic vitality despite the collaboration of many African rulers and traders in the process.

The three documents that follow, ranging from the fifteenth to the eighteenth centuries, suggest aspects of European-African interaction. They are taken from the east coast, where European activity was less intense than in parts of the west. Coastal settlements along the Indian Ocean already participated in an extensive trading network dominated by Arabs. The Islamic religion had won many adherents, and a written language, Swahili, develolped by the eighteenth century.

The first document, written around 1520 in Arabic, offers an unusual opportunity to glimpse directly African reactions to the first Portuguese explorers, colored of course by the Muslim author's hostility to Christianity. The second document, drawn from the same region on the coast around the port city of Kilwa Kisiwani, is a characteristic, though late, slave-trade treaty drawn up between a French adventurer and the Sultan of Kilwa. Around the same period a French ship's captain in the slave trade offered a businessman's approach to human trade, in which the view of slaves as profit-and-loss commodities comes through clearly.

While the documents sketch European activities in the period, they also allow some evaluation of diverse African reactions and the reasons why some Africans believed they profited from Western ventures.

I. REACTIONS TO THE FIRST PORTUGUESE ARRIVALS IN EAST AFRICA

During al-Fudail's reign there came news from the land of Mozambique that men had come from the land of the Franks. They had three ships, and the name of their captain was al-Mirati [Dom Vasco da Gama]. After a few days there came word that the ships had passed Kilwa and had gone on to Mafia. The lord of Mafia rejoiced, for they thought they [the Franks] were good and honest men. But those who knew the truth confirmed that they were corrupt and dishonest persons who had only come to spy out the land in order to seize it. And they determined to cut the anchors of their ships so that they should drift ashore and be wrecked by the Muslims. The Franks learnt of this and went on to Malindi. When the people of Malindi saw them, they knew they were bringers of war and corruption, and were troubled with very great fear. They gave them all they asked, water, food, firewood, and everything else. And the Franks asked for a pilot to guide them to India, and after that back to their own land—God curse it! All this took place in the year which began on a Tuesday, A.H. 905. Some say it was A.H. 904, which began on a Monday; but the writer of this book was born on the 2nd Shawwal A.H. 904, which began on a Monday, in the time of Sultan Fudail and Amir Ibrahim. The writer was called by the name of the writer we have already mentioned.

Then in the year A.H. 906, which began on a Wednesday, there came al-Kabitan Bidhararis [Dom Pedro Alvarez Cabral] with a fleet of ships. He asked the people of Kilwa to send water and firewood and desired that the sultan or his son should go on board to converse with him. The amir and the people of the land decided it was best to send him an important citizen. So they sent Sayyid Luqman ibn al-Malik al-Adil. They dressed him in royal robes and sent him over.

Then they wanted water, and the Kilwa people drew it in a number of waterskins, and the porters carried it to the shore. Then they called out to the Portuguese to come ashore and take it. As they were coming, one of the principal slaves of the Amir Hajj Ibrahim, who was surnamed Hajj Kiteta, ordered the water carriers [of Kilwa] to carry the water away. So they did so. When the Christians disembarked on shore to fetch water, they saw neither much nor little water, but none at all. So they went back to their ships in anger. They set off again—God curse them!—to Malindi, and received everything they wanted in the way of water, firewood and food. When the Franks went to their own land, they left seven convert Christians at Malindi. They told the people that two should remain there, and four were to be sent to Gujarat to Sultan Mahmud and one to Kilwa. Then the Portuguese left, and the four men went to India and were circumcised and became Muslims.

II. A SLAVE-TRADE AGREEMENT

A copy of M. Morice's Treaty with the King of Kilwa written in Arabic on the reverse side, with two identical octagonal seals inscribed in white in Arabic. On the front was the translation in these terms:

We the King of Kilwa, Sultan Hasan son of Sultan Ibrahim son of Sultan Yusuf the Shirazi of Kilwa, give our word to M. Morice, a French national, that we will give him a thousand slaves annually at twenty *piastres* each and that he [M. Morice] shall give the King a present of two *piastres* for each slave. No other but he shall be allowed to trade for slaves, whether French, Dutch, Portuguese, &c., until he shall have received his slaves and has no wish for more. This contract is made for one hundred years between him and us. To guarantee our word we give him the fortress in which he may put as many cannon as he likes and his Flag. The French, the Moors and the King of Kilwa will henceforth be one. Those who attack one of us we shall both attack. Made under our signs and seals the 14th X. 1776 signed Morice.

And further down is written:

We the undersigned Captain and Officer of the ship *Abyssinie,* commissioned by M. Morice, certify to all whom it may concern that the present treaty was made in our presence at Kilwa on the 14th X. 1776 signed Pichard, Pigné,—Bririard.

III. REPORT OF A FRENCH SLAVE-TRADER

The country is superb and pleasing once one has extricated oneself from the forests of half submerged trees called Mangroves. Judging from the ruins of stone-built houses, which can be seen not only on the island of Kilwa but also on the southern side of the pass, it appears that this was once a very important town and that it must have had a big trade; at Kilwa one can see the whole of a big mosque built in stone whose arches are very well constructed. Within the last three years a pagoda which stood at the southern extremity, and which was very curious looking, fell. Finally, this country produces millet, indigo, superb cotton, silkier even than the cotton produced on the Ile de Bourbon, sugar cane, gums in abundance, brown cowries of the second sort which are currency at Jiddah and in Dahomey, besides elephant ivory which is very common, as are elephants, and lastly negroes—superb specimens if they are selected with care. This selection we cannot make ourselves, being at the discretion of the traders, who are now aware of our needs and who know that it is absolutely essential for us to sail at a given season in order to round the Cape of Good Hope. In addition to competition amongst ourselves the expeditions have never been properly thought out and always left to chance, and so it happens that three or four ships find themselves in the same place and crowd each other out. This would not happen if there were a properly organized body and the expeditions were planned to fit in with the seasons and the quantity of cargo and the means of using up surplus also planned, since it is not the business of seamen to concern themselves with correspondence and administration. To my knowledge, the trading that has been done in this port for the last three years, without counting traders not personally known to me, is as follows:

La Pintade	Capt.		600	blacks	
La Victoire	"	La Touche	224	"	1st Voyage
Les bons amis	"	Beguet	336	"	
La Samaritaine	"	Herpin	254	"	
La Créolle	"	Crassons	176	"	
La Victoire	"	La Touche 3rd voyage 230 }	690	"	In his three voyages
[omitted]	"	Berton	233	"	
La Grande Victoire	"	Michel	289	"	
La Thémis	"	Bertau	450	"	
La Grande Victoire	"	Michel	289	"	
La Créolle	"	Crassons	211	"	
La Thémis 2nd voyage	"	Bertau	480	"	
La Gde. Victoire	"	Rouillard	250	"	
				"	
			4,193	"	

A total, to my knowledge, of 4,193, and certainly there must have been more in three years.

It is clear that if this number of captives, i.e. 4,193, who were traded for at least in this period of three years, cost forty *piastres* each, this represents a sum of 167,720 *piastres,* raised for the most part from the Ile de France and from Bourbon, or from France direct. It is therefore important not only to safeguard this trade but also to find a way of spending rather fewer *piastres,* which would be quite possible if one considers that the *piastres* which we give them for their captives do not remain long in their hands and that they almost immediately give them to the Moors and Arabs who provide them with their needs which are rice, millet, lambs, tunics, shirts, carpets, needles, swords, shoes, and silk materials for dresses and linings. The Arabs obtain most of these things from Surat, and why should we not get them direct from there ourselves? We should make the profit they make, and we should employ men and ships and we should keep a good number of our *piastres* which would remain in the Ile de France and in Bourbon; more certainly still, if privately owned ships from Europe or these islands could not go to the coast of Mozambique and if ships belonging to a private company sent out from Europe could participate in this trade only by means of *piastres* taken to Kilwa, it can be estimated how much we have paid into the hands of the Portuguese at Mozambique, Kerimba and . . . [omitted: Ibo] where they make us pay fifty or sixty *piastres* each for them. This does not include presents and tiresome vexations. What need is there to give our money to the Portuguese, when we have the means to operate among ourselves and when we can use our own industry and keep our money? I have heard for a long time talk of establishing a settlement or trading post in Madagascar. Truly, seeing the number of idle hands we have and the great number of poor and needy and foundlings in our almshouses it is surprising that we have not yet considered this plan, at least as far as that part of the island which we have most visited over a long period is concerned, and also, in certain ports which are particularly well situated, trading posts could be established without straining the resources of the state.

18

The Decades of Imperialism in Africa

The four documents in this section all date from the period 1880–1910. This was the great age of European imperialism in sub-Saharan Africa when virtually all available territory was swept up by the British, French, Germans, or Belgians. African political and economic life was transformed by the inescapable European presence.

The first document comes from German southwest Africa. It is unusual in having been written, in Swahili, by an African trader. A prosaic account of theft on a trip to an inland tribal village, the statement shows how some Africans and their new rulers could interact to apparent mutual benefit.

The second document briefly describes the new work system the Europeans brought. It uses the derogatory term "kaffir," taken from the Arab word for pagan, to describe labor in the British-controlled mines in South Africa, while at the same time it claims great benefits from the jobs. The vantage point is that of an owner and Westerner. What might the workers have thought of this system?

The third document, also from British-controlled southern Africa, describes a characteristic legal arrangement used to deprive African chiefs of their land. It was carried through by agents of Cecil Rhodes. By granting full powers to the

Selection I from "The Uses of Colonial Government," from: Lyndon Harries, ed. and trans., *Swahili Prose Texts: A Selection from the Material Collected by Carl Velten from 1893 to 1896* (Oxford: Oxford University Press, 1965), pp. 243–44. Copyright © 1965 by Oxford University Press. Reprinted by permission. Selection II from John Noble, *Official Handbook: History, Production, and the Resources of the Cape of Good Hope*, 2d ed. (Cape Town, 1886), pp. 194–95. Selection III from Sir Lewis Michell, *The Life of the Right Honourable Cecil John Rhodes*, Vol. 1 (London: 1910), pp. 244–45. Selection IV from John D. Hargreaves, ed., *France and West Africa* (London: St. Martin's Press, Inc., 1969), pp. 198–99. Copyright © 1969 by St. Martin's Press, Inc. Reprinted by permission.

concession holders, this land-use agreement made later incorporation into the British Empire possible.

The fourth document, from French-held Mali in the region below the Sahara, was issued in 1890 by a French military commander who let no African stand in his way. The arrangement described was meant to regularize a local government, in part by playing different groups against each other. While disclaiming French power, what roles were reserved for the imperialist forces?

Collectively, the documents on the imperialist impact raise a number of basic questions. How did the Europeans view Africans at this point? How did imperialist penetration and controls compare to earlier colonial outposts described in the previous section? And what accounts for the change? Finally, how would Africans perceive the new imperialism, and how might their reactions differ?

Imperialism is fresh in African history. Understanding its impact, its limitations, and the responses it provoked is vital to a grasp of African patterns even after imperialism subsided.

I. AN AFRICAN ACCOUNT: THE USES OF COLONIAL GOVERNMENT

We consulted together, saying, "Brothers, hadn't we better get going? We talk, and this pagan does not hear. Perhaps he will change his mind and seek to kill us? Our property is lost, and shall not our souls be lost?" Some said, "Shall we not go to Karema and inform the European, because Chata has robbed us? Now when shall we get out of here? It is no good leaving in the daytime, for perhaps the tribesmen will follow us to get us on the way and kill us; we had better go the Chief and tell him, We agree to what you say, keep our property safe, and we are going to look for Matumla."

We agreed and went to the Chief and told him what we intended, and he said, "Isn't that just what I wanted? Very well, take a hut and go to rest, do not be afraid; sleep until morning, let us take proper leave of one another, and I will give you food for the way (enough) until you arrive at your place (i.e. your destination)." And we sat disconsolately, being sorry for our property which was lost and for our brethren who were dead. It was without any proper reason.

In the morning we reached Karema, and we found the European still in bed. . . . So when the Bwana came, we told him, "Bwana, we have been attacked." And he asked, "Who has attacked you?" We replied, "Chata." And he said to us, "But haven't I said that all traders should first come to me! What did you go to do at the pagan's? But never mind, I will send soldiers to make enquiry why you traders have been robbed. And you provide one person from among you to go along with my soldier, so that he can listen to what my soldier says with Chata, and so that you yourselves may hear about it."

So they set off for Chata's place. The soldiers said to him, "You Chata, so now you have become a man who robs people of their property? Aren't you afraid of government rule?" And he said, "I did not attack them for nothing; I attacked them because of Matumla taking my property, twenty pieces of ivory." The soldiers told him, "Oh no, we don't agree, bring the traders' property, that is what the District Officer told us (you must do)." When he saw their superior strength he took out the stuff and gave it to the soldiers, and they brought it to Karema, all that was left of our goods.

When they reached Karema, the European called us (saying), "You traders, come here, come and look at your property, is this what Chata took?" We looked at it and told him, "Yes, Bwana, some more was lost in the fire." And he said, "Never mind, take this which is left."

II. AFRICAN WORK IN SOUTH AFRICA'S DIAMOND MINES

Kaffir labour is mainly employed in all the less responsible operations of the mines: in drilling holes for the dynamite cartridges, in picking and breaking up the ground in the claims and *trucking* it away from the depositing boxes and the margin on the mine and tipping it on the depositing floors, where it undergoes a variety of processes before it is ready for washing, and is again filled into trucks and driven to the machines. For every three truckloads of ground daily hauled out of the mine there is on an average one Kaffir labourer employed, and to every five Kaffirs there is one white overseer or artizan. In 1882 the number of native labourers at Kimberley mine was 4,000; but in 1884, owing to the serious stoppage of works, they had sunk to 1,500. These labourers are recruited from 16 or 20 different native tribes from various parts of the Colony and the Interior, the proportion of the several tribes at any time on the Fields varying greatly according to the internal state, whether of peace or war, of the district whence they hail. Out of 20,000 natives arriving in search of work in the first half of 1882, 8,000 were Secocoeni's Basutos, 6,000 Shangaans, 1,500 British Basutos, and 1,000 Zulus, the balance consisting of representatives of no less than 16 other different tribes and races. The market afforded for the employment of native labour and the consequent development of native trade is not the least of the incidental benefits conferred on South Africa by the discovery of the Diamond Fields.

III. AN IMPERIALIST CONTRACT: AN ECONOMIC PACT WITH A REGIONAL KING

Know all men by these presents, that whereas Charles Dunell Rudd, of Kimberley; Rochfort Maguire, of London; and Francis Robert Thompson, of Kimberley, hereinafter called the grantees, have covenanted and agreed, and do hereby covenant and agree, to pay to me, my heirs and successors, the sum of one hundred pounds sterling, British currency, on the first day of every lunar month; and, further, to deliver at my royal kraal one thousand Martini-Henry breech-loading rifles, together with one hundred thousand rounds of suitable ball cartridge, five hundred of the said rifles and fifty thousand of the said cartridges to be ordered from England forthwith and delivered with reasonable dispatch, and the remainder of the said rifles and cartridges to be delivered as soon as the said grantees shall have commenced to work mining machinery within my territory; and further, to deliver on the Zambesi River a steamboat with guns suitable for defensive purposes upon the said river, or in lieu of the said steamboat, should I so elect to pay to me the sum of five hundred pounds sterling, British currency. On the execution of these presents, I, Lo Bengula, King of Matabeleland, Mashonaland, and other adjoining territories, in exercise of my council of indunas, do hereby grant and assign unto the said grantees, their heirs, representatives, and assigns, jointly and severally, the complete and exclusive charge over all metals and minerals situated and contained in my kingdoms, principalities, and dominions, together with full power to do all things that they may deem necessary to win and procure the same, and to hold, collect, and enjoy the profits and revenues, if any, derivable from the said metals and minerals, subject to the aforesaid payment; and whereas I have been much molested [of] late by diverse persons seeking and desiring to obtain grants and concessions of land and mining rights in my territories, I do hereby authorise the said grantees, their heirs, representatives, and assigns, to take all necessary and lawful steps to exclude from my kingdom, principalities, and dominions all persons seeking land, metals, minerals, or mining rights therein, and I do hereby undertake to render them all such needful assistance as they may from time to time require for the exclusion of such persons, and to grant no concessions of land or mining rights from and after this date without their consent and concurrence; provided that, if at any time the said monthly payment of one hundred pounds shall cease [the agreement's end dates from] the last-made payment.

IV. THE FRENCH ARRANGE LOCAL GOVERNMENT

I have had you brought here to explain to you the French way of doing things. The French have not come to Ségou to take the country and govern it themselves, but with the intention of restoring it to the Bambaras, from whom it was stolen by the Tukolors. . . .

I am going to give Ségou to the son of your ancient kings. As from today your *Fama* will be Mari-Diara; but on certain conditions which will provide us with guarantees that the welfare of the country will be assured, that trade will be free, and that the Bambaras of the right bank will not be pillaged as were those of the left bank, where Mari-Diara was recently living.

To ensure this, the Commandant Supérieur will firstly station a white officer here, with troops. This Resident will reside in the *dionfoutou* of Ahmadu. Part of the fort will be demolished so that the Resident can have a private gate leading out of the village, and a view over the Niger.

The French Resident will not concern himself with administrative problems between the *Fama* and his villages. The *Fama* will exercise all his rights, will appoint or change chiefs as he thinks fit, but the Resident will have the right to be kept fully informed on all matters and to know everything that takes place.

He may help the *Fama* maintain order in the country by giving him military support, with his troops. . . . But the *Fama* will not have the right to make war or undertake negotiations in neighbouring countries without authorisation from the Resident. If such actions should be undertaken without the Resident's approval, the *Fama* would have to meet all the costs, and accept all the consequences. The Resident would not help him, but would report to the Commandant Supérieur, who is to decide whether the *Fama* has acted wisely or must be reprimanded. . . .

The Tukolors must leave the country within three days after the departure of the Commandant Supérieur; Major Colonna de Giovellina will protect their convoy. After that date the Bambaras may massacre those who remain behind.

19

The Interaction Between Western and African Cultures: Tradition "Falls Apart"

The history of European imperialism in Africa, if it does not focus simply on the activities of the German, British, or French leaders, typically dwells on the political and economic fallout. This involves the new boundaries and governments imposed on Africans and the reactions of African traditional leaders, and the heavy reliance on low-paid African wage labor to produce goods for the Western-dominated world economy. These are important aspects of the African side of imperialism's history. But the issue of cultural impact is receiving growing attention as well. Western government agents, teachers, and missionaries worked hard to modify or undermine traditional African religious values, beliefs about nature, property concepts, and family practices. African reactions to these attempts varied from stark rejection to assimilation, with a compromise position—accepting some introduced elements but retaining traditional elements too—probably most common. The theme of interaction with Western culture constitutes a major strand in African history from the later nineteenth century onward.

The following selection deals with Western-African cultural (though also political and economic) interaction around 1900. The material comes from a novel, the same one used in Volume I to provide a sense of traditional African religion. The author, the Nigerian Chinua Achebe, is deeply aware of the complex balance of gain and loss brought by changes away from tradition. He conveys the different types of Africans and different kinds of motives involved in at least partial adaptation to Western values and also the solemn validity (though the ultimate

From Chinua Achebe, *Things Fall Apart* (London: William Heinemann Ltd., 1959), pp. 138–41, 162, 163, 166–67, 186–88. Copyright © 1959 by Chinua Achebe. Reprinted by permission of William Heinemann Limited.

futility as well) of frontal resistance. This selection, though fictional and written after the fact, describes many real patterns. It cites the ways missionaries were received, the complex value system they imported, beyond Christianity including literacy itself, and a variety of African reactions. The selection ends with a resistance meeting, centered around the strong traditionalist figure of Okonkwo (whose son had converted to Christianity) and the arrival and death of a messenger sent by the English administration to prevent disorder. Overall, the selection invites understanding of why Africans divided in response to Western values—what motives some had for changing, what motives others had for refusing to change.

The missionaries spent their first four or five nights in the marketplace, and went into the village in the morning to preach the gospel. They asked who the king of the village was, but the villagers told them that there was no king. "We have men of high title and the chief priests and the elders," they said.

It was not very easy getting the men of high title and the elders together after the excitement of the first day. But the missionaries persevered, and in the end they were received by the rulers of Mbanta. They asked for a plot of land to build their church.

Every clan and village had its "evil forest." In it were buried all those who died of the really evil diseases, like leprosy and smallpox. It was also the dumping ground for the potent fetishes of great medicine men when they died. An "evil forest" was, therefore, alive with sinister forces and powers of darkness. It was such a forest that the rulers of Mbanta gave to the missionaries. They did not really want them in their clan, and so they made them that offer which nobody in his right senses would accept.

"They want a piece of land to build their shrine," said Uchendu to his peers when they consulted among themselves. "We shall give them a piece of land." He paused, and there was a murmur of surprise and disagreement. "Let us give them a portion of the Evil Forest. They boast about victory over death. Let us give them a real battlefield in which to show their victory." They laughed and agreed, and sent for the missionaries, whom they had asked to leave them for a while so that they might "whisper together." They offered them as much as the Evil Forest as they cared to take. And to their greatest amazement the missionaries thanked them and burst into song.

"They do not understand," said some of the elders. "But they will understand when they go to their plot of land tomorrow morning." And they dispersed.

The next morning the crazy men actually began to clear a part of the forest and to build their house. The inhabitants of Mbanta expected them all to be dead within four days. The first day passed and the second and third and fourth, and none of them died. Everyone was puzzled. And then it became known that the white man's fetish had unbelievable power. It was said that he wore glasses on his eyes so that he could see and talk to evil spirits. Not long after, he won his first three converts.

Although Nwoye had been attacted to the new faith from the very first day, he kept it secret. He dared not go too near the missionaries for fear of his father. But whenever they came to preach in the open marketplace or the village playground, Nwoye was there. And he was already beginning to know some of the simple stories they told.

"We have now built a church," said Mr. Kiaga, the interpreter, who was now in charge of the infant congregation. The white man had gone back to Umuofia, where he built his headquarters and from where he paid regular visits to Mr. Kiaga's congregation at Mbanta.

"We have now built a church," said Mr. Kiaga, "and we want you all to come in every seventh day to worship the true God."

On the following Sunday, Nwoye passed and repassed the little red-earth and thatch building without summoning enough courage to enter. He heard the voice of singing and although it came from a handful of men it was loud and confident. Their church stood on a circular clearing that looked like the open mouth of the Evil Forest. Was it waiting to snap its teeth together? After passing and re-passing by the church, Nwoye returned home.

It was well known among the people of Mbanta that their gods and ancestors were sometimes long-suffering and would deliberately allow a man to go on defying them. But even in such cases they set their limit at seven market weeks or twenty-eight days. Beyond that limit no man was suffered to go. And so excitement mounted in the village as the seventh week approached since the impudent missionaries built their church in the Evil Forest. The villagers were so certain about the doom that awaited these men that one or two converts thought it wise to suspend their allegiance to the new faith.

At last the day came by which all the missionaries should have died. But they were still alive, building a new red-earth and thatch house for their teacher, Mr. Kiaga. That week they won a handful more converts. And for the first time they had a woman. Her name was Nneka, the wife of Amadi, who was a prosperous farmer. She was very heavy with child.

Nneka had had four previous pregnancies and childbirths. But each time she had borne twins, and they had been immediately thrown away. Her husband and his family were already becoming highly critical of such a woman and were not unduly perturbed when they found she had fled to join the Christians. It was a good riddance. . . .

"Does the white man understand our custom about land?"

"How can he when he does not even speak our tongue? But he says that our customs are bad; and our own brothers who have taken up his religion also say that our customs are bad. How do you think we can fight when our own brothers have turned against us? The white man is very clever. He came quietly and peaceably with his religion. We were amused at his foolishness and allowed him to stay. Now he has won our brothers, and our clan can no longer act like one. He has put a knife on the things that held us together and we have fallen apart." . . .

There were many men and women in Umuofia who did not feel as strongly as Okonkwo about the new dispensation. The white man had indeed brought a lunatic religion, but he had also built a trading store and for the first time palm-oil and kernel became things of great price, and much money flowed into Umuofia. . . .

Mr. Brown [the missionary to the Ibo village] learned a good deal about the religion of the clan and he came to the conclusion that a frontal attack on it would not succeed. And so he built a school and a little hospital in Umuofia. He went from family to family begging people to send their children to his school. But at first they only sent their slaves or sometimes their lazy children. Mr. Brown begged and argued and prophesied. He said that the leaders of the land in the future would be men and women who had learned to read and write. If Umuofia failed to send her children to the school, strangers would come from other places to rule them. They could already see that happening in the Native Court, where the D.C. was surrounded by strangers who spoke his tongue. Most of these strangers came from the distant town of Umuru on the bank of the Great River where the white man first went.

In the end Mr. Brown's arguments began to have an effect. More people came to learn in his school, and he encouraged them with gifts of singlets and towels. They were not all young, these people who came to learn. Some of them were thirty years old or more. They worked on their farms in the morning and went to school in the afternoon. And it was not long before the people began to say that the white man's medicine was quick in working. Mr. Brown's school produced quick results. A few months in it were enough to make one a court messenger or even a court clerk. Those who stayed longer became teachers; and from Umuofia laborers went forth into the Lord's vineyard. New churches were established in the surrounding villages and a few schools with them. From they very beginning religion and education went hand in hand. . . .

"You all know why we are here, when we ought to be building our barns or mending our huts, when we should be putting our compounds in order. My father used to say to me: 'Whenever you see a toad jumping in broad daylight, then know that something is after its life.' When I saw you all pouring into this meeting from all the quarters of our clan so early in the morning, I knew that something was after our life." He paused for a brief moment and then began again:

"All our gods are weeping. Idemili is weeping, Ogwugwu is weeping, Agbala is weeping, and all the others. Our dead fathers are weeping because of the shameful sacrilege they are suffering and the abomination we have all seen with our eyes." He stopped again to steady his trembling voice.

"This is a great gathering. No clan can boast of greater numbers or greater valor. But are we all here? I ask you: Are all the sons of Umuofia with us here?" A deep murmur swept through the crowd.

"They are not," he said. "They have broken the clan and gone their several ways. We who are here this morning have remained true to our fathers, but our brothers have deserted us and joined a stranger to soil their fatherland. If we fight the stranger we shall hit our brothers and perhaps shed the blood of a clansman. But we must do it. Our fathers never dreamed of such a thing, they never killed their brothers. But a white man never came to them. So we must do what our fathers would never have done. Eneke the bird was asked why he was always on the wing and he replied: 'Men have learned to shoot without missing their mark and I have learned to fly without perching on a twig.' We must root out this evil. And if our brothers take the side of evil we must root them out too. And we must do it *now*. We must bale this water now that it is only ankle-deep. . . ."

At this point there was a sudden stir in the crowd and every eye was turned in one direction. There was a sharp bend in the road that led from the marketplace to the white man's court, and to the stream beyond it. And so no one had seen the approach of the five court messengers until they had come round the bend, a few paces from the edge of the crowd. Okonkwo was sitting at the edge. . . .

"What do you want here?"

"The white man whose power you know too well has ordered this meeting to stop."

In a flash Okonkwo drew his machete. The messenger crouched to avoid the blow. It was useless. Okonkwo's machete descended twice and the man's head lay beside his uniformed body.

The waiting backcloth jumped into tumultuous life and the meeting was stopped. Okonkwo stood looking at the dead man. He knew that Umuofia would not go to war. He knew because they had let the other messengers escape. They had broken into tumult instead of action. He discerned fright in that tumult. He heard voices asking: "Why did he do it?"

He wiped his machete on the sand and went away.

two

THE TWENTIETH CENTURY

Growing challenges to Western world dominance, sparked by growing nationalism and divisions within the West, produced new expressions of diversity in
the major world civilizations. Religion declined in some societies but was re-
asserted in others. Political structures varied from liberal-democratic to authoritarian to Communist, as new nations or revolutions yielded different patterns in
different parts of the globe. But amid renewed diversity, including widely-vary-
ing levels of economic well-being, were some common themes. Many civilizations sought ways to modify earlier political traditions—very few regimes in
place in 1914 still survived by the late 1980s. Changes in the outlook and
conditions of women marked fundamental social and personal upheaval.
Hardly uniform, the twentieth-century world also shared a need to come to
terms with some basic forces of innovation in the areas of technology, ideas,
and social forms.

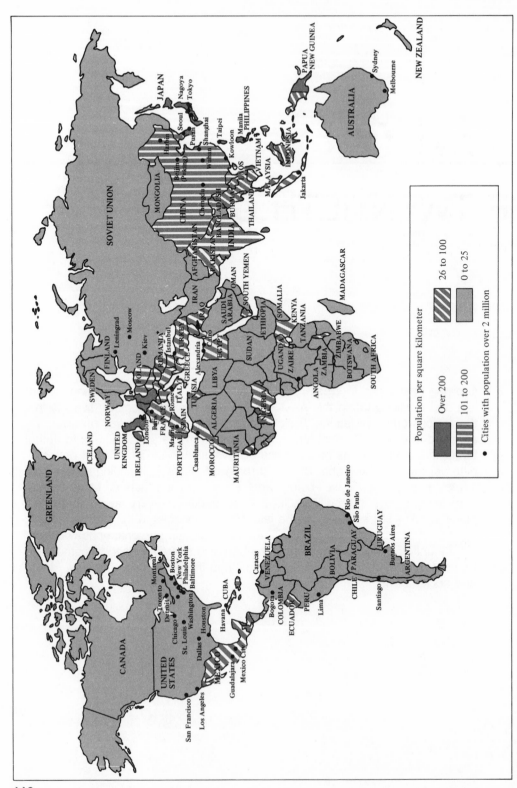

The Contemporary World

20

The Twentieth-Century Western State

One of the key new trends in Western society during the twentieth century has involved changes in the role of the state. Government powers expanded and contacts between state and ordinary citizen increased. Whether the form of government was democratic or not, voting was used to link individual and state. New ideologies and technologies alike expanded state activities. The growth of the Western state built on earlier trends, such as absolutism, and on the needs and capacities of industrial society. It was, nevertheless, a new creature.

The growth of this state power could take vitally different forms, however. Tensions in the Western political tradition, visible in the seventeenth and eighteenth centuries, emerged anew, focusing on the extent of government power as well as constitutional structure. Between the world wars, the most striking political development in the West was the rise of fascist or Nazi totalitarianism. The totalitarian state did not emerge everywhere in the West, but rather in nations where liberal traditions were relatively weak and the shocks of World War I particularly great. Hitler, the Nazi leader, defines the fascist worship of the state in his tract *Mein Kampf,* written in 1924.

The second main version of governmental growth was the welfare state, which became the common Western form after World War II. Britain, converting

Selection I from *Mein Kampf* by Adolf Hitler, translated by Ralph Manheim, pp. 443, 449–51. Copyright 1943 and copyright © renewed by Houghton Mifflin Company. Reprinted by permission of Houghton Mifflin Company. Selection II from "Report by Sir William Beveridge," *Social Insurance and Allied Services* (Cmd 6404), London, Her Majesty's Stationery Office, 1942, pages 6–8, 13, 158–59. British Crown copyright. Reproduced by the permission of the Controller of Her Britannic Majesty's Stationery Office.

from liberal suspicion of government to a desire for new social responsibility, clearly illustrated welfare-state principles. The British welfare-state concept was sketched in a vital wartime planning document, the "Beveridge Report," that was put into practice after 1945.

Both the Nazi and the "Beveridge Report" selections require some interpretation, for neither Hitler nor the Beveridge Commission spelled out a full definition of state functions in a tidy way. Hitler's writings were vague in most respects, featuring strong emotions more than careful programs. The "Beveridge Report" was a pragmatic planning exercise, not a statement of basic theory. A first task, then, is to figure out how state goals are defined and justified in each case—what Hitler means by state reliance on "personality"; what the welfare planners mean by state responsibility.

Nazi and welfare-state definitions obviously invite comparison. How did they differ in political ideals? How did each relate to earlier Western political standards? Why did the different state forms arise amid the crisis conditions of world wars and economic depression in the West, and how would each affect ordinary citizens? But also, in what ways did Nazi and welfare states reflect some similar trends and principles?

The Nazi version of the state seems to have been confined, in the West, to the special conditions of the 1920s and 1930s. Might these reemerge? Is the welfare state a more durable Western form? If so, why? Compared to contemporary political structures elsewhere in the world, has the twentieth-century Western state remained particularly distinctive?

I. HITLER DEFINES THE STATE

Anyone who believes today that a folkish National Socialist state must distinguish itself from other states only in a purely mechanical sense, by a superior construction of its economic life—that is, by a better balance between rich and poor, or giving broad sections of the population more right to influence the economic process, or by fairer wages by elimination of excessive wage differentials—has not gone beyond the most superficial aspect of the matter and has not the faintest idea of what we call a philosophy. All the things we have just mentioned offer not the slightest guaranty of continued existence, far less of any claim to greatness. A people which did not go beyond these really superficial reforms would not obtain the least guaranty of victory in the general struggle of nations. A movement which finds the content of its mission only in such a general leveling, assuredly just as it may be, will truly bring about no great and profound, hence real, reform of existing conditions, since its entire activity does not, in the last analysis, go beyond externals, and does not give the people that inner armament which enables it, with almost inevitable certainty I might say, to overcome in the end those weaknesses from which we suffer today. . . .

The folkish state must care for the welfare of its citizens by recognizing in all and everything the importance of the value of personality, thus in all fields preparing the way for that highest measure of productive performance which grants to the individual the highest measure of participation.

And accordingly, the folkish state must free all leadership and especially the highest—that is, the political leadership—entirely from the parliamentary principle of majority rule—in other words, mass rule—and instead absolutely guarantee the right of the personality.

From this the following realization results:

The best state constitution and state form is that which, with the most unquestioned certainty, raises the best minds in the national community to leading position and leading influence.

But as, in economic life, the able men cannot be appointed from above, but must struggle through for themselves, and just as here the endless schooling, ranging from the smallest business to the largest enterprise, occurs spontaneously, with life alone giving the examinations, obviously political minds cannot be "discovered." Extraordinary geniuses permit of no consideration for normal mankind.

From the smallest community cell to the highest leadership of the entire Reich, the state must have the personality principle anchored in its organization.

There must be no majority decisions, but only responsible persons, and the word "council" must be restored to its original meaning. Surely every man will have advisers by his side, but *the decision will be made by one man.*

The principle which made the Prussian army in its time into the most wonderful instrument of the German people must some day, in a transferred sense, become the principle of the construction of our whole state conception: *authority of every leader downward and responsibility upward.*

Even then it will not be possible to dispense with those corporations which today we designate as parliaments. But their councillors will then actually give counsel; responsibility, however, can and may be borne only by *one* man, and therefore only he alone may possess the authority and right to command.

Parliaments as such are necessary, because in them, above all, personalities to which special responsible tasks can later be entrusted have an opportunity gradually to rise up.

This gives the following picture:

The folkish state, from the township up to the Reich leadership, has no representative body which decides anything by the majority, but only *advisory bodies* which stand at the side of the elected leader, receiving their share of work from him, and in turn if necessary assuming unlimited responsibility in certain fields, just as on a larger scale the leader or chairman of the various corporations himself possesses.

As a matter of principle, the folkish state does not tolerate asking advice or opinions in special matters—say, of an economic nature—of men who, on the basis of their education and activity, can understand nothing of the subject. It, therefore, divides its representative bodies from the start into *political and professional chambers.*

In order to guarantee a profitable cooperation between the two, a special *senate* of the élite always stands over them.

In no chamber and in no senate does a vote ever take place. They are working institutions and not voting machines. The individual member has an advisory, but never a determining, voice. The latter is the exclusive privilege of the responsible chairman.

This principle—absolute responsibility unconditionally combined with absolute authority—will gradually breed an élite of leaders such as today, in this era of irresponsible parliamentarianism, is utterly inconceivable.

Thus, the political form of the nation will be brought into agreement with that law to which it owes its greatness in the cultural and economic field.

*   *   *

As regards the possibility of putting these ideas into practice, I beg you not to forget that the parliamentary principle of democratic majority rule has by no means always dominated mankind, but on the contrary is to be found only in brief periods of history, which are always epochs of the decay of peoples and states.

But it should not be believed that such a transformation can be accomplished by purely theoretical measures from above, since logically it may not even stop at the state constitution, but must permeate all other legislation, and indeed all civil life. Such a fundamental change can and will only take place through a movement which is itself constructed in the spirit of these ideas and hence bears the future state within itself.

Hence the National Socialist movement should today adapt itself entirely to these ideas and carry them to practical fruition within its own organization, so that some day it may not only show the state these same guiding principles, but can also place the completed body of its own state at its disposal.

II. BRITAIN PLANS THE WELFARE STATE (1942)

In proceeding from this first comprehensive survey of social insurance to the next task—of making recommendations—three guiding principles may be laid down at the outset.

The first principle is that any proposals for the future, while they should use to the full the experience gathered in the past, should not be restricted by consideration of sectional interests established in the obtaining of that experience. Now, when the war is abolishing landmarks of every kind, is the opportunity for using experience in a clear field. A revolutionary moment in the world's history is a time for revolutions, not for patching.

The second principle is that organisation of social insurance should be treated as one part only of a comprehensive policy of social progress. Social insurance fully developed may provide income security; it is an attack upon Want. But Want is one only of five giants on the road of reconstruction and in some ways the easiest to attack. The others are Disease, Ignorance, Squalor and Idleness.

The third principle is that social security must be achieved by co-operation between the State and the individual. The State should offer security for service and contribution. The State in organising security should not stifle incentive, opportunity, responsibility; in establishing a national minimum, it should leave room and encouragement for voluntary action by each individual to provide more than that minimum for himself and his family. . . .

Abolition of want requires, first, improvement of State insurance, that is to say provision against interruption and loss of earning power. All the principal causes of interruption or loss of earnings are now the subject of schemes of social insurance. If, in spite of these schemes, so many persons unemployed or sick or old or widowed are found to be without adequate income for subsistence according to the standards adopted in the social surveys, this means that the benefits amount to less than subsistence by those standards or do not last as long as the need, and that the assistance which supplements insurance is either insufficient in amount or available only on terms which make men unwilling to have recourse to it. None of the insurance benefits provided before the war were in fact designed with reference to the standards of the social surveys. Though unemployment benefit was not altogether out of relation to those standards, sickness and disablement benefit, old age pensions and widows' pensions were far below them, while workmen's compensation was below subsistence level for anyone who had family responsibilities or whose earnings in work were less than twice the amount needed for subsistence. To prevent interruption or destruction of earning power from leading to want, it is necessary to improve the present schemes of social insurance in three directions: by extension of scope to cover persons now excluded, by extension of purposes to cover risks now excluded, and by raising the rates of benefit.

Abolition of want requires, second, adjustment of incomes, in periods of earning as well as interruption of earning, to family needs, that is to say in one form or another it requires allowances for children. Without such allowances as part of benefit or added to it, to make provision for large families, no social insurance against interruption of earnings can be adequate. But, if children's allowances are given only when earnings are interrupted and are not given during earning also, two evils are unavoidable. First, a substantial measure of acute want will remain among the lower paid workers as the accompaniment of large families. Second, in all such cases, income will be greater during unemployment or other interruptions of work than during work.

· · ·

There is here an issue of principle and practice on which strong arguments can be advanced on each side by reasonable men. But the general tendency of public opinion seems clear. After trial of a different principle, it has been found to accord best with the sentiments of the British people that in insurance organised by the community by use of compulsory powers each individual should stand in on the same terms; none should claim to pay less because he is healthier or has more regular employment. In accord with that view, the proposals of the Report mark another step forward to the development of State insurance as a new type of human institution, differing both from the former methods of preventing or alleviating distress and from voluntary insurance. The term "social insurance" to describe this institution implies both that it is compulsory and that men stand together with their fellows. The term implies a pooling of risks except so far as separation of risks serves a social purpose. There may be reasons of social policy for adjusting premiums to risks, in order to give a stimulus for avoidance of danger, as in the case of industrial accident and disease. There is no longer an admitted claim of the individual citizen to share in national insurance and yet to stand outside it, keeping the advantage of his individual lower risk whether of unemployment or of disease or accident. . . .

A comprehensive national health service will ensure that for every citizen there is available whatever medical treatment he requires, in whatever form he requries it, domiciliary or institutional, general, specialist or consultant, and will ensure also the provision of dental, ophthalmic and surgical appliances, nursing and midwifery and rehabilitation after accidents. Whether or not payment towards the cost of the health service is included in the social insurance contribution, the service itself should

  (i) be organised, not by the Ministry concerned with social insurance, but by Departments responsible for the health of the people and for positive and preventive as well as curative measures;

 (ii) be provided where needed without contribution conditions in any individual case.

Restoration of a sick person to health is a duty of the State and the sick person, prior to any other consideration. The assumption made here is in accord with the definition of the objects of medical service as proposed in the Draft Interim Report of the Medical Planning Commission of the British Medical Association:

"(a) to provide a system of medical service directed towards the achievement of positive health, of the prevention of disease, and the relief of sickness;

 (b) to render available to every individual all necessary medical services, both general and specialist, and both domiciliary and institutional."

21

The Feminist Revolt

The publication of *The Second Sex* in 1949 by the noted French intellectual Simone de Beauvoir marked the beginning of postwar feminism in Western society. It was followed by works such as Betty Friedan's *The Feminine Mystique* that frankly acknowledged their debt to de Beauvoir and by a number of powerful women's political movements in the United States and Western Europe. The following selection from de Beauvoir's manifesto calls for an assessment of what contemporary feminism is all about—what goals it has, what its grievances are.

This feminist statement is of course phrased in rather theoretical terms. But it corresponded to a rapid change in the actual roles and aspirations of women in the West, marked by a rise in educational levels, a new reduction of the birth rate (though only after 1962, following a "baby boom" period), and above all a real revolution in work roles, as adult women—including wives and mothers— poured into the formal labor force. Women's lives, and their position in society and the family, constituted one of the areas of great change in Western social history during the twentieth century. While part of the change followed from shifts in the economy such as the rise of service jobs, part also followed from new goals—which brings us back to the feminism of intellectual leaders like de Beauvoir. What was going on in Western society to spur such intense desire for fundamental upheaval in what many people, women as well as men, had viewed as biological destiny?

Feminist movements had existed before in the West in the nineteenth and

Feminism—an international movement? American feminist leader Betty Friedan with Indian, Kenyan, and Egyptian representatives at the United Nations Conference on Women, 1984. [AP/Wide World Photos]

early twentieth centuries that culminated in women's suffrage, granted in most Western countries between 1900 and 1920 and in some, such as France, after World War II. De Beauvoir's feminism argued that earlier gains were insufficient, that a more thoroughgoing attack on tradition, including nineteenth-century family ideals, was vital. An understanding of de Beauvoir's views as representative of contemporary intellectual feminism goes far toward creating an understanding of basic currents among twentieth-century Western women more generally.

In the context of world history, the rise of Western women—important in its own right—raises larger issues. Western feminism was not matched in other civilizations, and indeed many societies, such as Latin America and the Middle East, were wary of even lesser changes in women's status. What combination of values and problems spurred the distinctive Western movement? And is it likely that as industrialization and other "modern" forces advance elsewhere, comparable feminist drives will surface? Already, from Africa to Japan, women's-rights advocates were stirring after World War II, though their movements lacked the sweep of those in the West. Will women's rights become part of an international agenda in the final years of the twentieth century? What general forces were prompting the new questions about what women were and what they should be doing?

The "feminine" woman in making herself prey tries to reduce man, also, to her carnal passivity; she occupies herself in catching him in her trap, in enchaining him by means of the desire she arouses in him in submissively making herself a thing. The emancipated woman, on the contrary, wants to be active, a taker, and refuses the passivity man means to impose on her. . . .

The innumerable conflicts that set men and women against one another come from the fact that neither is prepared to assume all the consequences of this situation which the one has offered and the other accepted. The doubtful concept of "equality in inequality," which the one uses to mask his despotism and the other to mask her cowardice, does not stand the test of experience: in their exchanges, woman appeals to the theoretical equality she has been guaranteed, and man the concrete inequality that exists. The result is that in every association an endless debate goes on concerning the ambiguous meaning of the words *give* and *take:* she complains of giving her all, he protests that she takes his all. Woman has to learn that exchanges—it is a fundamental law of political economy—are based on the value the merchandise offered has for the buyer, and not for the seller: she has been deceived in being persuaded that her worth is priceless. The truth is that for man she is an amusement, a pleasure, company, an inessential boon; he is for her the meaning, the justification of her existence. The exchange, therefore, is not of two items of equal value. . . .

But is it enough to change laws, institutions, customs, public opinion, and the whole social context, for men and women to become truly equal? "Women will always be women," say the skeptics. Other seers prophesy that in cutting off their femininity they will not succeed in changing themselves into men and they will become monsters. This would be to admit that the woman of today is a creation of nature; it must be repeated once more that in human society nothing is natural and that woman, like much else, is a product elaborated by civilization. The intervention of others in her destiny is fundamental: if this action took a different direction, it would produce a quite different result. Woman is determined not by her hormones or by mysterious instincts, but by the manner in which her body and her relation to the world are modified through the action of others than herself. The abyss that separates the adolescent boy and girl has been deliberately opened out between them since earliest childhood; later on, woman could not be other than what she *was made,* and that past was bound to shelter her for life. If we appreciate its influence, we see clearly that her destiny is not predetermined for all eternity.

We must not believe, certainly, that a change in woman's economic condition alone is enough to transform her, though this factor has been and remains the basic factor in her evolution; but until it has brought about the moral, social, cultural, and other consequences that it promises and requires, the new woman cannot appear. At this moment they have been realized nowhere, in Russia no more than in France or the United States; and this explains why the woman of today is torn between the past and the future. She appears most often as a "true woman" disguised as a man, and she feels herself as ill at ease in her flesh as in her masculine garb. She must shed her old skin and cut her own new clothes. This she could do only through a social solution. No single educator could fashion a *female human being* today who would be the exact homologue of the *male human being;* if she is raised like a boy, the young girl feels she is an oddity and thereby she is given a new kind of sex specification. Stendhal understood this when he said: "The forest must be planted all at once." But if we imagine, on the contrary, a society in which the equality of the sexes would be concretely realized, this equality would find new expression in each individual.

If the little girl were brought up from the first with the same demands and rewards, the same severity and the same freedom, as her brothers, taking part in the same studies, the same games, promised the same future, surrounded with women and men who seemed to her undoubted equals, the meanings of the castration complex and of the œdipus complex would be profoundly modified. Assuming on the same basis as the father the material and moral responsibility of the couple, the mother would enjoy the same lasting prestige; the child would perceive around her an androgynous world and not a masculine world. . . .

As a matter of fact, man, like woman, is flesh, therefore passive, the plaything of his hormones and of the species, the restless prey of his desires. And she, like him, in the midst of the carnal fever, is a consenting, a voluntary gift, an activity; they live out in their several fashions the strange ambiguity of existence made body. In those combats where they think they confront one another, it is really against the self that each one struggles, projecting into the partner that part of the self which is repudiated; instead of living out the ambiguities of their situation, each tries to make the other bear the abjection and tries to reserve the honor for the self. If, however, both should assume the ambiguity with a clear-sighted modesty, correlative of an authentic pride, they would see each other as equals and would live out their erotic drama in amity. The fact that we are human beings is infinitely more important than all the peculiarities that distinguish human beings from one another; it is never the given that confers superiorities: "virtue," as the ancients called it, is defined at the level of "that which depends on us." In both sexes is played out the same drama of the flesh and the spirit, of finitude and transcendence; both are gnawed away by time and laid in wait for by death, they have the same essential need for one another; and they can gain from their liberty the same glory. If they were to taste it, they would no longer be tempted to dispute fallacious privileges, and fraternity between them could then come into existence.

I shall be told that all this is utopian fancy, because woman cannot be "made over" unless society has first made her really the equal of man. Conservatives have never failed in such circumstances to refer to that vicious circle; history, however, does not revolve. If a caste is kept in a state of inferiority, no doubt it remains inferior; but liberty can break the circle. Let the Negroes vote and they become worthy of having the vote: let woman be given responsibilities and she is able to assume them. The fact is that oppressors cannot be expected to make a move of gratuitous generosity; but at one time the revolt of the oppressed, at another time even the very evolution of the privileged caste itself, creates new situations; thus men have been led, in their own interest, to give partial emancipation to woman: it remains only for women to continue their ascent, and the successes they are obtaining are an encouragement for them to do so. It seems almost certain that sooner or later they will arrive at a complete economic and social equality, which will bring about an inner metamorphosis.

However this may be, there will be some to object that if such a world is possible it is not desirable. When woman is "the same" as her male, life will lose its salt and spice. . . .

One can appreciate the beauty of flowers, the charm of women, and appreciate them at their true value; if these treasures cost blood or misery, they must be sacrificed.

But in truth this sacrifice seems to men a peculiarly heavy one; few of them really wish in their hearts for woman to succeed in making it; those among them who hold woman in contempt see in the sacrifice nothing for them to gain, those who cherish her see too much that they would lose. And it is true that the evolution now in progress threatens more than feminine charm alone: in beginning to exist for herself, woman will relinquish the function as double and mediator to which she owes her privileged place in the masculine universe; to man, caught between the silence of nature and the demanding presence of other free beings, a creature who is at once his like and a passive thing seems a great treasure. The guise in which he conceives his companion may be mythical, but the experiences for which she is the source or the pretext are none the less real: there are hardly any more precious, more intimate, more ardent. There is no denying that feminine dependence, inferiority, woe, give women their special character; assuredly woman's autonomy, if it spares men many troubles, will also deny them many conveniences; assuredly there are certain forms of the sexual adventure which will be lost in the world of tomorrow. But this does not mean that love, happiness, poetry, dream, will be banished from it.

Let us not forget that our lack of imagination always depopulates the future; for us it is only an abstraction; each one of us secretly deplores the absence there of the one who was himself. But the humanity of tomorrow will be living flesh and in its conscious liberty; that time will be its present and it will in turn prefer it. New relations of flesh and sentiment of which we have no conception will arise between the sexes; already, indeed, there have appeared between men and women friendships, rivalries, complicities, comradeships—chaste or sensual—which past centuries could not have conceived. To mention one point, nothing could seem to me more debatable than the opinion that dooms the new world to uniformity and hence to boredom. I fail to see that this present world is free from boredom or that liberty ever creates uniformity. . . .

It is nonsense to assert that revelry, vice, ecstasy, passion, would become impossible if man and woman were equal in concrete matters; the contradictions that put the flesh in opposition to the spirit, the instant to time, the swoon of immanence to the challenge of transcendence, the absolute of pleasure to the nothingness of forgetting, will never be resolved; in sexuality will always be materialized the tension, the anguish, the joy, the frustration, and the triumph of existence. To emancipate woman is to refuse to confine her to the relations she bears to man, not to deny them to her; let her have her independent existence and she will continue none the less to exist for him *also:* mutually recognizing each other as subject, each will yet remain for the other an *other.* The reciprocity of their relations will not do away with the miracles—desire, possession, love, dream, adventure—worked by the division of human beings into two separate categories; and the words that move us—giving, conquering, uniting—will not lose their meaning. On the contrary, when we abolish the slavery of half of humanity, together with the whole system of hypocrisy that it implies, then the "division" of humanity will reveal its genuine significance and the human couple will find its true form.

22

Lenin and the Russian Revolution

The year 1917 brought momentous change to Russia. Mass upheaval in the cities and the countryside, deriving in part from suffering associated with World War I, led to the destruction of key elements of the old order: The Romanov dynasty and the landlord class, each of which had deep roots in the Russian past, were swept away forever. These changes alone are important enough to place the Russian Revolution in the same category as the French Revolution. But the events of 1917 had an added significance, for the victorious Bolshevik revolutionaries did not seek to establish a Western-style middle-class society. Instead, they proclaimed socialism and communism as their goals.

If the meaning and legacy of the Russian Revolution have engendered much controversy, there is, nevertheless, widespread agreement on the central role played by V. I. Lenin (1870–1924), the indefatigable leader of the Bolshevik party and the first head of the new Soviet regime. Lenin's leading role in the Russian Revolution is traceable to the force of his ideas and his organizing ability, illustrated in the following selections from his works. In reading the following excerpts from Lenin's writings, note the way in which his thought embraces various tensions. Do you see elements of realism as well as utopianism in Lenin? Does his commitment to class struggle mesh with his desire to modernize Russia? Can Lenin's desire for democracy be reconciled with his belief in the

From V. I. Lenin, *Selected Works* (New York: International Publishers, 1971), p. 33. Copyright © 1971 by International Publishers. Reprinted by permission; Robert C. Tucker, ed., *The Lenin Anthology* (New York: W.W. Norton, 1975), pp. 76–77, 492–95, 743. Copyright © 1975 by W.W. Norton. Reprinted by permission; F. A. Golder, ed., *Documents of Russian History*, 1914–1917 (New York: Appleton, 1927), pp. 618–19.

necessity of authoritarian rule? Do you see any similarity between Lenin's ideas and those of nineteenth-century Asian thinkers like Fukuzawa and Jamal ad-Din?

OUR PROGRAMME (1899)

We take our stand entirely on the Marxist theoretical position: Marxism was the first to transform socialism from a utopia into a science, to lay a firm foundation for this science, and to indicate the path that must be followed in further developing and elaborating it in all its parts. It disclosed the nature of modern capitalist economy by explaining how the hire of the labourer, the purchase of labour power, conceals the enslavement of millions of propertyless people by a handful of capitalists, the owners of the land, factories, mines, and so forth. It showed that all modern capitalist development displays the tendency of large-scale production to eliminate petty production and creates conditions that make a socialist system of society possible and necessary. It taught us how to discern, beneath the pall of rooted customs, political intrigues, abstruse laws, and intricate doctrines—the *class struggle,* the struggle between the propertied classes in all their variety and the propertyless mass, the *proletariat,* which is at the head of all the propertyless. It made clear the real task of a revolutionary socialist party: not to draw up plans for refashioning society, not to preach to the capitalists and their hangers-on about improving the lot of the workers, not to hatch conspiracies, *but to organise the class struggle of the proletariat and to lead this struggle, the ultimate aim of which is the conquest of political power by the proletariat and the organisation of a socialist society. . . .*

LEADING A REVOLUTIONARY MOVEMENT (1902)

I assert that it is far more difficult to unearth a dozen wise men than a hundred fools. This position I will defend, no matter how much you instigate the masses against me for my "anti-democratic" views, etc. As I have stated repeatedly, by "wise men," in connection with organisation, I mean *professional revolutionaries,* irrespective of whether they have developed from among students or working men. I assert: (1) that no revolutionary movement can endure without a stable organisation of leaders maintaining continuity; (2) that the broader the popular mass drawn spontaneously into the struggle, which forms the basis of the movement and participates in it, the more urgent the need for such an organisation, and the more solid this organisation must be (for it is much easier for all sorts of demagogues to side-track the more backward sections of the masses); (3) that such an organisation must consist chiefly of people professionally engaged in revolutionary activity; (4) that in an autocratic state, the more we *confine* the membership of such an organisation to people who are professionally engaged in revolutionary activity and who have been professionally trained in the art of combating the political police, the more difficult will it be to unearth the organisation; and (5) the *greater* will be the number of people from the working class and from the other social classes who will be able to join the movement and perform active work in it. . . .

PROCLAIMING THE NEW SOVIET GOVERNMENT (NOVEMBER 1917)

Comrades, the workers' and peasants' revolution, the need of which the Bolsheviks have emphasized many times, has come to pass.

What is the significance of this revolution? Its significance is, in the first place, that we shall have a soviet government, without the participation of bourgeoisie of any kind. The oppressed masses will of themselves form a government. The old state machinery will be smashed into bits and in its place will be created a new machinery of government by the soviet organizations. From now on there is a new page in the history of Russia, and the present, third Russian revolution shall in its final result lead to the victory of Socialism.

One of our immediate tasks is to put an end to the war at once. But in order to end the war, which is closely bound up with the present capitalistic system, it is necessary to overthrow capitalism itself. In this work we shall have the aid of the world labor movement, which has already begun to develop in Italy, England, and Germany.

A just and immediate offer of peace by us to the international democracy will find everywhere a warm response among the international proletariat masses. In order to secure the confidence of the proletariat, it is necessary to publish at once all secret treaties.

In the interior of Russia a very large part of the peasantry has said: Enough playing with the capitalists; we will go with the workers. We shall secure the confidence of the peasants by one decree, which will wipe out the private property of the landowners. The peasants will understand that their only salvation is in union with the workers.

We will establish a real labor control on production.

We have now learned to work together in a friendly manner, as is evident from this revolution. We have the force of mass organization which has conquered all and which will lead the proletariat to world revolution.

We should now occupy ourselves in Russia in building up a proletarian socialist state.

Long live the world-wide socialistic revolution.

MODERNIZING RUSSIA (1920)

The essential feature of the present political situation is that we are now passing through a crucial period of transition, something of a zigzag transition from war to economic development. This has occurred before, but not on such a wide scale. This should constantly remind us of what the general political tasks of the Soviet government are, and what constitutes the particular feature of this transition. The dictatorship of the proletariat has been successful because it has been able to combine compulsion with persuasion. The dictatorship of the proletariat does not fear any resort to compulsion and to the most severe, decisive and ruthless forms of coercion by the state. The advanced class, the class most oppressed by capitalism, is entitled to use compulsion, because it is doing so in the interests of the working and exploited people, and because it possesses means of compulsion and persuasion such as no former classes ever possessed, although they had incomparably greater material facilities for propaganda and agitation than we have.

.   .   .

We have, no doubt, learnt politics; here we stand as firm as a rock. But things are bad as far as economic matters are concerned. Henceforth, less politics will be the best politics. Bring more engineers and agronomists to the fore, learn from them, keep an eye on their work, and turn our congresses and conferences, not into propaganda meetings but into bodies that will verify our economic achievements, bodies in which we can really learn the business of economic development.

. . .

While we live in a small-peasant country, there is a firmer economic basis for capitalism in Russia than for communism. That must be borne in mind. Anyone who has carefully observed life in the countryside, as compared with life in the cities, knows that we have not torn up the roots of capitalism and have not undermined the foundation, the basis, of the internal enemy. The latter depends on small-scale production, and there is only one way of undermining it, namely, to place the economy of the country, including agriculture, on a new technical basis, that of modern large-scale production. Only electricity provides that basis.

Communism is Soviet power plus the electrification of the whole country. Otherwise the country will remain a small-peasant country, and we must clearly realise that. We are weaker than capitalism, not only on the world scale, but also within the country. That is common knowledge. We have realised it, and we shall see to it that the economic basis is transformed from a small-peasant basis into a large-scale industrial basis. Only when the country has been electrified, and industry, agriculture and transport have been placed on the technical basis of modern large-scale industry, only then shall we be fully victorious. . . .

I recently had occasion to attend a peasant festival held in Volokolamsk Uyezd, a remote part of Moscow Gubernia, where the peasants have electric lighting. A meeting was arranged in the street, and one of the peasants came forward and began to make a speech welcoming this new event in the lives of the peasants. "We peasants were unenlightened," he said, "and now light has appeared among us, an 'unnatural light, which will light up our peasant darkness.' " For my part, these words did not surprise me. Of course, to the non-Party peasant masses electric light is an "unnatural" light; but what we consider unnatural is that the peasants and workers should have lived for hundreds and thousands of years in such backwardness, poverty and oppression under the yoke of the landowners and the capitalists. You cannot emerge from this darkness very rapidly. What we must now try is to convert every electric power station we build into a stronghold of enlightenment to be used to make the masses electricity-conscious, so to speak.

. . .

We must see to it that every factory and every electric power station becomes a centre of enlightenment; if Russia is covered with a dense network of electric power stations and powerful technical installations, our communist economic development will become a model for a future socialist Europe and Asia.

LAST REFLECTIONS (1923)

The general feature of our present life is the following: we have destroyed capitalist industry and have done our best to raze to the ground the medieval institutions and landed proprietorship, and thus created a small and very small peasantry, which is following the lead of the proletariat because it believes in the results of its revolutionary work. It is not easy for us, however, to keep going until the socialist revolution is victorious in more developed countries merely with the aid of this confidence, because economic necessity . . . keeps the productivity of labour of the small and very small peasants at an extremely low level. Moreover, the international situation, too, threw Russia back and, by and large, reduced the labour productivity of the people to a level considerably below pre-war. The West-European capitalist powers, partly deliberately and partly unconsciously, did everything they could to throw us back, to utilise the elements of the Civil War in Russia in order to spread as much ruin in the country as possible. It was precisely this way out of the imperialist war that seemed to have many advantages. They argued somewhat as follows: "If we fail to overthrow the revolutionary system in Russia, we shall, at all events, hinder its progress towards socialism." And from their point of view they could argue in no other way. In the end, their problem was half-solved. They failed to overthrow the new system created by the revolution, but they did prevent it from at once taking the step forward that would have justified the forecasts of the socialists, that would have enabled the latter to develop the productive forces with enormous speed, to develop all the potentialities which, taken together, would have produced socialism; socialists would thus have proved to all and sundry that socialism contains within itself gigantic forces and that mankind had now entered into a new stage of development of extraordinarily brilliant prospects. . . .

23

Stalin and the Soviet Union During the 1930s: Progress and Terror

Lenin's death in 1924 left a huge void at the head of the Soviet government. Gradually, however, over the next several years Joseph V. Stalin (1879–1953) emerged as the dominant force in the revolutionary regime. By the late 1920s Stalin was firmly in charge. The result was a "second revolution" during the following decade.

The key to Stalin's "revolution from above" was the all-out drive to industrialize the economy and make agriculture a collective process. These policies were accompanied by a massive expansion of schools and health-care facilities. While the net affect of these policies was to move Soviet society rapidly along the road to modernization, the human cost was enormous. Living standards in the 1930s were quite low; several million peasants are thought to have died from starvation in 1932–33. In addition, political repression reached an unparalleled peak. Between 1936 and 1938, 7 or 8 million Soviet citizens — many of them dedicated Communists — were arrested and imprisoned or executed.

The readings below illustrate important aspects of Stalin's policies and their consequences. The first selection is from a speech that Stalin made in 1931 at a conference of Soviet business executives. What is his basic point? How do his ideas compare with Lenin's? How might the leader of a Third World country today react to this speech? The second excerpt comes from the autobiography of Yevgeny Yevtushenko, the most famous poet in the contemporary Soviet Union. How

Selection I from J. V. Stalin, *Works,* Vol. XIII (Moscow: Foreign Languages Publishing House, 1955), pp. 38–51, 43–44. Selection II from Yevgeny Yevtushenko, *A Precocious Autobiography,* trans. Andrew R. MacAndrew (New York: E. P. Dutton, 1963), pp. 14–17. Copyright © 1963 by E. P. Dutton. Reprinted by permission.

does Yevtushenko help us understand Soviet attitudes toward Stalin and the 1930s?

I. STALIN SPEAKS IN 1931

About ten years ago a slogan was issued: "Since Communists do not yet properly understand the technique of production, since they have yet to learn the art of management, let the old technicians and engineers—the experts—carry on production, and you, Communists, do not interfere with the technique of the business; but, while not interfering, study technique, study the art of management tirelessly, in order later on, together with the experts who are loyal to us, to become true managers of production, true masters of the business." Such was the slogan. But what actually happened? The second part of this formula was cast aside, for it is harder to study than to sign papers; and the first part of the formula was vulgarised: non-interference was interpreted to mean refraining from studying the technique of production. The result has been nonsense, harmful and dangerous nonsense, which the sooner we discard the better. . . .

It is time, high time that we turned towards technique. It is time to discard the old slogan, the obsolete slogan of non-interference in technique, and ourselves become specialists, experts, complete masters of our economic affairs. . . .

This, of course, is no easy matter; but it can certainly be accomplished. Science, technical experience, knowledge, are all things that can be acquired. We may not have them today, but tomorrow we shall. The main thing is to have the passionate Bolshevik desire to master technique, to master the science of production. Everything can be achieved, everything can be overcome, if there is a passionate desire for it.

It is sometimes asked whether it is not possible to slow down the tempo somewhat, to put a check on the movement. No, comrades, it is not possible! The tempo must not be reduced! On the contrary, we must increase it as much as is within our powers and possibilities. . . .

To slacken the tempo would mean falling behind. And those who fall behind get beaten. But we do not want to be beaten. No, we refuse to be beaten! One feature of the history of old Russia was the continual beatings she suffered because of her backwardness. She was beaten by the Mongol khans. She was beaten by the Turkish beys. She was beaten by the Swedish feudal lords. She was beaten by the Polish and Lithuanian gentry. She was beaten by the British and French capitalists. She was beaten by the Japanese barons. All beat her—because of her backwardness, because of her military backwardness, cultural backwardness, political backwardness, industrial backwardness, agricultural backwardness. They beat her because to do so was profitable and could be done with impunity. You remember the words of the pre-revolutionary poet: "You are poor and abundant, mighty and impotent, Mother Russia." Those gentlemen were quite familiar with the verses of the old poet. They beat her, saying: "You are abundant," so one can enrich oneself at your expense. They beat her, saying: "You are poor and impotent," so you can be beaten and plundered with impunity. Such is the law of the exploiters—to beat the backward and the weak. It is the jungle law of capitalism. You are backward, you are weak—therefore you are wrong; hence you can be beaten and enslaved. You are mighty—therefore you are right; hence we must be wary of you.

That is why we must no longer lag behind.

In the past we had no fatherland, nor could we have had one. But now that we have overthrown capitalism and power is in our hands, in the hands of the people, we have a fatherland, and we will uphold its independence. Do you want our socialist fatherland to be beaten and to lose its independence? If you do not want this, you must put an end to its backwardness in the shortest possible time and develop a genuine Bolshevik tempo in building up its socialist economy. There is no other way. That is why Lenin said on the eve of the October Revolution: "Either perish, or overtake and outstrip the advanced capitalist countries."

We are fifty or a hundred years behind the advanced countries. We must make good this distance in ten years. Either we do it, or we shall go under. . . .

It is said that it is hard to master technique. That is not true! There are no fortresses that Bolsheviks cannot capture. We have solved a number of most difficult problems. We have overthrown capitalism. We have assumed power. We have built up a huge socialist industry. We have transferred the middle peasants on to the path of socialism. We have already accomplished what is most important from the point of view of construction. What remains to be done is not so much: to study technique, to master science. And when we have done that we shall develop a tempo of which we dare not even dream at present.

And we shall do it if we really want to.

II. YEVGENY YEVTUSHENKO REMEMBERS HIS CHILDHOOD

I was born on July 18, 1933, in Siberia, at Zima Junction, a small place near Lake Baikal. My surname, Yevtushenko, is Ukrainian.

Long ago, at the end of the last century, my great-grandfather, a peasant from the Zhitomir Province, was deported to Siberia for having "let out the red rooster" in his landlord's house. This is the Russian peasant way of saying that he had set fire to his house. That's probably the origin of my inclination to reach for that red rooster whenever I meet anyone with a landlord's mentality.

No one in our family uttered the word "Revolution" as if he were making a speech. It was uttered quietly, gently, a shade austerely. Revolution was the religion of our family.

My grandfather, Yermolay Yevtushenko, a soldier who could barely read, was one of the organizers of the peasant movement in the Urals and in eastern Siberia. Later, under the Soviet regime he studied at a military academy, became a brigade commander, and held the important post of deputy commander of artillery in the Russian Republican Army. But even in his commander's uniform he remained the peasant he had always been and kept his religious faith in Revolution.

I last saw him in 1938. I was five then. I remember our conversation very well.

My grandfather came into my room. I had already undressed and was lying in bed. He sat down on the edge of my bed. He had in his hands a box of liqueur-filled chocolates. His eyes, usually mischievous and smiling, that night looked at me from under his gray prickly crew-cut with a tired and sad expression. He offered me the box of chocolates and then pulled a bottle of vodka out of the pocket of his cavalry breeches.

"I want us to have a drink together," he said. "You have the candy and I'll have the vodka."

He slapped the bottom of the bottle with the flat of his hand and the cork shot out. I fished a chocolate out of the box.

"What shall we drink to?" I asked, trying hard to sound grown-up.

"To the Revolution," my grandfather said with grim simplicity.

We touched glasses—that is, my candy touched his bottle—and we drank.

"Now go to sleep," Grandfather said.

He switched off the light but remained sitting on my bed.

It was too dark for me to see his face but I felt that he was looking at me.

Then he began to sing softly. He sang the melancholy songs of the chain gangs, the songs of the strikers and the demonstrators, the songs of the Civil War.

And listening to them I went to sleep. . . .

I never saw my grandfather again. My mother told me he had gone away for a long trip. I didn't know that on that very night he had been arrested on a charge of high treason. I didn't know that my mother stood night after night in that street with the beautiful name, Marine Silence Street, among thousands of other women who were also trying to find out whether their fathers, husbands, brothers, sons were still alive. I was to learn all this later.

Later I also found out what had happened to my other grandfather, who similarly had vanished. He was Rudolph Gangnus, a round-shouldered gray-bearded mathematician of Latvian origin, whose textbooks were used to teach geometry in Soviet schools. He was arrested on a charge of spying for Latvia.

But at this time I knew nothing.

I went with my father and mother to watch the holiday parades, organized workers' demonstrations, and I would beg my father to lift me up a little higher.

I wanted to catch sight of Stalin.

And as I waved my small red flag, riding high in my father's arms above that sea of heads, I had the feeling that Stalin was looking right at me.

I was filled with a terrible envy of those children my age lucky enough to be chosen to hand bouquets of flowers to Stalin and whom he gently patted on the head, smiling his famous smile into his famous mustache.

To explain away the cult of Stalin's personality by saying simply that it was imposed by force is, to say the least, rather naive. There is no doubt that Stalin exercised a sort of hypnotic charm.

Many genuine Bolsheviks who were arrested at that time utterly refused to believe that this had happened with his knowledge, still less on his personal instructions. Some of them, after being tortured, traced the words "Long live Stalin" in their own blood on the walls of their prison.

Did the Russian people understand what was really happening?

I think the broad masses did not. They sensed intuitively that something was wrong, but no one wanted to believe what he guessed at in his heart. It would have been too terrible.

The Russian people preferred to work rather than to think and to analyze. With a heroic, stubborn self-sacrifice unprecedented in history they built power station after power station, factory after factory. They worked in a furious desperation, drowning with the thunder of machines, tractors, and bulldozers the cries that might have reached them across the barbed wire of Siberian concentration camps.

24

"To Combine Motherhood with Active Participation in Labor": Family and Gender in the Contemporary Soviet Union

Concern over the well-being of the Soviet family has been an important topic of public discussion in the USSR for the past twenty years. Two key trends relating to the family have worried Soviet authorities. First, the divorce rate has been rising steadily since the 1950s; today only the United States leads the Soviet Union in the rate of marriages ending in divorce. Second, the Soviet birth rate — which began to fall following the 1917 Revolution — has continued to decline in recent decades. In the cities of the European USSR the single-child family is now the norm. Because the scarcity of labor remains a major problem for the Soviet economy, this trend toward smaller families has disquieting implications for the future.

Underlying these crucial developments in family life is one of the most significant characteristics of contemporary Soviet society: Half of the workers and employees are women. Since the end of World War II, the USSR has led other industrial societies in the percentage of the labor force that is female. (The Soviet rate has hovered around 50 percent for the entire postwar period.) Thus Soviet women, more than women in any other modern society, have had to struggle with the "double burden" of lifelong participation in the labor force combined with the responsibilities of motherhood.

Below are two readings from the contemporary Soviet press that illustrate how the authorities in the USSR are attempting to come to grips with the prob-

Selection I from *Izvestia*, 31 August 1985, p. 6; in *The Current Digest of the Soviet Press*, Vol. XXXVII, No. 35 (September 25, 1985), pp. 27–28. Selection II from *Pravda*, 29 May 1986, p. 2, *Izvestia*, n.d., pp. 1–2; in *The Current Digest of the Soviet Press*, Vol. XXXVIII, No. 22 (July 2, 1986), pp. 4–5. Reprinted by permission of *The Digest*, published weekly at Columbus, Ohio.

lems families face. How do the Soviet leaders hope to strengthen the family? How are these efforts likely to affect gender relations? Also consider the comparison between family and gender trends in the Soviet Union and those in the twentieth-century West, marked—among other things—by the feminist movement. How might Soviet and Western societies be more similar than their political forms indicate?

I. A TELEVISION SERIES ON THE FAMILY

[*Izvestia*] *Editors' Note.*—On Sept. 4 [1985] Central Television's Second Program will offer viewers the first broadcast in the series "The Ethics and Psychology of Family Life." Moderator of the series and one of the authors, Prof. I. V. Bestuzhev-Lada, Doctor of History, head of the department for the management of social processes and head of the social-forecasting section of the USSR Academy of Science's Institute of Sociological Research, tells us who this program is aimed at and why the need for it arose.

. . .

A course called "The Ethics and Psychology of Family Life" is being introduced as a required subject in the upper grades of the country's schools this year. But the difficulty is that young people—the potential mothers and fathers—react with a certain skepticism toward the efforts of adults to explain to them certain factors of their present and future lives. It's as if they were saying: "We don't interfere in your lives, so you had better leave us alone, too." How can we overcome this barrier? No doubt the best way is to avoid pronouncing truisms of any sort and to try to think through, together with the upper-grade students, the questions of marriage and family—questions that are not simple, as I'm sure you'll agree.

Based on this premise, Central Television decided to do a series of lecture-conversations that we hope will help the upper-grade students to approach the new subject with greater awareness.

What is the topic of the first program? It primarily deals with the question of why far from everyone gains admission to an institution that everyone without exception wants to get into—the institution of the happy family. (Note that in the large cities almost a third of the population under 30 is single, and this third is made up equally of men and women.) To put it briefly, this is primarily attributable to the past two or three decades' mass migration from country to city, with the transition to an urban lifestyle. It also has to do with the gradual disappearance of the former patriarchal family, in which children often inherited not only their parents' occupations but their family traditions as well. As a result, a situation unprecedented in human history has now come about, in which the attainment of sexual maturity does not correlate with psychological and social maturity. Can this gap be bridged? We must think about that together with the upper-grade students.

A second set of questions has to do with the fact that the problems of the family are not just individual problems but are also problems of the country and the society. What will happen, what are the prospects for society if the number of divorces increases still further, while the number of children decreases? If two parents in each succeeding generation are replaced by a single person? If, finally, there are fewer people who are happy in their personal lives and more who are unhappy? We will try—once again, together with the young people—to think through these questions as well.

Every such conversation—and eight are planned (at the rate of one a month)—will be accompanied by excerpts from feature and documentary films and theatrical productions, and will include interviews with upper-grade students and their parents. Finally, we are putting great hopes in young people's letters, because thinking about questions of the family and marriage is impossible without reliable and, most important, sincere feedback.

II. A RESOLUTION OF THE SOVIET PRESIDIUM

In the past few years there has been some increase in the birth rate in the [Latvian] republic, and several other indicators of social and demographic development have improved.

At the same time, the work being conducted in the Latvian republic on compliance with legislation strengthening the family and increasing its responsibility for children's upbringing still does not meet the requirements of the 27th CPSU Congress. For many Soviet and economic agencies, labor collectives and public organizations, concern for using all possible means to strengthen and assist the family in fulfilling its social functions has not yet become a matter of paramount state importance. Work to create the necessary opportunities for women to combine motherhood with active participation in labor and public activity needs to be improved. Preferential work schedules for women are not used often enough.

In the cities of Jelgava and Jurmala, and in Kuldiga District and certain others, questions of expanding the network and strengthening the material and technical base of obstetric and pediatric treatment and preventive-care institutions are being resolved too slowly. Many families experience difficulties in placing children in preschool institutions. Yet plans for the opening of kindergartens and nursery schools regularly go unfulfilled in the republic. The proper attention is not devoted to improving the housing conditions of young families. Trade and consumer services for families with children need further improvement. The demand for baby food, specific types of sewn goods, knit underwear and shoes is not being fully met.

Work to establish the norms and principles of communist morality and a healthy moral climate in all places needs to be significantly increased. This work lacks sufficient concreteness and individualization, and unity of the upbringing process at work, in educational institutions and at home does not exist. Work with so-called "difficult" adolescents is characterized by stereotyped approaches and formalism. There are still a great many disadvantaged families that do a poor job of rearing children.

Some labor collectives, such as the Rigas Manufaktura Production Association, Liepaja's Lauma Accessories Association and others, make poor use of the powers granted to them by law to participate in creating conditions that help to strengthen the family and improve the upbringing of children. The interests of the family and the need to strengthen it are still frequently ignored in club and sports work, and in scheduling summer vacations. Young men and women's moral preparation for starting families needs fundamental improvement. The contribution of educational institutions and public organizations to the formation of a feeling of responsibility to the family among young people is insufficient. The press, television and radio still devote little attention to propagandizing the intellectually and morally healthy family.

The educational and preventive work done by people's courts when hearing cases involving marital and family relations is on a low level. They often display unjustifiable haste in rendering decisions on dissolution of marriages.

[At a May 23 meeting,] the Presidium of the USSR Supreme Soviet [adopted a resolution requiring] the Presidium of the Latvian Republic Supreme Soviet, the Latvian Republic Council of Ministers, and the executive committees of the republic's local Soviets:

to adopt effective measures to eliminate shortcomings in compliance with the requirements of legislation on strengthening the family and increasing parents' responsibility for children's upbringing. . . . To intensify work aimed at strengthening the family, providing it all-round assistance in fulfilling its social functions, and improving working and living conditions for women; and to ensure closer cooperation between economic agencies, public organizations and labor collectives in this matter;

to work to achieve the necessary expansion in construction by enterprises and organizations of cooperative housing for young families, dormitories for young student families and young people's housing complexes, the creation of incentive funds to provide material aid to young families with children, and the extension of the practice of issuing them interest-free loans for cooperative and individual housing construction;

to work out and implement additional measures aimed at completely satisfying, during the current five-year plan, the demand for children's preschool institutions, and to ensure the prompt and high-quality fulfillment of plans for the commissioning of obstetric and pediatric treatment and preventive-care institutions, the strengthening of their material and technical base, their staffing, and a rise in the quality of their work;

to take into fuller consideration the population's demographic structure and the needs of families with children in planning and organizing the production of consumer goods and developing the consumer service sphere, with an eye to expanding production, improving the selection and raising the quality of children's goods, and adopting effective measures to prevent a reduction in the output of inexpensive and sturdy goods for children;

to assist in the organization of family and marriage counseling services and of psychological, legal and other forms of assistance to citizens in strengthening their families, ordering their lives and bringing up their children.

The Latvian Republic Soviets and their executive and administrative agencies, in conjunction with trade-union and Young Communist League organizations, women's councils and other public organizations, are instructed:

to increase the responsibility of enterprise and organization executives to create favorable conditions for women to combine motherhood with active participation in labor and public activity, and to set up work for them on part-time and flexible schedules, as well as work to be done at home. To adopt additional measures to develop the network of facilities for trade, public catering, consumer and other services at the workplace, especially at enterprises and organizations employing primarily women, and to introduce more widely the types of services that make housekeeping easier;

to step up the participation of labor collectives in creating conditions that help to strengthen the family and improve children's upbringing, and to increase the demands on individuals who are not fulfilling their parental duties;

to ensure the more effective utilization of cultural and sports institutions and the further strengthening of their material and technical base, to assist in organizing amateur family clubs, workshops, and amateur associations, in allocating space for these purposes, in outfitting them with the necessary equipment and in staffing these institutions, and to develop and support in every way possible the population's initiative and independent efforts to build sports fields and facilities where they live;

to step up efforts to introduce new socialist ceremonies, to organize public festivities, cultural and sporting events, and joint leisure-time activities for families, to honor labor dynasties, and to instill in young people the experience of the older generations;

to intensify efforts to prevent lawbreaking among juveniles, to identify disadvantaged families, to increase the effectiveness of the struggle against drunkenness and alcoholism, and to improve coordination of the activities of law-enforcement agencies, public education and public health institutions, commissions on juvenile affairs and on the struggle against alcoholism, and agencies staffed by volunteers.

25

Mao Tse-tung and the Chinese Revolution

The twentieth century has been one of the most tumultuous in the history of China. Buffeted by the shocks from Western (and Japanese) imperialism and unable to deal effectively with China's many internal problems, the Manchu dynasty collapsed in 1911. A protracted period of instability and confusion followed. For more than a decade warlords fought for control of the country. Beginning in 1927, Chiang Kai-shek—the conservative leader of the Kuomintang, or Nationalist Party—attempted to govern from Nanking. However, the invasion of the Japanese in 1937 and the simultaneous rise of the rural-based Communist movement overwhelmed Chiang's regime. Following the end of the Second World War—a struggle which some estimate took the lives of 10 million Chinese—the conflict between Chiang's forces and the Communists became a full-scale civil war. In 1949 the Communists swept to power and have governed the country ever since.

Mao Tse-tung (1891–1976) was the central figure in the rise of Chinese communism. The son of a Hunan peasant, Mao was one of the founders of the Chinese Communist Party in 1921. He emerged as the leader of the party during the 1930s and was the moving force in the Communist regime from 1949 until his death. The following passages from Mao's writings illustrate important aspects of his thinking, including the ways he challenged earlier Chinese political traditions. How do Mao's writings help explain the success of the Communists up to 1949? Do you see any differences between Mao's thinking before 1949 and after? What is the significance of Mao's remarks on mistakes made in "other socialist countries"? What is the importance of his comments on social classes and bureaucracy?

THE PEASANTS OF HUNAN (1927)

During my recent visit to Hunan I conducted an investigation on the spot into the conditions in the five counties of Siangtan, Siangsiang, Hengshan, Liling and Changsha. In the thirty-two days from January 4 to February 5, in villages and in county towns, I called together for fact-finding conferences experienced peasants and comrades working for the peasant movement, listened attentively to their reports and collected a lot of material. . . .

All kinds of arguments against the peasant movement must be speedily set right. The erroneous measures taken by the revolutionary authorities concerning the peasant movement must be speedily changed. Only thus can any good be done for the future of the revolution. For the rise of the present peasant movement is a colossal event. In a very short time, in China's central, southern and northern provinces, several hundred million peasants will rise like a tornado or tempest, a force so extraordinarily swift and violent that no power, however great, will be able to suppress it. They will break all trammels that now bind them and rush forward along the road to liberation. They will send all imperialists, warlords, corrupt officials, local bullies and bad gentry to their graves. All revolutionary parties and all revolutionary comrades will stand before them to be tested, and to be accepted or rejected as they decide.

To march at their head and lead them? Or to follow at their rear, gesticulating at them and criticising them? Or to face them as opponents?

Every Chinese is free to choose among the three alternatives, but circumstances demand that a quick choice be made. . . .

A revolution is not the same as inviting people to dinner, or writing an essay, or painting a picture, or doing fancy needlework; it cannot be anything so refined, so calm and gentle, or so mild, kind, courteous, restrained and magnanimous. A revolution is an uprising, an act of violence whereby one class overthrows another. A rural revolution is a revolution by which the peasantry overthrows the authority of the feudal landlord class. If the peasants do not use the maximum of their strength, they can never overthrow the authority of the landlords which has been deeply rooted for thousands of years. In the rural areas, there must be a great, fervent revolutionary upsurge, which alone can arouse hundreds and thousands of the people to form a great force. . . .

MARXISM (1939)

Marxism consists of thousands of truths, but they all boil down to the one sentence, "It is right to rebel." For thousands of years, it had been said that it was right to oppress, it was right to exploit, and it was wrong to rebel. This old verdict was only reversed with the appearance of Marxism. This is a great contribution. It was through struggle that the proletariat learned this truth, and Marx drew the conclusion. And from this truth there follows resistance, struggle, the fight for socialism.

Snow (1944–45)

The northern scene:
A thousand leagues locked in ice,
A myriad leagues of fluttering snow.
On either side of the Great Wall
Only one vastness to be seen.
Up and down this broad river
Torrents flatten and stiffen.
The mountains are dancing silver serpents
And hills, like waxen elephants, plod on the plain,
Challenging heaven with their heights.
A sunny day is needed
For seeing them, with added elegance,
In red and white.
Such is the beauty of these mountains and rivers
That has been admired by unnumbered heroes—
The great emperors of Ch`in and Han
Lacking literary brilliance,
Those of T`ang and Sung
Having but few romantic inclinations,
And the prodigious Gengis Khan
Knowing only how to bend his bow and shoot at vultures.
All are past and gone!
For men of vision
We must seek among the present generation.

ECONOMIC POLICY (1956)

Heavy industries are the center of gravity and their development should be given the first priority. We all agree with this. In dealing with the relationship between heavy and light industries and between industry and agriculture, we have not committed any fundamental mistake. We have not repeated the mistakes of some socialist countries which attached excessive importance to heavy industries at the expense of light industries and agriculture. The results [of their mistakes] were an insufficient supply of goods for the market, a shortage of means of living, and an instability of the currency. We have given comparatively greater importance to light industries and agriculture. Unlike the market situation in some countries, immediately after a revolution, goods in our markets have been more plentiful. We cannot say that our daily necessities are abundant, but they are not in short supply. Furthermore, their prices, and the value of the *jen-min-pi* [the Chinese legal tender] are stable. This is not to say that no problems remain. There *are* problems—e.g. greater attention to light industries and agriculture than before, and adequate readjustment of the rates of investment in heavy and light industries and in industry and agriculture to give a comparatively greater weight to the investment in light industries and agriculture. . . .

As to agriculture, the experience of some socialist countries has proved that bad management could fail to raise production even after collectivization. Some other countries have failed to raise agricultural output because their agrarian policies were doubtful. They put too heavy a tax burden on the peasants and they lowered agricultural prices in terms of industrial prices. When we develop industries, especially heavy ones, we must give a proper place to agriculture and adopt a correct agricultural tax and price policy.

CHINA'S FUTURE (1962)

. . . In the seventeenth century, a number of European countries were already in the process of developing capitalism. It has taken over 300 years for capitalist productive forces to develop to their present pattern. Socialism is superior in many respects to capitalism, and the economic development of our country may be much faster than that of capitalist countries. But China has a large population, our resources are meagre, and our economy backward so that in my opinion, it will be impossible to develop our productive power so rapidly as to catch up with, and overtake, the most advanced capitalist countries in less than one hundred years. If it requires only a few decades, for example only fifty years as some have conjectured, then that will be a splendid thing, for which heaven and earth be praised. But I would advise, comrades, that it is better to think more of the difficulties and so to envisage it as taking a longer period. It took from three to four hundred years to build a great and mighty capitalist economy; what would be wrong with building a great and mighty socialist economy in our country in about fity or a hundred years? The next fifty or hundred years from now will be an epic period of fundamental change in the social system of the world, an earth-shaking period, with which no past era can be compared. Living in such a period, we must be prepared to carry out great struggles, differing in many respects from the forms of struggle of previous periods. In order to carry out this task, we must do our very best to combine the universal truth of Marxism-Leninism with the concrete reality of Chinese socialist construction and with the concrete reality of future world revolution and, through practice, gradually come to understand the objective laws of the struggle. We must be prepared to suffer many defeats and set-backs as a result of our blindness, thereby gaining experience and winning final victory. When we see things in this light, then there are many advantages in envisaging it as taking a long period; conversely, harm would result from envisaging a short period. . . .

SOCIALISM AND CLASS STRUGGLE (1962)

Now then, do classes exist in socialist countries? Does class struggle exist? We can now affirm that classes do exist in socialist countries and that class struggle undoubtedly exists. . . .

The bourgeois revolutions in Europe in such countries as England and France had many ups and downs. After the overthrow of feudalism there were several restorations and reversals of fortune. This kind of reversal is also possible in socialist countries. An example of this is Yugoslavia which has changed its nature and become revisionist, changing from a workers' and peasants' country to a country ruled by reactionary nationalist elements. In our country we must come to grasp, understand and study this problem really thoroughly. We must acknowledge that classes will continue to exist for a long time. We must also acknowledge the existence of a struggle of class against class, and admit the possibility of the restoration of reactionary classes. We must raise our vigilance and properly educate our youth as well as the cadres, the masses and the middle- and basic-level cadres. Old cadres must also study these problems and be educated. Otherwise a country like ours can still move towards its opposite.

TWENTY MANIFESTATIONS OF BUREAUCRACY (1970)

. . .

2. They are conceited, complacent, and they aimlessly discuss politics. They do not grasp their work; they are subjective and one-sided; they are careless; they do not listen to people; they are truculent and arbitrary; they force orders; they do not care about reality; they maintain blind control. This is authoritarian bureaucracy.

3. They are very busy from morning until evening; they labor the whole year long; they do not examine people and they do not investigate matters; they do not study policies; they do not rely upon the masses; they do not prepare their statements; they do not plan their work. This is brainless, misdirected bureaucracy. In other words, it is routinism.

4. Their bureaucratic attitude is immense; they can not have any direction; they are egoistic; they beat their gongs to blaze the way; they cause people to become afraid just by looking at them; they repeatedly hurl all kinds of abuse at people; their work style is crude; they do not treat people equally. This is the bureaucracy of the overlords.

. . .

14. The greater an official becomes, the worse his temperament gets; his demands for supporting himself become higher and higher; his home and its furnishings become more and more luxurious; and his access to things becomes better and better. The upper strata gets the larger share while the lower gets high prices; there is extravagance and waste; the upper and lower and the left and right raise their hands. This is the bureaucracy of putting on official airs.

. . .

16. They fight among themselves for power and money; they extend their hands into the party; they want fame and fortune; they want positions, and if they do not get it they are not satisfied; they choose to be fat and to be lean; they pay a great deal of attention to wages; they are cozy when it comes to their comrades but they care nothing about the masses. This is the bureaucracy that is fighting for power and money.

. . .

19. Their revolutionary will is weak; their politics has degenerated and changed

its character; they act as if they are highly qualified; they put on official airs; they do not exercise their minds or their hands. They eat their fill every day; they easily avoid hard work; they call a doctor when they are not sick; they go on excursions to the mountains and to the seashore; they do things superficially; they worry about their individual interests, but they do not worry whatsoever about the national interest. This is degenerate bureaucracy.

26

A Chinese Peasant
Maps His Road to Wealth

The death of Mao in 1976 led to major changes in Chinese life. Within two years Deng Xiaoping (b. 1904), once denounced by Mao as an "unrepentant capitalist roader," emerged as China's new leader. Reversing many of Mao's policies, Deng has sought to lead China toward the "four modernizations" of agriculture, industry, science-technology, and national defense. Centralized economic planning has been modified to make room for free-market economics. Foreign investment is now welcome in China. The controls over intellectual life, which were extraordinarily restrictive during the Cultural Revolution (1966–76), have been relaxed.

The results of Deng's policies have been mixed. Agricultural productivity has greatly increased, contributing to an overall rise in the standard of living. In addition, Chinese universities have made great strides in repairing the damage the Cultural Revolution caused. However, inflation, unemployment, and growing regional and social inequality have emerged as potentially serious problems in China. What these various trends mean for the future of the world's most populous country is unclear.

The author of the following selection is a peasant who has lived through the turmoil of the last four decades and benefited from Deng's economic policies. Indeed, in 1984, Wang Xin's family was one of the twenty-two richest in China, having an income in excess of ten thousand *yuan* (approximately $17,500). What did the 1949 Revolution mean to Wang and his family? How did they fare during the period up to the death of Mao? Is Wang a capitalist? How does Wang compare with the peasants that Mao observed in Hunan in 1927?

From Wang Xin with Yang Xiaobing, "A Peasant Maps His Road to Wealth," *Beijing Review,* 27 (12 November 1984), pp. 28–30. Reprinted by permission.

There is a long story behind my family's prosperity. My family's history is closely linked with the history of the Chinese society. So let me start my story with the rise and fall of the country.

In 1941, I was born to a poor peasant family in Pinggu County. At the time, my family had 10 members from three generations, but we had no farmland at all. My grandpa and his brother had to work for the landlord. My father and his brother wove at home and traded their coarse cloth at the market for some food. While peddling their handmade cloth, they had to be alert and evasive to avoid being forced to bribe the police.

One winter day, my grandpa's brother had two fingers bit off while feeding cattle for the landlord. The landlord simply dismissed him when he saw he was no longer useful. This made our lives even worse. My grandma had no other way to earn money but to pick wild jujubes in the mountains, which were ground up and mixed with wild herbs to make something like a bun.

At the time, my grandparents and parents wanted to work hard and get rich. Their desire, however, was merely a dream.

BRIGHT DAWN

In 1949 New China was founded and we peasants became masters of the country. Land reform was carried out, with feudalist land ownership abolished and farmland returned to the tillers. All the 300 peasant families in my village got shares of farmland, averaging 0.2 hectare per person. For us peasants, this really meant something to live on.

During the land reform, the landlords' surplus rooms were confiscated and the extra rooms were distributed among the poor. My family moved from a three-room thatched house into a tile-roofed house with seven rooms. Though only a small child at the time, I clearly remember how happy the peasants were.

In 1951 the agricultural collectivization movement got underway in my village. We first got organized into mutual-aid production teams and then into elementary agricultural co-operatives, pooling our land and sharing the dividends. In 1956 we switched to the advanced agricultural co-operatives and put our farmland into public ownership. The principle of "to each according to his work" was followed. The removal of land boundary stakes made it possible to develop a unified farming plan on a larger scale and created favourable conditions for water conservation projects and agricultural mechanization.

With the land under public ownership, all the villagers met to discuss how to use their farmland and how to distribute the income. This was completely different from preliberation days when we had no land at all.

During those years, since everyone worked hard and the government provided the co-operative with preferential loans and farm tools, production grew rapidly. The grain output, for instance, grew from 2,250 kg per hectare before 1949 to 4,225 kg in 1956. I remember my family got more than enough wheat that year. We lived quite well during those years.

In July of 1957, our village was hit by a hailstorm. With crops ruined, old people worried that they would have to go begging as they had in the past when natural disasters struck. But when the government heard about our problems, it exempted us from agricultural taxes for that whole year, shipped in grain seeds and potato seedlings and urged us to tide over the difficulty while developing production. By relying on the collective strength of the village and everybody's hard work, no one ran short of food.

In 1957 something important happened to me. I was enrolled in the county's middle school after I graduated from the primary school in my village. Before me, for generations all my family had been illiterate.

TWISTS AND TURNS

In 1958 we got organized into the people's commune, which brought about some desirable changes, but also resulted in some baffling developments.

A people's commune usually consisted of several villages (a village was usually an advanced co-operative). To see many people working on a vast expanse of land was really a spectacular view. Soon after the founding of the people's commune, a tractor station was set up to oversee ploughing and sowing.

The year of 1959, however, was chaotic. Some people said we had arrived at real communism. All the people in my village ate at the same canteen, free of charge. We produced hundreds of thousands of kilogrammes of sweet potatoes. But nobody wanted them. The result was that all the potatoes rotted in the fields. Some people were prone to boasting and exaggeration. There was a 0.13 hectare plot of farmland by my middle school. About 2,500 kg of wheat seeds were sown and people said it would yield 100,000 kg. But, in reality, it produced only 250 kg (because far too many seeds were sown). Though the Central Committee of the Chinese Communist Party later criticized this mistake of being boastful and exaggerating, much of wealth had already been wasted. The negative impacts of such actions were felt for years.

The people's commune authorities also gave some arbitrary and impractical orders. Our village had a piece of land which should have been planted with soybeans. Some cadres of the people's commune, however, ordered us to grow carrots. Another piece of land which had already been planted with sweet potatoes was designated for soybeans. All these illogical orders resulted in sizeable losses.

It now becomes clear that the inclination to boast and give arbitrary orders came from "Leftist" thinking.

Of course, the people's commune did some good. The most visible improvements were the water conservation projects. I myself took part in building several big projects.

In 1960 I came back home after graduation from junior middle school. My family of 10 members was then broken up into several small ones. I moved in with my uncle and his wife. Peasants from surrounding villages were then building the Haizi Reservoir, which would irrigate almost 10,000 hectares, one-third of the county's total farmland. The builders, in addition to getting subsidies from the state, were paid in cash by the people's commune and received food rations. This made it attractive work and made it possible for the people's commune to mobilize enough people to build the big projects. The water conservaton projects on which I worked are still benefiting the people.

I got married in 1962 and later had two sons and one daughter. More mouths need more money. I managed to increase the income for my family. The next year, I spent my spare time collecting firewood in the winter and growing melons on my family's private plot in the summer. The extra work brought in more than 400 yuan. Our life was pretty good.

In 1966, the chaotic "cultural revolution" began. I could no longer collect firewood or grow melons because these were seen as capitalist undertakings. We peasants, unlike workers who have regular wages, had to work in the fields or we would have had nothing to eat. So our agricultural production continued as usual.

In retrospect, my life improved steadily after I began working. But I always thought I could have done much better. I was held back. In 1969, I was elected deputy leader of the brigade in charge of sideline production. One day I bought some eggs from a state chicken farm in order to hatch chickens for the brigade. I sold some of the surplus eggs and made 100 yuan for the brigade. I was shocked when I was criticized for selling the eggs. I was labelled a capitalist speculator.

AFFLUENCE BEGINS

It is only in recent years that I have been able to work hard and grow prosperous without restrictions.

In 1979 I learnt from newspapers and broadcasts that the Party had adopted flexible policies in the countryside. The contract responsibility system, which guaranteed more pay for more work, became popular in my village. The new policies allowed us peasants to become the real masters of agriculture and set us free to work hard and make more money. I wondered what I could do to get wealthy.

In 1981, I chose to raise chickens. I spent 380 yuan to buy 500 chicks. I was then a Communist Party member and the brigade's deputy leader. What I did raised some eyebrows in the village, but it didn't affect my job. The policy supported me. I got rich by working hard. Nothing wrong. I earned 850 yuan that year.

I then expanded the scope of my chicken business. The state credit co-operative offered me loans and encouraged me to forge ahead. I read books and studied to learn how to raise chickens scientifically. I also learnt how to treat chicken diseases such as diarrhoea and typhoid fever. In 1982, I sold the state 6,000 chickens for 9,000 yuan. With my income from the brigade and other household sidelines. I earned a total of more than 10,000 yuan, a figure larger than my combined income for the previous 10 years. The county recognized my achievements and rewarded me.

The Party policy is to bring into full play everyone's enthusiasm for production. It creates more wealth for the country and provides a good life for the peasants. Being among the first in my county to get rich, I'd like to lead others to prosperity.

Wang Shuchen has eight family members, but only two are able men. They have had a hard time. I explained the Party's policy to him and asked if he would like to raise chickens, too. I lent him 580 yuan, saying, "Please use this money to raise chickens. If the chickens die, I won't ask for the money back." Because he was less experienced in raising chickens, I went to his home several times every day to help him write observation notes, make plans for buying chicken feed, keep balance sheets and cure chicken diseases. Last year Wang earned more than 5,000 yuan from his chicken business alone.

So far, I have encouraged 80 families to raise chickens. Last year alone, I lent the families 5,800 yuan free of interest. In addition, I took time to help them treat chicken diseases and teach them how to raise chickens. I was always available whenever I was asked.

My family's life has improved very much in recent years. However, I spent only 400 yuan buying a radio cassette recorder for my daughter to study a foreign language for her college examinations. Other than that, I have spent not a single penny for other electric appliances for my family. I'd rather spend my money expanding production. I bought a walking tractor that cost more than 3,000 yuan.

Not long ago, I was elected secretary of the village Party branch. Since the Party job took much of my time, my chicken business suffered. But it is worth it, because we are helping more people become prosperous.

I am now wondering how to boost enthusiasm even more so that we can turn our village into a village which specializes in chicken raising. We also want to develop other sideline business and to raise other livestock in order to make our village more competitive in commodity production. Our village cadres have decided that whoever comes up with a practical plan to make more than 10,000 yuan next year will be the first to get material assistance from the village.

27

Gender and Age in Contemporary Japan

Japan's emergence as a modern industrial society has been one of the most important developments in the second half of the twentieth century. At the end of the Second World War the country lay in ruins. However, postwar economic growth—the Japanese "miracle"—quickly overcame the war's destructiveness. By 1965 the Japanese economy was nearly four times as productive as it had been during the 1930s. In the late 1980s the country's gross national product is one of the highest worldwide. Japanese leadership in the manufacture of auto-mobiles, consumer electronics, and computer chips is well known, and Japanese living standards are approaching those of the West.

As the following reading reveals, the process of modernization has had major implications for gender relations in Japan. Among men (and many women), patriarchal attitudes remain strong. Japanese women who seek careers in the corporate world or in academia face formidable obstacles. At the same time, changing social conditions—a low birth rate and a greatly increased life expectancy—are compelling Japanese women to rethink traditional roles.

Higuchi Keiko, the author of the selection below, is a well-known Japanese feminist. What changes does she see occurring in the attitudes of Japanese women? Are the experiences of middle-class women different from those of other women? What does Higuchi have to say about the attitudes of men? What are the implications of a lengthened life expectancy for women and men? It is also important to compare Japanese trends with those elsewhere: why are many

From Higuchi Keiko, "Japanese Women in Transition," *Japan Quarterly,* 29 (July–September 1982): 311, 313–18.

changes among Japanese women similar to those in the West and the Soviet Union? Are there any major differences?

"The Age of Women"—so ran the catch-phrase adorning a Japanese newspaper advertisement on New Year's Day 1979, the eve of the 80s. The ad went on in part to say: "Dazzling—simply dazzling, the women of today. Mothers and daughters taking off suddenly on trips abroad, or giving up their diets and going in for yoga instead. Expressing themselves freely, without fear or hesitation, these are women who know the art of enjoying life to the full . . . Today's women are off the sidelines to stay."

The slogan notwithstanding, this message is probably best understood as a gift of flattery from male salesmen to female buyers. Beginning with this advertisement, the decade of the 80s has come with increasing frequency to be called "the age of women." And yet one has the distinct sense that before yielding any substantial results, the term was quickly taken over by the advertising industry as a piece of "fashion." In any case, the emergence of language such as this in newspaper advertising is surely a sign of change in the situation of Japanese women. . . .

The consciousness of Japanese women is now in a state of transition. Their attitude toward the idea that "men should work outside the home, women inside" has changed greatly in the last 10 years. In a 1972 survey of attitudes on women's issues undertaken by the Prime Minister's Office, over 80 percent of women respondents agreed with the idea as stated above. But in a similar survey conducted in 1976, the year after International Women's Year, those concurring that "men work, and women stay home" were 49 percent, while 40 percent disagreed and 11 percent were undecided. The wording of the question as well as the range of possible answers vary, making simple comparisons difficult, but it would seem clear at any rate that doubts regarding the traditional idea of sex-differentiated work roles are rapidly growing. In 1979 the Prime Minister's Office conducted another survey posing the same questions as in 1976, but this time, in response to the assertion that "men work and women stay home," pollees were evenly divided among "agree," "disagree" and "don't know," with each answer drawing a response in the 30th percentile. When the question pertains to "men" and "women," people are somewhat likely to go against the traditional view, but when the words "husbands" and "wives" are substituted, resistance declines. Acceptance of sex-differentiated work roles is still deep-rooted in Japan.

Among the younger generation, however, there is possibility for more rapid change. In the 1979 survey by the Prime Minister's Office, the assertion by 25 percent of unmarried women that they had "no wish to marry" attracted wide notice. Japanese have a high marriage rate, so much so that they have been called a people "fond of marrying": by age 50, 97 percent of both men and women have been married at least once. The Prime Minister's Office asked the same question in 1972, but at that time only 14 percent of women declared themselves uninterested in marrying. In the 1979 survey, a mere 12 percent of men selected the same response, thus revealing a gap in attitudes toward marriage between the sexes. Moreover, women responding that "a woman's happiness lies in marriage" went down from 40 percent to 32 percent.

Yearly surveys by Nippon Recruit Center, an employment agency, on "attitudes of female university students toward employment" show that until the late 70s, even among graduates of four-year colleges, those desiring to work "until retirement age" amounted to scarcely 20 percent. In the 1981 survey, however, 41 percent of respondents (19 percent for junior college graduates) gave that answer. The most frequently given answer was to work "until a child is born, then again after the child is older" (58.7 percent). Significantly, those who said simply "until marrying" or "until a child is born"—thus relegating work to a brief period early in their lifetimes—were in the minority for the first time at 25.3 percent or one quarter of the sample. For Japan, where women are held to be at a particular disadvantage in combining marriage and a career, and where long-term female employment is much rarer than in Europe and America, such a shift in attitudes is truly remarkable. . . .

In the Tokyo residential area where I live, around 10 every morning housewives clad in short, above-the-knee outfits get on their bikes, tennis rackets in baskets, and pedal off in a row for the local tennis court. A conspicuous change in the last 10 years has been the phenomenal growth in large cities nationwide of housewives' hobby and culture centers, sponsored by newspapers, broadcasting companies, department stores and even big businesses. Women in their 30s and 40s, freed from the burden of caring for small children, flock to tennis courts and culture centers out of a desire to be with others like themselves—a hunger, perhaps, for companionship—as they seek the pattern for the latter half of their lives. In the past, Japanese women were referred to by their husbands as *kanai,* meaning literally "inside the house"—and that is exactly where they stayed. Today, as women step out more and more in search of entertainment, education and a wide variety of activities, one sometimes hears a man say of his wife, "She's no *kanai;* she's my *kagai* ('outside the house')."

But housewives commuting to tennis courts and cultural enrichment centers are, after all, outnumbered by those commuting to work. The number of female employees is steadily increasing, and at present nearly 70 percent are married. In addition, more than half of all unemployed housewives aged 40 and above "would like to work." By far their biggest motivation is to bring the family budget out of the red. Although real earnings of household heads have declined in the last few years, the standard of living has held its own, thanks largely to increases in wives' earnings.

Not long ago, when I was in a department store, two clerks called out to me one after the other. They told me they had heard me speak at a lecture meeting sponsored by a grade-school PTA. Both of them are active as PTA members while holding down part-time jobs in a department store. The day of the lecture meeting, they said, they had taken off work to attend. I could not help feeling struck by this clear example of change. It wasn't many years ago that at PTA meetings one frequently heard the complaint that "so many women have jobs nowadays, there's nobody to work for the PTA." Some ladies even went so far as to take part-time jobs only when officers' elections came around, and then plead work as an excuse to decline. Now many women manage successfully to juggle work outside the home with active participation in community affairs. Working housewives have become so commonplace that it can no longer be said that "PTA is for mothers who don't work."

Toward the end of April 1982, the Ministry of Labor published results of a "Basic survey on Wage Structure in 1981." According to these results, although until recently male workers attained their top earning power in their 50s, now male wages have begun to peak earlier, in the 45–50 age bracket. "My husband's earnings will peak when he's in his 40s—so I'd better go to work to help out the budget." This sort of determination appears to be spreading rapidly among Japanese women.

Women in Japan are stepping out of the house in ever-swelling numbers. Yet men persist in clinging to the notion that "women's work is in the home." Those most critical of sex-differentiated labor roles are not men, but women. It appears inevitable, therefore, that discord will arise between the sexes.

Conflict between husband and wife is apt to arise from the work overload of working wives. The belief that household affairs are the wife's exclusive responsibility is deeply ingrained in Japanese society, and many women would in fact regard their husband's entrance into the kitchen as an unwelcome intrusion. According to a 1976 research survey by the Prime Minister's Office on "Lifestyles in Society," unemployed housewives spend an average of five hours and 54 minutes each day on housework and childcare, compared to three hours and 29 minutes for those with outside jobs. Husbands of unemployed wives, for their part, contribute an average of seven minutes daily to the same tasks, while for husbands of working women the figure is an astounding six minutes. Thus, utterly betraying the expectation that "it is only natural for the husband to help out around the house if the wife works too," Japenese married men reign as *shujin* ("husband"; literally, "master") in their homes, and whether or not the wife has an outside job they do virtually no housework.

The husband expects his wife to look after the home, and in the home he seeks a place of recreation and relaxation in which to garner strength for the coming day's work. This is the view of the wife's role, and of the function of the home, given often in Japanese textbooks for the lower, compulsory levels of school. The husband, behaving exactly as the textbooks predict he will, hands over his pay envelope to his wife without even looking inside. Most big corporations nowadays transfer paychecks directly to employees' bank accounts, but the wife remains firmly in charge of home finances. The husband sees the act of turning over his entire salary to his wife simultaneously as an expression of love and a fulfillment of obligation. The wife, however, has begun to entertain misgivings about an existence spent for the most part waiting passively at home for her husband's return.

The profound changes in the lifestyles of Japanese women surely have few precedents anywhere in the world. It is well known that Japanese women expend more love and energy on their children than on their husbands. But the children who are objects of so much maternal devotion have decreased drastically in number per family while average life expectancies have continued to rise. In 1940, a woman whose youngest child had just entered school had only 7.6 years of life remaining; in 1978, the number of years she could count on had jumped to 44. After the youngest child marries, moreover, she and her husband can still look forward to nearly a score of years of married life. . . .

The new women's liberation movement which spread to Japan in the early 70s brought pressure for change in the lives of both men and women. And the U.N.'s Decade for Women forced the Japanese government to face up to many of the issues involved. At the same time, the extremely rapid aging of Japanese society—a phenomenon without precedent or equal in the world—is forcing upon us, willy-nilly, a reevaluation of relationships between the sexes, married and unmarried alike.

Aged people (those 65 years old and above) now comprise a mere 9 percent of the population of Japan, but in the coming 30 to 40 years it is anticipated that their numbers will swell to more than 23 percent. No advanced nation has yet experienced a society in which one out of every four people is elderly.

The life span of Japanese women is approaching 80 years. The question of how middle-aged Japanese women are to spend the latter half of this extended lifetime is one that must be asked. With marriage as the single-minded goal of their youth, followed by harried years of caring for husband and children, they have had little time for self-reflection; now, realizing after their children are grown or their husband retires that without a personal goal they will be unable to face the loneliness of widowhood, these women are full of consternation. Among Japanese aged 65 and over, those whose spouse is living account for 80 percent of the men, but only one in three of women. Soon there will be one million old people living alone in Japan, 80 percent of them female. Their income, moreover, is less than half that of men. And of those looking after elderly invalids in their own homes, as many as 90 percent are women. Lately the idea that "the problems of old age are women's problems" is voiced more and more often at women's gatherings. . . .

The traditional life-patterns for Japanese men and women—until very recently thought natural and common-sensical—are now, under the pressures of a highly developed, rapidly aging industrial society, in a period of transition, as people seek to put them in a new frame of reference.

28

Gandhi and Modern India

No individual has been more important to the history of modern India than Mohandas K. Gandhi (1869–1948). The son of a prosperous Hindu official in western India, Gandhi studied law in England. He then spent twenty years in South Africa, where he led the Indian minority in a struggle against discrimination from white rulers. Returning to India in 1915, Gandhi plunged into the nationalist movement. From the end of the First World War until his assassination nearly three decades later, he led his people to establish Indian home rule.

Gandhi's legacy is both rich and ambiguous. For Indian patriots his greatest achievement was transforming the Indian National Congress from a middle-class organization into a mass movement; indeed, there is general agreement that it was the Mahatma (Great Soul) who won the commoners of India to the nationalist cause, thereby compelling the British to eventually withdraw from the subcontinent. Many also admire Gandhi's commitment to *satyagraha* (soul force or passive resistance) as well as his vigorous efforts on behalf of the untouchables and his quest for Hindu-Muslim unity. On the other hand, Gandhi's critics charge that his hostility to modernity and his opposition to mass insurrection contributed to the survival of much that is archaic in India today.

Below are excerpts from the work that best summarizes Gandhi's basic ideas, his 1909 booklet *Hind Swaraj* (Indian Home Rule). It is written in the form of a dialogue between an editor (Gandhi himself) and an anonymous reader. What is Gandhi's criticism of modern civilization? What does he admire about

From M. K. Gandhi, *The Collected Works of Mahatma Gandhi,* Vol. X (Ahmedabad: Navijivan Press, 1963), pp. 18–21, 36–38, 48–49, 51–53.

traditional India? How does Gandhi define passive resistance? Compare Gandhi's ideas with those of Lenin and Mao found elsewhere in this volume (see selections 22 and 25).

Editor: If India copies England, it is my firm conviction that she will be ruined.

Reader: To what do you ascribe this state of England?

Editor: It is not due to any peculiar fault of the English people, but the condition is due to modern civilization. It is a civilization only in name. Under it the nations of Europe are becoming degraded and ruined day by day.

Reader: Now you will have to explain what you mean by civilization. . . .

Editor: Let us first consider what state of things is described by the word "civilization." Its true test lies in the fact that people living in it make bodily welfare the object of life. We will take some examples. The people of Europe today live in better-built houses than they did a hundred years ago. This is considered an emblem of civilization, and this is also a matter to promote bodily happiness. Formerly, they wore skins, and used spears as their weapons. Now, they wear long trousers, and, for embellishing their bodies, they wear a variety of clothing, and, instead of spears, they carry with them revolvers containing five or more chambers. If people of a certain country, who have hitherto not been in the habit of wearing much clothing, boots, etc., adopt European clothing, they are supposed to have become civilized out of savagery. Formerly, in Europe, people plowed their lands mainly by manual labor. Now, one man can plow a vast tract by means of steam engines and can thus amass great wealth. This is called a sign of civilization. Formerly, only a few men wrote valuable books. Now, anybody writes and prints anything he likes and poisons people's minds. Formerly, men traveled in wagons. Now, they fly through the air in trains at the rate of four hundred and more miles per day. This is considered the height of civilization. It has been stated that, as men progress, they shall be able to travel in airships and reach any part of the world in a few hours. Men will not need the use of their hands and feet. They will press a button, and they will have their clothing by their side. They will press another button, and they will have their newspaper. A third, and a motor-car will be in waiting for them. They will have a variety of delicately dished up food. Everything will be done by machinery. Formerly, when people wanted to fight with one another, they measured between them their bodily strength; now it is possible to take away thousands of lives by one man working behind a gun from a hill. This is civilization. Formerly, men worked in the open air only as much as they liked. Now thousands of workmen meet together and for the sake of maintenance work in factories or mines. Their condition is worse than that of beasts. They are obliged to work, at the risk of their lives, at most dangerous occupations, for the sake of millionaires. Formerly, men were made slaves under physical compulsion. Now they are enslaved by temptation of money and of the luxuries that money can buy. . . .

This civilization is irreligion, and it has taken such a hold on the people in Europe that those who are in it appear to be half-mad. They lack real physical strength or courage. They keep up their energy by intoxication. They can hardly be happy in solitude. Women, who should be the queens of households, wander in the streets or they slave away in factories. For the sake of a pittance, half a million women in England alone are laboring under trying circumstances in factories or similar institutions. This awful fact is one of the causes of the daily growing suffragette movement.

This civilization is such that one has only to be patient and it will be self-destroyed. According to the teaching of Mahomed this would be considered a Satanic Civilization. Hinduism calls it the Black Age. I cannot give you an adequate conception of it. It is eating into the vitals of the English nation. It must be shunned. . . .

Reader: What then, is [true] civilization?

Editor: Civilization is that mode of conduct which points out to man the path of duty. Performance of duty and observance of morality are convertible terms. To observe morality is to attain mastery over our mind and our passions. So doing, we know ourselves. The Gujarati equivalent for civilization means "good conduct."

If this definition be correct, then India, as so many writers have shown, has nothing to learn from anybody else, and this is as it should be. We notice that the mind is a restless bird; the more it gets the more it wants, and still remains unsatisfied. The more we indulge our passions the more unbridled they become. Our ancestors, therefore, set a limit to our indulgences. They saw that happiness was largely a mental condition. A man is not necessarily happy because he is rich, or unhappy because he is poor. The rich are often seen to be unhappy, the poor to be happy. Millions will always remain poor. Observing all this, our ancestors dissuaded us from luxuries and pleasures. We have managed with the same kind of plow as existed thousands of years ago. We have retained the same kind of cottages that we had in former times and our indigenous education remains the same as before. We have had no system of life-corroding competition. Each followed his own occupation or trade and charged a regulation wage. It was not that we did not know how to invent machinery, but our forefathers knew that, if we set our hearts after such things, we would become slaves and lose our moral fibre. They, therefore, after due deliberation decided that we should only do what we could with our hands and feet. They saw that our real happiness and health consisted in a proper use of our hands and feet. They further reasoned the large cities were a snare and a useless encumbrance and that people would not be happy in them, that there would be gangs of thieves and robbers, prostitution, and vice flourishing in them and that poor men would be robbed by rich men. They were, therefore, satisfied with small villages. They saw that kings and their swords were inferior to the sword of ethics, and they, therefore, held the sovereigns of the earth to be inferior to the Rishis and the Fakirs. . . .

Now you see what I consider to be real civilization. Those who want to change conditions such as I have described are enemies of the country and are sinners.

·   ·   ·

Editor: Passive resistance is a method of securing rights by personal suffering; it is the reverse of resistance by arms. When I refuse to do a thing that is repugnant to my conscience, I use soul-force. For instance, the government of the day has passed a law which is applicable to me. I do not like it. If by using violence I force the government to repeal the law, I am employing what may be termed body-force. If I do not obey the law and accept the penalty for its breach, I use soul-force. It involves sacrifice of self.

Everybody admits that sacrifice of self is infinitely superior to sacrifice of others. Moreover, if this kind of force is used in a cause that is unjust, only the person using it suffers. He does not make others suffer for his mistakes. Men have before now done many things which were subsequently found to have been wrong. No man can claim that he is absolutely in the right or that a particular thing is wrong because he thinks so, but it is wrong for him so long as that is his deliberate judgment. It is therefore meet that he should not do that which he knows to be wrong, and suffer the consequence whatever it may be. This is the key to the use of soul-force. . . .

Whether I go beyond . . . [the laws] or whether I do not is a matter of no consequence. . . . We simply want to find out what is right and to act accordingly. The real meaning of the statement that we are a law-abiding nation is that we are passive resisters. When we do not like certain laws, we do not break the heads of law-givers but we suffer and do not submit to the laws. That we should obey laws whether good or bad is a new-fangled notion. There was no such thing in former days. The people disregarded those laws they did not like and suffered the penalties for their breach. It is contrary to our manhood if we obey laws repugnant to our conscience. Such teaching is opposed to religion and means slavery. If the government were to ask us to go about without any clothing, should we do so? If I were a passive resister, I would say to them that I would have nothing to do with their law. But we have so forgotten ourselves and become so compliant that we do not mind any degrading laws.

A man who has realized his manhood, who fears only God, will fear no one else. Man-made laws are not necessarily binding on him. Even the government does not expect any such thing from us. They do not say: "You must do such and such a thing," but they say: "If you do not do it, we will punish you." We are sunk so low that we fancy that it is our duty and our religion to do what the law lays down. If man will only realize that it is unmanly to obey laws that are unjust, no man's tyranny will enslave him. This is the key to self-rule or home-rule. . . .

Passive resistance is an all-sided sword, it can be used anyhow; it blesses him who uses it and him against whom it is used. Without drawing a drop of blood it produces far-reaching results. It never rusts and cannot be stolen. Competition between passive resisters does not exhaust. The sword of passive resistance does not require a scabbard. . . .

To become a passive resister is easy enough but it is also equally difficult. I have known a lad of fourteen years become a passive resister; I have known also sick people do likewise; and I have also known physically strong and otherwise happy people unable to take up passive resistance. After a great deal of experience it seems to me that those who want to become passive resisters for the service of the country have to observe perfect chastity, adopt poverty, follow truth, and cultivate fearlessness.

Chastity is one of the greatest disciplines without which the mind cannot attain requisite firmness. A man who is unchaste loses stamina, becomes emasculated and cowardly. He whose mind is given over to animal passions is not capable of any great effort. This can be proved by innumerable instances. What, then, is a married person to do is the question that arises naturally; and yet it need not. When a husband and wife gratify the passions, it is no less an animal indulgence on that account. Such an indulgence, except for perpetuating the race, is strictly prohibited. But a passive resister has to avoid even that very limited indulgence because he can have no desire for progeny. A married man, therefore, can observe perfect chastity. This subject is not capable of being treated at greater length. Several questions arise: How is one to carry one's wife with one? what are her rights? and other similar questions. Yet those who wish to take part in a great work are bound to solve these puzzles.

Just as there is necessity for chastity, so is there for poverty. Pecuniary ambition and passive resistance cannot well go together. Those who have money are not expected to throw it away, but they *are* expected to be indifferent about it. They must be prepared to lose every penny rather than give up passive resistance.

Passive resistance has been described in the course of our discussion as truth-force. Truth, therefore, has necessarily to be followed and that at any cost. In this connection, academic questions such as whether a man may not lie in order to save a life, etc., arise, but these questions occur only to those who wish to justify lying. Those who want to follow truth every time are not placed in such a quandry; and if they are, they are still saved from a false position.

Passive resistance cannot proceed a step without fearlessness. Those alone can follow the path of passive resistance who are free from fear, whether as to their possessions, false honor, their relatives, the government, bodily injuries or death. . . .

29

Nehru and India During the Second World War

If it is difficult to overestimate Gandhi's impact on modern India, the same can be said of the Mahatma's successor as leader of the Indian people, Jawaharlal Nehru (1889–1964). The son of a Brahmin lawyer and a graduate of England's best schools, Nehru emerged as a major figure in the Indian National Congress during the 1920s; by the 1930s he was widely seen as Gandhi's heir apparent. In 1947 Nehru became independent India's first prime minister, a position he held until his death in 1964. During his years as India's head of state, Nehru was one of the most influential leaders of the Third World.

In the following excerpts from one of his best-known books—written while he was in a British prison—Nehru recalls one of the great turning points in the Indian struggle against the British. In 1942, angry at the British for having taken India into the Second World War without prior consultation, Gandhi and the Indian National Congress called on their colonial masters to "quit India" immediately. The British responded by arresting the leading Congress activists, some sixty thousand in all. Below is Nehru's recollection of the protest and repression that followed, including his account of the severe famine of 1943.

As you read these pages, keep the following questions in mind: Do the events of 1942 suggest that Gandhi's commitment to nonviolence was unworkable? How does Nehru explain the causes of the 1943 famine? How do Nehru's life and thought illustrate the contradictory impact that the British had on India?

In the early morning of August 9, 1942, numerous arrests were made all over India. What happened then? Only scraps of news trickled through after many weeks to us, and even now we can form only an incomplete picture of what took place. All the prominent leaders had been suddenly removed and no one seemed to know what should be done. Protests, of course, there had to be, and there were spontaneous demonstrations. These were broken up and fired upon and tear gas bombs were used, and all the usual channels of giving expression to public feeling were stopped. And then all these suppressed emotions broke out and crowds gathered in cities and rural areas and came in conflict with the police and the military. They attacked espcially what seemed to them the symbols of British authority and power, the police stations, post offices, and railway stations; they cut the telegraph and telephone wires. These unarmed and leaderless mobs faced police and military firing, according to official statements, on 538 occasions, and they were also machine-gunned from low-flying aircraft. For a month or two or more these disturbances continued in various parts of the country, and then they dwindled away and gave place to sporadic occurrences. "The disturbances," said Mr. Churchill in the House of Commons, "were crushed with all the weight of the Government," and he praised "the loyalty and steadfastness of the brave Indian police as well as the Indian official class generally whose behaviour has been deserving of the highest praise." He added that "larger reinforcements have reached India and the number of white troops in that country is larger than at any time in the British connection." These foreign troops and the Indian police had won many a battle against the unarmed peasantry of India and crushed their rebellion; and that other main prop of the British Raj in India, the official class, had helped, actively or passively, in the process.

This reaction in the country was extraordinarily widespread, both in towns and villages. In almost all the provinces and in a large number of the Indian states there were innumberable demonstrations, in spite of official prohibition. There were hartals, closure of shops and markets, and a stoppage of business, everywhere, varying in duration from a number of days to some weeks and in a few cases to over a month. So also labor strikes. More orgainzed and used to disciplined action, industrial workers in many important centers spontaneously declared strikes in protest against government action in arresting national leaders. A notable instance of this was at the vital steel city of Jamshedpur, where the skilled workers, drawn from all over India, kept away from work for a fortnight and only agreed to return on the management's promising that they would try their best to get the Congress leaders released and a national government formed. In the great textile center of Ahmadabad there was also a sudden and complete stoppage of work in all the numerous factories without any special call from the trade union. This general strike in Ahmadabad continued peacefully for over three months in spite of all attempts to break it. It was a purely political and spontaneous reaction of the workers and they suffered greatly, for it was a time of relatively high wages. They received no financial help whatever from outside during this long period. At other centers the strikes were of briefer duration, lasting sometimes only for a few days. . . .

And so, for the first time since the great revolt of 1857, vast numbers of people again rose to challenge by force (but a force without arms!) the fabric of British rule in India. It was a foolish and inopportune challenge, for all the organized and armed force was on the other side, and in greater measure indeed than at any previous time in history. However great the numbers of the crowd, it cannot prevail in a contest of force against armed forces. It had to fail unless those armed forces themselves changed their allegiance. But those crowds had not prepared for the contest or chosen the time for it. It came upon them unawares, and in their immediate reaction to it, however unthinking and misdirected it was, they showed their love of India's freedom and their hatred of foreign domination.

Though the policy of nonviolence went under, for the time being at least the long training that the people had received under it had one important and desirable result. In spite of the passions aroused, there was very little, if any, racial feeling, and on the whole there was a deliberate attempt on the part of the people to avoid causing bodily injury to their opponents. There was a great deal of destruction of communications and governmental property, but even in the midst of this destruction care was taken to avoid loss of life. This was not always possible or always attempted, especially in actual conflicts with the police or other armed forces. According to official reports, so far as I have been able to find them, about one hundred persons were killed by mobs in the course of the disturbances all over India. This figure is very small considering the extent and area of the disturbances and the conflicts with the police. One particularly brutal and distressing case was the murder of two Canadian airmen by a mob somewhere in Bihar. But generally speaking, the absence of racial feeling was very remarkable.

Official estimates of the number of people killed and wounded by police or military firing in the 1942 disturbances are: 1,028 killed and 3,200 wounded. These figures are certainly gross underestimates, for it has been officially stated that such firing took place on at least 538 occasions, and besides this, people were frequently shot at by the police or the military from moving lorries. It is very difficult to arrive at even an approximately correct figure. Popular estimates place the number of deaths at 25,000, but probably this is an exaggeration. Perhaps 10,000 may be nearer the mark.

· · ·

India was very sick, both in mind and body. While some people had prospered during the war, the burden on others had reached the breaking point, and as an awful reminder of this came famine, a famine of vast dimensions affecting Bengal and east and south India. It was the biggest and most devastating famine in India during the past 170 years of British dominion, comparable to those terrible famines which occurred from 1766 to 1770 in Bengal and Bihar as an early result of the establishment of British rule. Epidemics followed, especially cholera and malaria, and spread to other provinces, and even today they are taking their toll of scores of thousands of lives. Millions have died of famine and disease, and yet that specter hovers over India and claims its victims.

This famine unveiled the picture of India as it was below the thin veneer of the prosperity of a small number of people at the top—a picture of poverty and ugliness and human decay after all these generations of British rule. That was the culmination and fulfillment of British rule in India. It was no calamity of nature or play of the elements that brought this famine, nor was it caused by actual war operations and enemy blockade. Every competent observer is agreed that it was a man-made famine which could have been foreseen and avoided. Everyone is agreed that there was amazing indifference, incompetence, and complacency shown by all the authorities concerned. Right up to the last moment, when thousands were dying daily in the public streets, famine was denied and references to it in the press were suppressed by the censors. When the *Statesman* of Calcutta published gruesome and ghastly pictures of starving and dying women and children in the streets of Calcutta, a spokesman of the Government of India, speaking officially in the Central Assembly, protested against the "dramatization" of the situation; to him apparently it was a normal occurrence for thousands to die daily from starvation in Inida. Mr. Amery, of the India Office in London, distinguished himself especially by his denials and statements. And then, when it became impossible to deny or cloak the existence of widespread famine, each group in authority blamed some other group for it. The government of India said it was the fault of the provincial government—which itself was merely a puppet government functioning under the governor and through the civil service. They were all to blame, but most of all, inevitably, that authoritarian government which the viceroy represented in his person and which could do what it chose anywhere in India. In any democratic or semi-democratic country such a calamity would have swept away all the governments concerned with it. Not so in India, where everything continued as before. . . .

India, it is often said, is a land of contrasts, of some very rich and many very poor, of modernism and medievalism, of rulers and ruled, of the British and Indians. Never before had these contrasts been so much in evidence as in the city of Calcutta during those terrible months of famine in the latter half of 1943. The two worlds, normally living apart, almost ignorant of each other, were suddenly brought physically together and existed side by side. The contrast was startling, but even more startling was the fact that many people did not realize the horror and astonishing incongruity of it and continued to function in their old grooves. What they felt, one cannot say; one can only judge them by their actions. For most Englishmen this was perhaps easier, for they had lived their life apart, and caste-bound as they were, they could not vary their routine, even if some individuals felt the urge to do so. But those Indians who functioned in this way showed the wide gulf that separated them from their own people, which no considerations even of decency and humanity could bridge. . . .

Though the famine was undoubtedly due to war conditions and could have been prevented, it is equally true that its deeper causes lay in the basic policy which was impoverishing India and under which millions lived on the verge of starvation. In 1933 Major General Sir John Megaw, the director-general of the Indian Medical Service, wrote in the course of a report on public health in India: "Taking India as a whole the dispensary doctors regard 39 per cent of the people as being well nourished, 41 per cent as poorly nourished, and 20 per cent as very badly nourished. The most depressing picture is painted by the doctors of Bengal who regard only 22 per cent of the people of the province as being well nourished while 31 per cent are considered to be very badly nourished."

The tragedy of Bengal and the famines in Orissa, Malabar, and other places are the final judgment on British rule in India. The British will certainly leave India and their Indian empire will become a memory, but what will they leave when they have to go, what human degradation and accumulated sorrow? Tagore saw this picture as he lay dying three years ago: "But what kind of India will they leave behind, what stark misery? When the stream of their centuries' administration runs dry at last, what a waste of mud and filth they will leave behind them!"

30

Family and Gender in Contemporary India

From earliest times to the present day the family has been both the smallest and the most significant social unit in Indian society. Functioning simultaneously as the focus of economic, religious, and emotional life, the Hindu family has been even more important than caste in shaping the lives of most Indian people.

As suggested by earlier readings in Volume I, the traditional Indian family was formed by strongly patriarchal attitudes. From the sixth century, the term *sati* (true wife) was used to honor widows who committed suicide by throwing themselves on their deceased husband's funeral pyre—a practice that, though uncommon, was outlawed only in the nineteenth century. In addition, *purdah,*—the veiling and nearly complete seclusion of women, a custom that probably developed in north India following the coming of the Muslims—kept many Indian women from venturing beyond their own courtyard at any time in their lives.

The other important characteristic of the Hindu family was that it included not only the husband, his wife, and their children but also the husband's close relatives on the paternal side (his uncles and aunts, cousins, nephews, and nieces). The principal advantage of this joint-family arrangement was the security it provided to people who were highly vulnerable to economic distress.

In the following article from a recent issue of the *Times of India,* Viji Srinivasan indicates that the traditional family remains significant in her country today. Indeed, the joint or extended family is still overwhelmingly dominant on the subcontinent. However, as Srinivasan makes clear, the "modern" nuclear fam-

From Viji Srinivasan, "My Son, My Son," *The Times of India* (Bombay), *Sunday Review,* 11 May 1985, p. I.

ily has emerged as an important institution in contemporary India. How do you explain this development? What problems are associated with the continued survival of the traditional family? How has the rise of the nuclear family affected gender relations?

Durga Devi cries as if her heart would break. "We lived happily for 15 years, my husband and I. Then he began to live with his younger brother's widow in front of my eyes . . . now, the work in Sewa-Mithila helps me to get over the grief."

Sarayu Devi is petrified. "I am a child-widow. From the age of 12. I have been living with my husband's elder brother's family as an unpaid drudge, wearing only white saris, no jewellery, not even a glass bangle. Yesterday I returned home from my first day's work at Sewa-Mithila. My brother-in-law's eyes were bloodshot. He had spread a mattress in the open courtyard. He held a pot of sindhur in his hand and lunged at me. You will go to work and lie with someone there? No, I'll lie with you first, right here. Then at least my younger brother's soul will rest in peace."

Both of them are poor women painters in Madhubani district of Bihar, and are members of the Self-Employed Women's Association, Mithila.

I interview 65 of Sewa-Mithila's women painters . . . slowly a pattern emerges . . . every problem in the world seems to be represented here—their husbands are alcoholic, or mentally ill, or, had tuberculosis or leprosy and had hidden it: or are deceitful, or manipulative, or irresponsible, or promiscuous. Only two painters say they are happy.

This profile comes up again and again, wherever poor women's organisations and organisations working against violence on women in India, document women's lives— the Annapurnas of Bombay; the lace-makers of Narsapur; the fisherwomen of Madras; the painters of Madhubani; the victims of dowry harassment in Delhi; the clerical women's union in Trivandrum.

And gradually a pattern emerges, as I think through the lives of the thousands of women I have interviewed. . . .

What do all these men and women have in common? [E]specially the lowest income, low-income and lower middle class Hindu families? *They are caste-centred families*. They are characterised by being joint families which participate in the ritualistic basis of the Hindu religion; having respect for the kin-group and a fear of kin-group censure; having socio-religious obligations towards the caste-community, and deference towards male authority; seeing support of parents as a moral duty for sons; and, last, but not least, having a domestic status for women, lacking a basic dignity.

These basic characteristics are certainly found to a greater or lesser degree in the lower and the lowest income groups, from the uppermost castes to the lowermost castes.

It may be argued that the lowest castes do not have these characteristics—their women are more free to divorce and remarry, their women cannot afford to be "secluded" etc. But it is also true that as these castes move upwards economically, their value-system changes into the value-system of typical caste-centred families.

As the group moves slightly upwards in economic terms (lower middle class), the basic characteristics of caste-centred families hold good, but additional characteristics emerge—the role of the woman is seen as being subordinate to the man's: there are invisible fears of going against this subordination; the joint family is viewed as being symbolic of the ethical framework of a Hindu household; there is the Hindu ideal that a husband is next only to God; there is family solidarity which in [times] of distress supports individuals on a long-term basis; women's self-effacement, self-sacrifice, complete subordination to male authority [and] submissiveness are seen as virtues. The older generation demands respect and concern based on their traditional position and they exercise power on the same basis, in important decisions such as education, taking up jobs, arranging marriages, etc.; the husband-wife relationship is not seen as pivotal, the wife is not dependent on the husband for companionship; she keeps a low profile with respect to her in-laws; and, in addition, concepts such as pollution with regard to women, avoidance, child marriage, widow's situation viewed as being unlucky, etc., flourish.

As opposed to this, as one moves upwards classwise, there is a multicaste secular society with "secular" families (e.g., the urban middle class, the urban elite). Its characteristics are: a nuclear family; children are brought up without the ritualistic basis of the Hindu religion; girls and women receive a somewhat western-oriented higher education; women use their education to establish their individual sphere of influence in the outside world. The secular families give her greater freedom of choice and scope for expression. Parental authority over her is present but diminishing. She is too confident to regard male authority as final, and she is not disciplined enough to subordinate herself entirely to male authority. But she has a distant admiration for self-sacrifice, subordination, timidity and modesty and values and cherishes the traditional wife ideal. She is modest, quiet, yet self-reliant, is job-worthy and has new skills.

These traits prepare her for two different roles, not compatible with each other, and she is extremely vulnerable to the competing demands of these two roles.

She is less tolerant of domination by in-laws, her independence is enhanced, she retains or tries to retain control over her income, she sees her husband and children in an exclusive relationship; the child-parent relationship is more equal. She wants to develop her interests and personality. She is not willing to accept a marriage on the basis of subjugation of her own interests. She has a sense of her own identity as separate from that of the man and has a personal desire to live fully and express herself fully. She is prepared to take second place in the husband-wife relationship, only if given with respect and consideration. She is not prepared to accept one standard of behaviour for the man and another for the woman. She has a greater sense of her rights.

But, often, she has very little competitiveness with respect to her husband, she is not ambitious for herself, and is not interested in competing with his ambition: she is willing to consider him as the head of the family. . . .

The modern Indian woman has a work-ethic, has efficiency and self-reliance; has discipline; but she is also non-individualistic, non-competitive, does not want complete freedom of action. She has a commitment to marriage, a commitment to the family. She is willing to serve men without fear or loss of self-respect, but wants respect and understanding.

But, a man in a secular family wants his wife to be non-aggressive and non-assertive in relation to him and his family. He still prefers not to recognise the change in women's psychology once they are equal partners in supporting a family. He does not want a challenge to his supremacy, he does not want a relationship of mutual respect, he wants a mere vehicle of his wishes, he wants a passive partner with no demands of her own. He is not psychologically prepared to set aside his comforts. He is unable to profit from the liberal attitudes of secular society.

The older generation still views the daughter-in-law as wholly subordinate to their wishes. They demand respect and concern based on their traditional position and they exercise power on the same basis. . . .

The logic of modern ideas is selectively accepted by Hindu men to the detriment of Hindu women. The man expects her to be completely traditional and pliable, to fit in with his own standards of feminine behaviour; to accept an unfair distribution of work, unreasonable dowry demands. He feels that he has to be obeyed; that it is his privilege to decide what his wife can do. He has been exposed to "modern" conflicts longer than women. He has been able to "manage" different demands by dominating his wife in a non-rational manner. He counts on the absolute stability of his marriage, which can be shaken only by him. In spite of being highly educated and responsible, he has not yet accurately judged the mental makeup of the modern Indian woman.

We bring up our daughters with an understanding of the discipline required in day-to-day life and for a self-reliant way of life; we give them confidence, we give them strength. We give our daughters modesty, humility, self-sacrifice, a commitment to marriage, a commitment to family—as we have always done in the old way of life. But now we also give our daughters skills, and a work-ethic; we give her a modern education—we give her the capabilities to be independent—this is the new way of life. . . .

But we "spoil" our sons. We bring them up saying: "You are so important. You will live with us and take care of us in our old age. Your sisters will go away to another home. You will bring a daughter-in-law to our home. She will bring a dowry. Your sisters have to be given a dowry—so they are a burden.

"But you are our wealth. Your wife will take care of you. You have no need to step into the kitchen. There is no need for you to learn to cook, to sew, to bring water, to bring fuel and fodder, to sweep and clean, to wash dirty vessels and clothes, to wash cows, to make cow-dung cakes, she will do it all. Your role is different. You are the one to do our funeral rites, you are the one to offer *pinda* to us and to our ancestors. Without you there is no salvation for us. You are crucial and you are wonderful . . . Of course, we love your sisters, but differently." . . .

Indian society is still in a painful transition from the old world to the new. Indian women are achieving the transition with strength and dignity. Let us bring up at least the new generations of our sons and daughters to face the transition with courage. Then only will Indian women and men realize their full potential.

31

The Emergence of Arab Nationalism: Two Views from the 1930s

The First World War made a deep impact on the Middle East. One major consequence of that war was the final disintegration of the Ottoman Empire, a victim of its alliance with the defeated Central Powers. By the mid-1920s the newly constituted Repulic of Turkey had emerged as the region's first modern national state, under the authoritarian leadership of Kemal Ataturk.

However, postwar events in the Arab lands vacated by the Turks became increasingly volatile. During the war the British had promised to recognize the independence of the Arabs in return for their support against the Turks. The Arabs had upheld their part of the bargain, but when the war ended, the British and French moved into Arab lands under the authority of the League of Nations. While countries such as Egypt and Iraq won formal independence during the 1930s, the Europeans remained dominant in the region between the two world wars.

These are the circumstances that gave rise to modern Arab nationalism, early examples of which are illustrated in the two readings below. In the first selection, Sami Shawkat, the Iraqi director-general of education, addresses Baghdad students in 1933. What is Shawkat's basic point? Note his references to Prussia and to the Arab past. How do you explain the violence in Shawkat's views? The second selection is the manifesto issuing from the First Arab Students' Congress, held in Paris in 1938. How do the students define what it means to be an Arab? Do you see any problems with their definition? Note the students'

Selections I and II from Sylvia G. Haim, ed., *Arab Nationalism: An Anthology* (Berkeley, Calif.: University of California Press, 1962), pp. 97–102. Copyright © 1962 The Regents of the University of California. Reprinted by permission.

hostility to the Jews in Palestine, an issue to be considered more fully in the next selection.

I. SAMI SHAWKAT (1933)

Tomorrow, your headmaster Mr. Darwish al-Miqdadi will visit the Ministry of Defense to discuss with its senior officials the curriculum of your military studies. Do you know what these studies are and why they are introduced this year into the curricula of our schools? I have called you together today to explain this point.

We often hear and read that there is no political independence without economic independence, or that there can be no independence without knowledge. But Egypt, whose income has for many years now exceeded her expenditure by millions of pounds, and who has the best universities and schools and the greatest scholars in the Near East, has had her independence delayed up to now. The treasuries of the Indian rajas contain hundreds of millions of gold pieces and vast numbers of precious stones; India herself has more than twenty-five large universities from which graduate annually thousands of young men with diplomas in higher studies. Yet India is a colony. The proportion of the educated in Syria amounts to 76 per cent, and the majority of her population is not different in progress, civilization or culture from the peoples of southern Europe, but in spite of this, unfortunately, we still find her deprived of independence. On the other hand, the Afghans, who lead the life of the fourteenth century and whose treasuries have never been filled with gold, are independent. And here is our neighbor, the Kingdom of Saudi Arabia, whose inhabitants live on dates and camels' milk, in whose schools no modern arts are taught, and whose culture has not crossed the boundaries of religion; she too is independent. And Arab Yemen is also independent, in spite of her lack of money.

Money and learning, therefore, are not all that is needed for the independence of nations, nor are they the only axe with which to strike down the walls of imperialism and sever the chains of humiliation.

But . . .

There is something else more important than money and learning for preserving the honor of a nation and for keeping humiliation and enslavement at bay.

That is strength.

Strength is the soil on which the seed of justice burgeons; the nation which has no strength is destined to humiliation and enslavement. Riches without strength are a cause of humiliation and enslavement; as for knowledge without strength, it only produces crying and weeping on the part of the weak, and mockery on the part of the strong. This weeping and mocking will sometimes go on for tens, even hundreds, of years, as has happened in India and other countries.

Strength, as I use the word here, means to excel in the Profession of Death.

The nation which does not excel in the Profession of Death with iron and fire will be forced to die under the hooves of the horses and under the boots of a foreign soldiery. If to live is just, then killing in self-defense is also just. Had Mustafa Kemal not had, for his revolution in Anatolia, forty thousand officers trained in the Profession of Death, we would not have seen Turkey restoring in the twentieth century the glories of Yavouz Sultan Selim. Had not Pahlavi had thousands of officers well versed in the sacred profession we would not have seen him restoring the glory of Darius. And had Mussolini not had tens of thousands of Black Shirts well versed in the Profession of Death he would not have been able to put on the temples of Victor Emmanuel the crown of the first Caesars of Rome.

In the Balkans, the Albanian nation is independent, and in the Near East Arab Iraq is independent; in Albania the reed has prospered and in Iraq the cedar. The reed bush casts its shade over no more than a few centimeters of ground, no matter how tall it grows; but the cedar tree, after only a few years of growth, casts its shade over tens and hundreds of meters. Iraq's horizon of hope extends to all the Arab countries, whereas it is not in the power of Albania to look beyond its boundaries. Sixty years ago, Prussia used to dream of uniting the German people. What is there to prevent Iraq, which fulfilled her desire for independence ten years ago, from dreaming to unite all the Arab countries?

On the banks of this great river which we see morning and evening Harun al-Rashid established his throne, and from this sandy shore he ruled more than 200 million souls. We will not deserve to take pride in him and to claim that we are his descendants if we do not restore what he built and what the enemies of the Arabs destroyed. The spirit of Harun al-Rashid and the spirit of al-Ma'mun want Iraq to have in a short while half a million soldiers and hundreds of airplanes. Is there in Iraq a coward who will not answer their call? Your military studies this year, oh youths, are those lessons of strength which the country needs and which our glorious history demands. If we do not want death under the hooves of the horses and the boots of the foreign armies, it is our duty to perfect the Profession of Death, the profession of the army, the sacred military profession. This year, the lessons will be confined to the Central Secondary School in the capital, but in the future they will extend to all the secondary schools in the country, as well as to all the teachers' training colleges.

On then, oh young men, to Strength. On to the perfection of the sacred Profession of Death. Lift up high the banner of Faisal, the successor of Harun al-Rashid.

II. THE FIRST ARAB STUDENTS' CONGRESS, 1938
I. Our National Pact

I am an Arab, and I believe that the Arabs constitute one nation. The sacred right of this nation is to be sovereign in her own affairs. Her ardent nationalism drives her to liberate the Arab homeland, to unite all its parts, and to found political, economic, and social institutions more sound and more compatible than the existing ones. The aim of this nationalism is to raise up the standard of living and to increase the material and the spiritual good of the people; it also aspires to share in working for the good of the human collectivity; it strives to realize this by continuous work based on national organization.

I pledge myself to God, that I will strive in this path to my utmost, putting the national interest above any other consideration.

II. First Principles

The Arabs: All who are Arab in their language, culture, and loyalty, . . . those are the Arabs. The Arab is the individual who belongs to the nation made up of those people.

The Arab Homeland: It is the land which has been, or is, inhabited by an Arab majority, in the above sense, in Asia and Africa. As such it is a whole which cannot be divided or partitioned. It is a sacred heritage no inch of which may be trifled with. Any compromise in this respect is invalid and is national treason.

Arab Nationalism: It is the feeling for the necessity of independence and unity which the inhabitants of the Arab lands share. . . . It is based on the unity of the homeland, of language, culture, history, and a sense of the common good.

The Arab Movement: It is the new Arab renaissance which pervades the Arab nation. Its motive force is her glorious past, her remarkable vitality and the awareness of her present and future interests. This movement strives continuously and in an organized manner toward well-defined aims. These aims are to liberate and unite the Arab home-land, to found political, economic, and social organizations more sound than the existing ones, and to attempt afterward to work for the good of the human collectivity and its progress. These aims are to be realized by definite means drawn from the preparedness of the Arabs and their particular situation, as well as from the experience of the West. They will be realized without subscribing to any particular creed of the modern Western ones such as Fascism, Communism, or Democracy.

The Arab National Idea: It is a national idea which proscribes the existence of racial, regional, and communal fanaticisms. It respects the freedom of religious observance, and individual freedoms such as the freedom of opinion, work, and assembly, unless they conflict with the public good. The Arab national idea cannot be contradictory to the good of real racial and religious minorities; it aims rather at treating all sincere patriots on the principle of equality of rights and duties.

III. Foreign Elements in the Arab Countries

We have said that the Arab countries belong to the Arabs and that benefits therefrom must accrue to them. By Arabs we mean those whom the political report has included under this appellation. As for those elements who are not Arabized and who do not intend to be Arabized but are, rather, intent on putting obstacles in the way of the Arab nation, they are foreign to the Arab nation. The most prominent problem of this kind is that of the Jews in Palestine.

If we looked at the Jews in Palestine from an economic angle we would find that their economy is totally incompatible with the Arab economy. The Jews are attempting to build up a Jewish state in Palestine and to bring into this state great numbers of their kind from all over the world. Palestine is a small country, and they will therefore have to industrialize it so that this large number of inhabitants can find subsistence. And in order to make their industry a success they will have to find markets for their products. For this they depend on the Arab market; their products will therefore flood the Arab countries and compete with Arab industries. This is very harmful to the Arabs.

Moreover, Palestine, placed as it is between the Arab countries in Asia and Africa, occupies an important position in land, sea, and air communications. A foreign state in Palestine will impede these communications and have a harmful effect on commerce. And even if the Jews in Palestine presented no danger other than the economic, this would be enough for us to oppose them and to put an end to their intrigues, so that we may ensure for our country a happy and glorious future.

Among the dangerous alien elements in the Arab countries are the foreign colonies such as the Italians in Tripolitania, the French, and the Frenchified Jews in Tunisia, Algeria, and Morocco. The danger of these elements is akin to that of the Jews in Palestine, even though less prominent and less critical.

32

Middle Eastern Dreams in Conflict: Two Views

The Arab-Israeli conflict that so troubles the contemporary Middle East is rooted in two powerful and contradictory claims to the same "homeland," each side invoking history and love of the land in defense of its position. Beginning in the 1890s European Jews, responding to antisemitic prejudice, organized the Zionist movement in order to establish a "national home" in Palestine. At that time Palestine was a part of the Ottoman Empire and inhabited largely by Arabs. The proclamation of the state of Israel in 1948 was the realization of that Zionist dream.

Palestine, however, had been a part of the Arab world since the seventh century. Palestinian Arabs bitterly resented the coming of the Zionists, and they opposed the founding of the new Jewish state. In 1948–49, when the Israeli army defeated the forces of its Arab neighbors in the first Arab-Israeli war, hundreds of thousands of Palestinians went into exile. Vowing to return to their homeland one day, the aspirations of the Palestinians have come to constitute a kind of Zionism in reverse.

Below are two sources that help illuminate the thinking of the early Zionists and the contemporary Palestinian exiles. In the first selection, Nahum Goldman, a leading Zionist, describes his background and recalls his first visit to Palestine. What did Goldman find important about Palestine? What was his reaction to the

Selection I from Nahum Goldman, *The Autobiography of Nahum Goldman: Sixty Years of a Jewish Life* (New York: Holt, Rinehart and Winston, 1969), pp. 38–42, 44. Copyright © 1969 by Holt, Rinehart and Winston. Reprinted by permission. Selection II from Fawaz Turki, *The Disinherited: Journal of a Palestinian Exile* (New York: Monthly Review Press, 1972), pp. 43–45, 47–48, 54. Copyright © 1972 by Monthly Review Press. Reprinted by permission.

Arabs? In the second selection, Fawaz Turki remembers his family's flight from Palestine in 1948 and his childhood as an exile. How would you characterize Turki's attitudes? Does the term "Zionism in reverse" capture his thinking? Do the accounts of Goldman and Turki provide any hope for a solution to the Arab-Israeli conflict?

I. NAHUM GOLDMAN

As I have said, I was not a very diligent student and spent a lot of time during the academic year with my parents in Frankfurt and in excursions to the Odenwald or the Neckar Valley. All in all my relationship to the university was not very close, and when the chance of going to Palestine was offered to me in 1913, I jumped at it. A group of students was going there on a visit organized and led by Theodor Zlocisti, one of the oldest German Zionists in Berlin, a physician by profession and a man of literary interests. I was asked if I would like to go along; my expenses would be paid by a wealthy friend of the family. The trip was supposed to last four weeks, but I stayed five months and skipped a whole semester at Heidelberg. . . .

I left the group, which was returning to Germany shortly in any case, and decided really to get to know the country. Although I have been in Palestine probably more than a hundred times since then, I have never again had the opportunity to discover it at such a leisurely yet intensive pace. Free of the group's daily hikes, receptions, and ceremonies and having decided to stay several months, I could dispose of my time as I pleased.

I spent several weeks in Tel Aviv, which then consisted of only a few streets, several more in Rishon le-Zion and Rehovot, and a week in Rosh Pina in Galilee. But most of my time I spent in Jerusalem, where I rented, in what was then the Russian apartment-house complex, a romantic attic with a balcony. I used to sleep on the balcony when the weather got warm.

A detailed account of colonization in those days is beyond the scope of this book, but it was all in quite a primitive stage, except for a few old-established settlements such as Petah Tiqva, Rishon le-Zion, and one or two others. I was especially impressed by kibbutzim, such as Deganyah and Kinneret, and by the type of young *halutz,* or pioneer, Zionists I encountered for the first time. In Jerusalem I tried to get to know the old *yishuv,* the pre-Zionist Orthodox Jewish community, as well as the new one and had some very impressive encounters with kabbalists and mystics in the Meah Shearim quarter of Jerusalem. . . .

I often used to take long moonlight rides with friends and once, on our way back, we were surrounded by a Bedouin band. They would certainly have robbed us and left us naked on the road if one of my companions, who was familiar with the country, had not advised us to act naturally, to sing and occasionally pat our hip pockets as if we were carrying guns. Apparently this produced the desired effect. After riding along with us for about ten minutes, the Bedouin suddenly scattered. Another time I found myself in a precarious situation when my Arab guide in Jericho arranged for me to be a hidden spectator at an Arab wedding and at the bride's dancing—something forbidden to foreigners under Bedouin law. I had already watched several dances, unforgettable in their wild passion, when my guide rushed up to me, pale with fear, and said that one of the bride's relatives had noticed something and was looking for me. We disappeared as fast as we could and got back to the hotel before it was too late. . . .

But even more than the people and the early achievements of Jewish colonization, the country itself impressed me. Never again was Palestine to have such an impact upon me. For one thing I was younger and more sensitive to such impressions and less distracted by other responsibilities than I was during later visits. The exceptional quality of this curious little territory, which has acquired a unique significance in human history not to be explained by its natural resources or geopolitical situation—what I would like to call its mystical meaning—was brought home to me then as never again. Later it became much more difficult to sense that special aura; one was too distracted by what was happening in and to the country. But at that time Palestine was still untouched. You felt the presence of the mountains without having to think about the settlements that would be established on them. You rode across the plains unmarred by buildings and highways. You traveled very slowly; there were no cars and only a few trains; you usually rode on horseback or in a cart. It took two days to get from Haifa to Jerusalem. One saw the country clearly as if emerging from thousands of years of enchantment. The clearness of the air, the brilliance of the starry sky, the mystery of the austere mountains, made it seem as though its history had grown out of the landscape. In those days it was an extraordinarily peaceful, idealistic country, absorbed in a reverie of its own unique past. In the atmosphere lingered something of the prophets and the great Talmudists, of Jesus and the Apostles, of the Safed kabbalists, and the singers of bygone centuries. . . .

When I left Palestine my Zionism had been enriched by a momentous factor, the country itself. Until then Zionism had been an abstract idea to me, and I had no real conception of what the return of the Jews meant in any concrete sense. My visit gave me that feeling for the soil without which Zinoism is bound to remain quite unsubstantial. From then on I began to understand what it means, not merely negatively in terms of leaving the Diaspora behind, but also positively, as a new beginning in a Jewish homeland.

II. FAWAZ TURKI

A breeze began to blow as we moved slowly along the coast road, heading to the Lebanese border—my mother and father, my two sisters, my brother and I. Behind us lay the city of Haifa, long the scene of bombing, sniper fire, ambushes, raids, and bitter fighting between Palestinians and Zionists. Before us lay the city of Sidon and indefinite exile. Around us the waters of the Mediterranean sparkled in the sun. Above us eternity moved on unconcerned, as if God in his heavens watched the agonies of men, as they walked on crutches, and smiled. And our world had burst, like a bubble, a bubble that had engulfed us within its warmth. From then on I would know only crazy sorrow and watch the glazed eyes of my fellow Palestinians burdened by loss and devastated by pain.

April 1948. And so it was the cruelest month of the year; but there were crueler months, then years. . . .

After a few months in Sidon, we moved again, a Palestinian family of six heading to a refugee camp in Beirut, impotent with hunger, frustration, and incomprehension.

But there we encountered other families equally helpless, equally baffled, who like us never had enough to eat, never enough to offer books and education to their children, never enough to face an imminent winter. In later years, when we left the camp and found better housing and a better life outside and grew up into our early teens, we would complain about not having this or that and would be told by our mothers: "You are well off, boy! Think of those still living there in the camps. Just think of them and stop making demands." We would look out the window and see the rain falling and hear the thunder. And we would remember. We would understand. We would relent as we thought "of those still living there."

Man adapts. We adapted, the first few months, to life in a refugee camp. In the adaptation we were also reduced as men, as women, as children, as human beings. At times we dreamed. Reduced dreams. Distorted ambitions. One day, we hoped, our parents would succeed in buying two beds for me and my sister to save us the agonies of asthma, intensified from sleeping on blankets on the cold floor. One day, we hoped, there would be enough to buy a few pounds of pears or apples as we had done on those special occasions when we fought and sulked and complained because one of us was given a smaller piece of fruit than the others. One day soon, we hoped, it would be the end of the month when the UNRWA rations arrived and there was enough to eat for a week. One day soon, we argued, we would be back in our homeland.

The days stretched into months and those into a year and yet another. Kids would play in the mud of the winters and the dust of the summers, while "our problem" was debated at the UN and moths died around the kerosene lamps. A job had been found for me in a factory not far from the camp, where I worked for six months. I felt pride in the fact that I was a bread earner and was thus eligible to throw my weight around the house, legitimately demand an extra spoonful of sugar in my tea, and have my own money to spend on comic books and an occasional orange on the side. I had even started saving to buy my own bed, but I was fired soon after that.

A kid at work had called me a two-bit Palestinian and a fist fight ensued. The supervisor, an obese man with three chins and a green stubble that covered most of his face and reached under his eyes, came over to stop the fight. He decided I had started it all, slapped me hard twice, deducted three lira from my wages for causing trouble (I earned seven lira a week), paid me the rest, called me a two-bit Palestinian, and, pointing to my blond hair, suggested I had a whore mother and shoved me out the door.

I went to the river and sat on the grass to eat my lunch. I was shaken more by the two-bit-Palestinian epithet than by the plight of being unemployed. At home and around the camp, we had unconsciously learned to be proud of where we came from and to continue remembering that we were Palestinians. If this was stigmatic outside, there it was an identity to be known, perpetuated, embraced. My father, reproaching us for an ignoble offense of some kind, would say: "You are a Palestinian." He would mean: as a Palestinian one is not expected to stoop that low and betray his tradition. If we came home affecting a Lebanese accent, our mother would say: "Hey, what's wrong with your own accent? You're too good for your own people or something? You want to sound like a foreigner when we return to Haifa? What's wrong with you, hey?"

.   .   .

Our Palestinian consciousness, instead of dissipating, was enhanced and acquired a subtle nuance and a new dimension. It was buoyed by two concepts: the preservation of our memory of Palestine and our acquisition of education. We persisted in refusing the houses and monetary compensation offered by the UN to settle us in our host countries. We wanted nothing short of returning to our homeland. And from Syria, Lebanon, and Jordan, we would see, a few miles, a few yards, across the border, a land where we had been born, where we had lived, and where we felt the earth. "This is my land," we would shout, or cry, or sing, or plead, or reason. And to that land a people had come, a foreign community of colonizers, aided by a Western world in a hurry to rid itself of guilt and shame, demanding independence from history, from heaven, and from us.

33

The Resurgence of Islam in the Contemporary Middle East

One of the dominant trends in the Middle East today is the renewed vitality of Islam. For the past decade or so mosque attendance and the dissemination of religious literature have been increasing throughout the region. Traditional Islamic dress for women has made a comeback, and the popularity and influence of Islamic student organizations in Middle Eastern universities are at an all-time high.

Islam has also made a dramatic imprint on the political life of the region in recent years, most notably in Iran, where, in 1979, Shiite Muslims toppled the regime of Shah Muhammed Reza Pahlavi (r. 1941–1979). In 1981 Anwar Sadat, the head of the Egyptian government, was assassinated by Muslim fundamentalists in the Egyptian army. During the mid-1980s, the Qaddafi regime in Lybia continued to offer the rest of the Middle East the model of Islam fused with radical socialism.

The readings below illustrate key aspects of this Islamic resurgence. The first selection is by Hasan al-Banna (1906–1949), the Egyptian activist who founded the Muslim Brotherhood, a secret organization that has had a major impact on the politics of the region since the Second World War. The product of an earlier period, al-Banna's ideas nevertheless anticipate and underlie the thinking of many of today's Muslim intellectuals. What reasons does al-Banna give

Selection I from Kemal Karpat, ed., *Political and Social Thought in the Contemporary Middle East* (New York: Fredrick A. Praeger, 1968), pp. 118–21. Copyright © 1968 by Praeger Publishers. Reprinted by permission. Selection II from John J. Donohue and John L. Esposito, eds., *Islam in Transition: Muslim Perspectives* (New York: Oxford University Press, 1982), pp. 308–13. Copyright © 1982 by Oxford University Press. Reprinted by permission.

for the renewal of Islamic fervor? In the second excerpt Ayatullah Murtada Mutahhari, a leader of the 1979 Iranian Revolution, sheds light on the thinking of the Shiite revolutionaries. According to Mutahhari, what is singular about the Islamic movement in Iran? What were the Shiite objections to the Pahlavis? What are the aims of the Iranian revolutionaries? Compare the two readings above with the earlier selections on Arab nationalism. Do you see any conflicts?

I. HASAN AL-BANNA

When we observe the evolution in the political, social, and moral spheres of the lives of nations and peoples, we note that the Islamic world—and, naturally, in the forefront, the Arab world—gives to its rebirth an Islamic flavor. This trend is ever-increasing. Until recently, writers, intellectuals, scholars, and governments glorified the principles of European civilization, gave themselves a Western tint, and adopted a European style and manner; today, on the contrary, the wind has changed, and reserve and distrust have taken their place. Voices are raised proclaiming the necessity for a return to the principles, teachings, and ways of Islam, and, taking into account the situation, for initiating the reconciliation of modern life with these principles, as a prelude to a final "Islamization."

This development worries a good number of governments and Arab powers, which, having lived during the past generations in a state of mind that had retained from Islam only lessons of fanaticism and inertia, regarded the Muslims only as weak drudges or as nations easily exploitable by colonialism. In trying to understand the new movement . . . these governments have produced all sorts of possible interpretations: "It is the result," said some, "of the growth of extremist organizations and fanatical groups." Others explained that it was a reaction to present-day political and economic pressures, of which the Islamic nations had become aware. Finally, others said, "It is only a means whereby those seeking government or other honors may achieve renown and position."

Now all these reasons are, in our opinion, as far as possible from the truth; for this new movement can only be the result of the following three factors, which we will now examine.

The first of the three is the failure of the social principles on which the civilization of the Western nations has been built. The Western way of life—bounded in effect on practical and technical knowledge, discovery, invention, and the flooding of world markets with mechanical products—has remained incapable of offering to men's minds a flicker of light, a ray of hope, a grain of faith, or of providing anxious persons the smallest path toward rest and tranquillity. Man is not simply an instrument among others. Naturally, he has become tired of purely materialistic conditions and desires some spiritual comfort. But the materialistic life of the West could only offer him as reassurance a new materialism of sin, passion, drink, women, noisy gatherings, and showy attractions which he had come to enjoy. Man's hunger grows from day to day: he wants to free his spirit, to destroy this materialistic prison and find space to breathe the air of faith and consolation.

The second factor—the decisive factor in the circumstances—is the discovery by Islamic thinkers of the noble, honorable, moral, and perfect content of the principles and rules of this religion, which is infinitely more accomplished, more pure, more glorious, more complete, and more beautiful than all that has been discovered up till now by social theorists and reformers. For a long time, Muslims neglected all this, but once God had enlightened their thinkers and they had compared the social rules of their religion with what they had been told by the greatest sociologists and the cleverest leading theorists, they noted the wide gap and the great distance between a heritage of immense value on one side and the conditions experienced on the other. Then, Muslims could not but do justice to the spirit and the history of their people, proclaiming the value of this heritage and inviting all peoples—nonpracticing Muslims or non-Muslims—to follow the sacred path that God had traced for them and to hold to a straight course.

The third factor is the development of social conditions between the two murderous world wars (which involved all the world powers and monopolized the minds of regimes, nations, and individuals) which resulted in a set of principles of reform and social organization that certain powers, in deciding to put them into practice, have taken as an instructional basis. . . .

Thus, German Nazism and Italian Fascism rose to the fore; Mussolini and Hitler led their two peoples to unity, order, recovery, power, and glory. In record time, they ensured internal order at home and, through force, made themselves feared abroad. Their regimes gave real hope, and also gave rise to thoughts of steadfastness and perseverance and the reuniting of different, divided men around the words "chief" and "order." In their resolutions and speeches, the Führer and the Duce began to frighten the world and to upset their epoch. . . .

The star of socialism and Communism, symbol of success and victory, shone with an increasing brilliance; Soviet Russia was at the head of the collectivist camp. She launched her message and, in the eyes of the world, demonstrated a system which had been modified several times in thirty years. The democratic powers—or, to use a more precise expression, the colonialist powers, the old ones worn out, the new ones full of greed—took up a position to stem the current. The struggle intensified, in some places openly, in others under cover, and nations and peoples, perplexed, hesitated at the crossroads, not knowing which way was best; among them were the nations of Islam and the peoples of the Qur`ān; the future, whatever the circumstances, is in the hands of God, the decision with history, and immortality with the most worthy.

This social evolution and violent, hard struggle stirred the minds of Muslim thinkers; the parallels and the prescribed comparisons led to a healthy conclusion: to free themselves from the existing state of affairs, to allow the necessary return of the nations and peoples to Islam.

II. AYATULLAH MURTADA MUTAHHARI

Scholars and knowledgeable persons in contemporary history concede that in the second half of our century in almost all or at least in a large number of Islamic countries Islamic movements have been in ascent openly or secretly. These are practically directed against despotism, capitalist colonialism or materialistic ideologies subscribing to colonialism in its new shape. Experts on political affairs acknowledge that after having passed through a period of mental crisis the Muslims are once again struggling to reestablish their "Islamic identity" against the challenges of capitalist West and the communist East. But in no Islamic country has this type of movement gained as much of depth and extent as in Iran since the year 1960. Nor is there a parallel to the proportions which the Iranian movement has obtained. It, therefore, becomes necessary to analyze this remarkably significant event of history.

Like all natural occurrences, social and political events also tend to differ from one another in their behaviours. All historical movements cannot be considered identical in their nature. The nature of the Islamic movement is in no case similar to the French revolution or to the great October revolution of Russia.

The current Iranian movement is not restricted to any particular class or trade union. It is not only a labour, an agrarian, a student, an intellectual or a bourgeois movement. Within its scope fall one and all in Iran, the rich and the poor, the man and the woman, the school boy and the scholar, the warehouse man and the factory labourer, the artisan and the peasant, the clergy and the teacher, the literate and the illiterate, one and all. An announcement made by the preceptor of the highest station guiding the movement is received in the length and breadth of the country with equal enthusiasm by all classes of the people. . . .

This movement is one of the glaring historical proofs which falsifies the concept of materialistic interpretation of history and that of the dialectics of materialism according to which economy is recognised as the cornerstone of social structure and a social movement is considered a reflection of class struggle. . . .

The awakened Islamic conscience of our society has induced it to search for Islamic values. This is the conscience of the cumulative enthusiasms of all classes of people, including perhaps some of the hereby dissident groups, which has galvanized them into one concerted upsurge.

The roots of this movement shall have to be traced in the events that occurred during the last half century in our country [during the reign of the Pahlavi shahs, 1925–1979] and the way these events came into conflict with the Islamic spirit of our society.

It is evident that during the last half century, there have been events which adopted a diametrically opposite direction as far as the nobler objectives of Islam were concerned and which aimed at nullifying the aspirations of the well-meaning reformers for the last century. This state of affairs could not continue for long without reaction.

What happened in Iran during the last half century may be summed up as under:

1. Absolute and barbaric despotism.
2. Denial of freedom of every kind.
3. A new type of colonialism meaning an invisible and dangerous colonialism embracing political, economic and cultural aspects of life.
4. Maintaining distance between religion and politics. Rather, divorcing politics from religion.
5. An attempt at leading Iran back to the age of ignorance of pre-Islamic days. . . .
6. Effecting a change and corrupting the rich Islamic culture and replacing it with the ambiguous Iranian culture.
7. Gruesome killing of Iranian Muslims, imprisonment and torture of the alleged political prisoners.

8. Ever increasing discrimination and cleavage among the classes of society despite so-called reforms.
9. Domination of non-Muslim elements over the Muslim elements in the government and other institutions.
10. Flagrant violation of Islamic laws either directly or by perpetrating corruption in the cultural and social life of the people.
11. Propaganda against Persian literature (which has always been the protector and upholder of Islamic spirit) under the pretext of purifying the Persian language of foreign terminology.
12. Severing relations with Islamic countries and flirting with non-Islamic and obviously with anti-Islamic countries like Israel.

· · ·

What is the objective pursued by the movement and what does it want? Does it aim at democracy? Does it want to liquidate colonialism from our country? Does it rise to defend what is called in modern terminology as human rights? Does it want to do away with discrimination, inequality? Does it want to uproot oppression? Does it want to undo materialism and so forth and so on?

In view of the nature of the movement and its roots as already brought under consideration and also in view of the statements and announcements given out by the leaders of the movement, what one may gather as an answer to these questions is "Yes" as well as "No."

"Yes" because all the objectives mentioned above form the very crux of it. And "No" because the movement is not limited to only these or any one of these objectives. An Islamic movement cannot, from the point of its objective, remain a restricted affair, because Islam, in its very nature, is "an indivisible whole" and with the realization of any of the objectives set before it, its role does not cease to be.

· · ·

No movement can be led successfully without leadership. But who should be the leader or the group of leaders when the movement is an Islamic one in its nature and when its objective is exclusively Islam?

Evidently the leadership should, in the first place, fulfill the general conditions of the task before it. Then the leaders must be deeply Islamic, fully conversant with the ethical, social, political and spiritual philosophy of Islam. They must have the knowledge of Islam's universal vision, its insight about empirical matters like the creation, the origin, the creator of the universe, the need for creation of the universe, etc. They must have the deep knowledge of Islam's views and stipulations on man and his society. It is of great importance that the leaders must have a clear picture of the Islamic ideology of man's relations with his society; his manner and method of framing the social order; his abilities of defending and pursuing certain things and resisting others; his ultimate objectives and the means of attaining those objectives, etc.

It is obvious that only such persons can lead as have been brought up under the pure Islamic culture having perfectly mastered the branches of religious learning and Islamic sciences, the Qur`ān, tradition, jurisprudence, etc. It is, therefore, only ecclesiastics who qualify for the leadership of such a movement.

34

Twentieth-Century Latin American Politics: The Revolutionary Challenge

Since their independence from Spain and Portugal (1810–1825), Latin American republics have experienced periods of severe political instability. From the 1830s to the 1860s, local military leaders left over from the Independence wars, known as *caudillos,* often seized national office, pillaged the treasury, and were in turn deposed by others. During the late nineteenth century, when Latin America began exporting raw materials (metals, fertilizers) and food (sugar, coffee, wheat, bananas), oligarchical elites closely linked to the export economy consolidated stable political regimes. This stability was purchased by limiting the exercise of political power to a narrow few and excluding commoners through voting restrictions. At the beginning of the twentieth century, population growth plus immigration from Europe greatly swelled the ranks of laborers, professionals, clerical people, and the urban poor. Most remained apolitical, but key groups such as railroad workers, dockworkers, and meatpackers formed unions, while professionals, small property owners, and clerical people formed middle-class political parties.

Social unrest along with often inflexible political regimes have led to a series of revolutions and other upheavals in twentieth-century Latin America. The following selections deal with three of the major episodes. All express some of the

Selection I from Emiliano Zapata, *The Plan of Ayala* (29 November 1911), translated by Erick D. Langer. Reprinted by permission. Selection II from Angel Perelman, *Como Hicimo el 17 de Octobre* (Buenos Aires: Editorial Coyoacan, 1961), pp. 44–46, translated in Joseph R. Barager, ed., *Why Peron Came to Power. The Background to Peronism in Argentine* (New York: Alfred A. Knopf, 1968), pp. 200–2. Copyright © 1968, Alfred A. Knopf. Reprinted by permission. Selection III from Fidel Castro, *History Will Absolve Me, Moncada Trial Defence Speech Santiago de Cuba, October, 16, 1956* (London: Jonathan Cape, 1958), pp. 40–45. First published in Cuba in 1967, and published in Great Britain in 1968 by Jonathan Cape Limited. Reprinted by permission.

basic social grievances that have created unrest, thus suggesting answers to the question of why Latin America has been so productive of political turmoil in our century. The documents also offer a comparison with earlier grievances, when Latin American nations struggled for political independence (see selection 15, above). What has changed among the goals and actors on center stage?

Selection I comes from the Mexican Revolution of 1910. It was issued by the most radical peasant leader, Emiliano Zapata. Zapata never seized control of the Mexican Revolution, but the radical economic demands of his Plan of Ayala influenced the course of Mexican social development for the next thirty years.

Selection II reflects a new kind of strongman rule that characterized several major Latin states during the twentieth century. Juan Peron, in Argentina, resembled revolutionaries in seeking to avoid foreign (in this case almost entirely economic) domination. Peron, a middle-class military man, appealed to working people neglected by earlier civilian governments. This selection shows how union leaders—in this case the head of the metal workers' union—had become disenchanted with Communist control and preferred a military ruler who could get things done for the workers. This decision resulted in state control of unions after Peron became president, from 1946 to 1955, and an enduring attachment of many Argentine workers to an authoritarian, but populist, government. How do the goals of Peronist workers resemble as well as differ from more literally revolutionary currents in Latin America?

A new round of revolutionary activity emerged during the 1950s, building on social and economic problems similar to those in Mexico earlier on. The lone successful change came in 1959, with Fidel Castro in Cuba, but his example then spurred other guerrilla movements which, particularly in Central America, have continued to the present day; later on it also helped inspire outright revolution in Nicaragua.

Although he bacame a symbol of Communist insurrection, Castro viewed his revolution as authentically Cuban. Looking back into Cuba's past, Castro saw a deformed nation. At each moment, when a true nationalist sought political power, he was either blocked by foreign intervention, or he betrayed the cause. José Marti, the intellectual spirit of the Cuban independence movement against Spain in 1895, was an authentic Cuban hero. Yet his political program was never realized because of the intervention of the United States during the Spanish-American War of 1898. From that year until Castro seized power in 1959, the United States dominated Cuba politically and economically, despite Cuba's nominal independence. Presidents of Cuba, such as Batista (1940–44, 1952–58) talked of reform but used their offices to become wealthy, especially by diverting U.S. loans into their own pockets. Meanwhile, the majority of the Cuban people— the poor—were neglected. For Cuba to take control of her destiny, Castro saw the necessity of revolution. After the failure of his first military operation on July 26, 1953, Castro—while in jail—described what the revolution was being fought for and what he would do once in power. The spirit that animates this document (selection III) is the same spirit that guides revolutionaries in other parts of Latin America. According to Castro, socialism was the necessary outcome of implementing these goals. Do you agree? Does this document support Castro's claim?

I. THE PLAN OF AYALA

The liberating Plan of the sons of the State of Morelos, affiliated with the Insurgent Army which defends the fulfillment of the Plan of San Luis Potosí, with the reforms which they have believed necessary to add for the benefit of the Mexican Fatherland.

We, the subscribers [to this Plan], constituted in a Revolutionary Council . . . declare solemnly before the countenance of the civilized world which judges us and before the Nation to which we belong and love, the principles which we have formulated to terminate the tyranny which oppresses us and redeem the Fatherland from the dictatorships which are imposed on us, which are determined in the following Plan:

1. [Accuses Francisco I. Madero, the leader of the 1910 revolution and President of Mexico, of betraying the Revolution and allying himself with the oppressive old guard in the State of Morelos.]
2. Francisco I. Madero is disavowed as Chief of the Revolution and as President of the Republic, for the above reasons, [and we will] endeavor to overthrow this official.
3. The illustrious General Pascual Orozco, second of the *caudillo* Don Francisco I. Madero, is recognized as Chief of the Liberating Revolution, and in case he does not accept this delicate post, General Emiliano Zapata is recognized as Chief of the Revolution.
4. The Revolutionary Junta of the State of Morelos manifests the following formal points . . . and will make itself the defender of the principles that it will defend until victory or death.
5. The Revolutionary Junta of the State of Morelos will not admit transactions or political compromises until the overthrow of the dictatorial elements of Porfirio Díaz and Francisco I. Madero, since the Nation is tired of false men and traitors who make promises as liberators but once in power, forget them and become tyrants.
6. As an additional part of the Plan which we invoke, we assert that: the fields, woodland, and water which the haciendados [landlords], *científicos* or bosses in the shadow of tyranny and venal justice have usurped, will revert to the possession of the towns or citizens who have their corresponding titles to these properties. [These properties] have been usurped through the bad faith of our oppressors, who maintained all along with arms in hand the above mentioned possession. The usurpers who feel they have the right [to ownership], will demonstrate this before special tribunals which will be established when the Revolution triumphs.
7. In virtue of the fact that the immense majority of the towns and Mexican citizens are not masters of the soil they step upon, suffering horrors of misery without being able to better their social condition at all nor dedicate themselves to industry or agriculture because of the monopoly in a few hands of the land, woodlands, and waters, for this reason [the lands] will be expropriated, with indemnity of the third part of these monopolies to their powerful owners, so that the towns and citizens of Mexico can obtain common lands (*ejidos*), colonies, and legitimate resources for towns or agricultural fields and that above all the lack of prosperity and wellbeing of the Mexican people is improved.
8. The haciendados, *científicos* or bosses who oppose directly or indirectly the present plan, will have their possessions nationalized and two thirds of what

they own will be destined for war indemnities, [and] pensions for the widows and orphans of the victims who succumb in the fight for this Plan.

9. To regulate the procedures in regard to the items mentioned above, the laws of disentailment and nationalization will be applied as is appropriate. [The laws] put into effect by the immortal Juarez regarding Church lands can serve as a guide and example, which set a severe example to the despots and conservatives who at all times have tried to impose the ignominious yoke of oppression and backwardness.

10. The insurgent military chiefs of the Republic, who rose up in armed revolt at the behest of Francisco I. Madero to defend the Plan of San Luis Potosí and who now oppose by force the present Plan, are to be judged traitors to the cause they defended and to the Fatherland, given the fact that in actuality many of them to please the tyrants for a handful of coins, or for bribes, are spilling the blood of their brethren who demand the fulfillment of the promises which don Francisco I. Madero made to the Nation.

[11–14. Details the payment of the expenses of war, the administration of the country after the Plan's success, and bids Madero to step down voluntarily.]

15. Mexicans: Consider that the cleverness and the bad faith of one man is spilling blood in a scandalous manner because of his inability to govern; consider that his system of government is putting the Fatherland in chains and by brute force of bayonets trampling under foot our institutions; and as we raised our arms to elevate him to power, today we turn them against him for having gone back on his agreements with the Mexican people and having betrayed the Revolution he initiated; we are not personalists, we are believers in principles, not in men.

People of Mexico: Support with your arms in hand this Plan and you will create prosperity and happiness for the Fatherland.

Justicia y ley.
Ayala, 28 of November, 1911.

II. PERONISM

Once the resistance of the [Communist] directors was overcome, we arranged with the Secretariat of Labor to convoke a meeting at which Perón would speak to the metal workers. The date fixed, we calculated that we could fill the assembly hall of the Deliberating Council, where the Secretariat of Labor and Social Welfare was located.

We had no resources for publicizing this meeting. Until noon of the day of the gathering, we were still sticking together some posters announcing the convocation. It was a great surprise when, by the time of the meeting, the meeting hall was completely filled, and an enormous multitude of nearly 20,000 metal workers was concentrated outside in the Diagonal Roca. The shops they came from were identified by improvised placards and reflected the enormous reprecussion the growth of industry was having on the working class at that time. . . .

Colonel Perón, in one of the salient parts of his discourse, told us that he was gratified to see the metal workers enter the house of the workers and that he had assumed that, since they were one of the last unions to come together there, they must be very well paid. But he added that, as a result of the remarks of the comrade who had preceded him on the platform, it appeared that this was not so, and consequently he was urging the metal workers to form a powerful union to defend their rights and the country's sovereignty. At this moment a metal worker interrupted to shout: "Thus speaks a *criollo!*" [true Argentine] Banners and posters fluttered approval of the metal worker's remark. We went out of that meeting with the conviction that the metal workers' union would soon be transformed into a very powerful labor organization. And in effect it was; from a membership of 1,500 we transformed that union "of form" into the present Union of Metal Workers (UOM) with 300,000 workers in the fold. So profound was the need for the country to defend its political independence and economic sovereignty, and for the working class to organize at last its unions on a grand scale, that, faced by the treason of the parties of the left, this need had to be embodied in a military man who had come from the ranks of the Army.

And we came to constitute then that ideological tendency known by many people as the "national left." In our union activities at the end of 1944 we witnessed unbelievable happenings: labor laws neglected in another era were being carried out; one did not need recourse to the courts for the granting of vacations; such other labor dispensations as the recognition of factory delegates, guarantees against being discharged, etc., were immediately and rigorously enforced. The nature of internal relations between the owners and the workers in the factories was completely changed. The internal democratization imposed by the metal workers' union resulted in factory delegates constituting the axis of the entire organization and in the direct expression of the will of the workers in each establishment. The owners were as disconcerted as the workers were astounded and happy. The Secretariat of Labor and Social Welfare was converted into an agency for the organization, development, and support of the workers. It did not function as a state regulator for the top level of the unions; it acted as a state ally of the working class. Such were the practical results that constituted the basis for the political shift of the Argentine masses and that were manifested in the streets on October 17, 1945. [Date when a massive demonstration took place that secured Peron's release from prison.]

III. CASTRO'S PROGRAM

When we speak of the people we do not mean the comfortable ones, the conservative elements of the nation, who welcome any regime of oppression, any dictatorship, any despotism, prostrating themselves before the master of the moment until they grind their foreheads into the ground. When we speak of struggle, the people means the vast unredeemed masses to whom all make promises and whom all deceive; we mean the people who yearn for a better, more dignified and more just nation; who are moved by ancestral aspirations of justice, for they have suffered injustice and mockery generation after generation; who long for great and wise changes in all aspects of their life; people who, to attain the changes, are ready to give even the very last breath of their lives, when they believe in something or in someone, especially when they believe in themselves. . . . The people we counted on in our struggle were these:

Seven hundred thousand Cubans without work, who desire to earn their daily bread honestly without having to emigrate in search of a livelihood.

Five hundred thousand farm labourers inhabiting miserable shacks (*bohíos*), who work four months of the year and starve during the rest, sharing their misery with their children; who have not an inch of land to till, and whose existence would move any heart not made of stone.

Four hundred thousand industrial labourers and stevedores whose retirement funds have been embezzled, whose benefits are being taken away, whose homes are wretched quarters, whose salaries pass from the hands of the boss to those of the money-lender (*garrotero*), whose future is a pay reduction and dismissal, whose life is eternal work and whose only rest is in the tomb.

One hundred thousand small farmers who live and die working on land that is not theirs, looking at it with sadness as Moses looked at the promised land, to die without ever owning it; who, like feudal serfs, have to pay for the use of their parcel of land by giving up a portion of its products; who cannot love it, improve it, beautify it, nor plant a lemon or an orange tree on it, because they never know when a sheriff will come with the rural guard to evict them from it.

Thirty thousand teachers and professors who are so devoted, dedicated and necessary to the better destiny of future generations and who are so badly treated and paid.

Twenty thousand small business men, weighted down by debts, ruined by the crisis and harangued by a plague of grafting and venal officials.

Ten thousand young professionals: doctors, engineers, lawyers, veterinarians, school teachers, dentists, pharmacists, newspapermen, painters, sculptors, etc., who come forth from school with their degrees, anxious to work and full of hope, only to find themselves at a dead end with all doors closed, and where no ear hears their clamour or supplication.

These are the people, the ones who know misfortune and, therefore, are capable of fighting with limitless courage!

To the people whose desperate roads through life have been paved with the bricks of betrayals and false promises, we were not going to say: "We will eventually give you what you need," but rather—"Here you have it, fight for it with all your might, so that liberty and happiness may be yours!"

In the brief of this case, the five revolutionary laws that would have been proclaimed immediately after the capture of the Moncada Barracks and would have been broadcasted to the nation by radio should be recorded. It is possible that Colonel Chaviano may deliberately have destroyed these documents, but even if he has done so I remember them.

The First Revolutionary Law would have returned power to the people and proclaimed the Constitution of 1940 the supreme Law of the State, until such time as the people should decide to modify or change it. And, in order to effect its implementation and punish those who had violated it, there being no organization for holding elections to accomplish this, the revolutionary movement, as the momentous incarnation of this sovereignty, the only source of legitimate power, would have assumed all the faculties inherent in it, except that of modifying the Constitution itself: in other words, it would have assumed the legislative, executive and judicial powers. . . .

The Second Revolutionary Law would have granted property, non-mortgageable and non-transferable, to all planters, non-quota planters, lessees, share-croppers, and squatters who hold parcels of five *caballerías* of land or less, and the State would indemnify the former owners on the basis of the rental which they would have received for these parcels over a period of ten years.

The Third Revolutionary Law would have granted workers and employees the right to share thirty per cent of the profits of all the large industrial, mercantile and mining enterprises, including the sugar mills. The strictly agricultural enterprises would be exempt in consideration of other agrarian laws which would be implemented.

The Fourth Revolutionary Law would have granted all planters the right to share fifty-five per cent of the sugar production and a minimum quota of forty thousand *arrobas* for all small planters who have been established for three or more years.

The Fifth Revolutionary Law would have ordered the confiscation of all holdings and ill-gotten gains of those who had committed frauds during previous regimes, as well as the holdings and ill-gotten gains of all their legatees and heirs. To implement this, special courts with full powers would gain access to all records of all corporations registered or operating in this country, in order to investigate concealed funds of illegal origin, and to request that foreign governments extradite persons and attach holdings rightfully belonging to the Cuban people. Half of the property recovered would be used to subsidize retirement funds for workers and the other half would be used for hospitals, asylums and charitable organizations.

35

Searching for the Soul of the Latin American Experience

Essayists and novelists have struggled to capture the uniqueness of Latin America. Although their descriptions are set in specific countries and locations, they tend toward common themes. For example, the Mexican essayist Octavio Paz, in search of his identity as well as that of his nation, wrote about the "labyrinth of solitude." The Colombian novelist Gabriel García Márquez examined the experiences of a family and a town through "one hundred years of solitude." The common theme of solitude becomes for these two men the chief vehicle for understanding Latin American civilization.

For Octavio Paz the feeling of solitude derives from the realization that Latin Americans are profoundly different from North Americans and Europeans. His search for an accurate interpretation of Latin American reality led him to examine the behavior of Mexicans living in the United States, an extreme type toward which all Mexicans were heading (selection I). When Paz contemplated writing a book about the meaning of Latin American culture as a whole, he again returned to a comparison with North America as its starting point (selection II). The great disparity between the developed and underdeveloped worlds, between one's material strength and the other's weakness, led directly to feelings of acute isolation and abandonment. Indeed, according to Paz, Latin America's entire past was alien since it represented Spanish domination rather than indigenous expres-

Selection I from Octavio Paz, *The Labyrinth of Solitude, Life, and Thought in Mexico*, translated by Lysander Kemp (New York: Grove Press, Inc., 1961), pp. 12–15. Copyright © 1961 by Grove Press. Reprinted by permission. Selection II from Octavio Paz, *The Other Mexico: Critique of the Pyramid*, translated by Lysander Kemp (New York: Grove Press, Inc., 1972), pp. viii–x. Copyright © 1972 by Grove Press, Inc. Reprinted by permission.

sions. Paz's plea is for the best minds of Latin America to overcome the past in order to create their own, new and socially just society. Yet imagine the difficulties in constructing a new society when one cannot call upon past traditions for help.

The concern about identity in Latin America reflects an important facet of Latin American culture, but this is not unique. Other twentieth-century civilizations worry about identity issues; these Latin American reflections can thus be compared to the issues of identity in societies such as sub-Saharan Africa. Why does the theme of defining identity echo in both African and Latin American civilizations? Is it in effect the same theme?

I. LABYRINTH OF SOLITUDE

The minority of Mexicans who are aware of their own selves do not make up a closed or unchanging class. They are the only active group, in comparison with the Indian-Spanish inertia of the rest, and every day they are shaping the country more and more into their own image. And they are also increasing. They are conquering Mexico. We can all reach the point of knowing ourselves to be Mexicans. It is enough, for example, simply to cross the border: almost at once we begin to ask ourselves, at least vaguely, the same questions that Samuel Ramos asked in his *Profile of Man and Culture in Mexico*. I should confess that many of the reflections in this essay occurred to me outside of Mexico, during a two-year stay in the United States. I remember that whenever I attempted to examine North American life, anxious to discover its meaning, I encountered my own questioning image. That image, seen against the glittering background of the United States, was the first and perhaps the profoundest answer which that country gave to my questions. Therefore, in attempting to explain to myself some of the traits of the present-day Mexican, I will begin with a group for whom the fact that they are Mexicans is a truly vital problem, a problem of life or death.

When I arrived in the United States I lived for a while in Los Angeles, a city inhabited by over a million persons of Mexican origin. At first sight, the visitor is surprised not only by the purity of the sky and the ugliness of the dispersed and ostentatious buildings, but also by the city's vaguely Mexican atmosphere, which cannot be captured in words or concepts. This Mexicanism—delight in decorations, carelessness and pomp, negligence, passion and reserve—floats in the air. I say "floats" because it never mixes or unites with the other world, the North American world based on precision and efficiency. It floats, without offering any opposition; it hovers, blown here and there by the wind, sometimes breaking up like a cloud, sometimes standing erect like a rising skyrocket. It creeps, it wrinkles, it expands and contracts; it sleeps or dreams; it is ragged but beautiful. It floats, never quite existing, never quite vanishing.

Something of the same sort characterizes the Mexicans you see in the streets. They have lived in the city for many years, wearing the same clothes and speaking the same language as the other inhabitants, and they feel ashamed of their origin; yet no one would mistake them for authentic North Americans. I refuse to believe that physical features are as important as is commonly thought. What distinguishes them, I think, is their furtive, restless air: they act like persons who are wearing disguises, who are afraid of a stranger's look because it could strip them and leave them stark naked. When you talk with them, you observe that their sensibilities are like a pendulum, but a pendulum that has lost its reason and swings violently and erratically back and forth. This spiritual condition, or lack of a spirit, has given birth to a type known as the *pachuco*. The *pachucos* are youths, for the most part of Mexican origin, who form gangs in Southern cities; they can be identified by their language and behavior as well as by the clothing they affect. They are instinctive rebels, and North American racism has vented its wrath on them more than once. But the *pachucos* do not attempt to vindicate their race or the nationality of their forebears. Their attitude reveals an obstinate, almost fanatical will-to-be, but this will affirms nothing specific except their determination—it is an ambiguous one, as we will see—not to be like those around them. The *pachuco* does not want to become a Mexican again; at the same time he does not want to blend into the life of North America. His whole being is sheer negative impulse, a tangle of contradictions, an enigma. Even his very name is enigmatic: *pachuco,* a word of uncertain derivation, saying nothing and saying everything. It is a strange word with no definite meaning; or, to be more exact, it is charged like all popular creations with a diversity of meanings. Whether we like it or not, these persons are Mexicans, are one of the extremes at which the Mexican can arrive.

Since the *pachuco* cannot adapt himself to a civilization which, for its part, rejects him, he finds no answer to the hostility surrounding him except this angry affirmation of his personality. Other groups react differently. The Negroes, for example, oppressed by racial intolerance, try to "pass" as whites and thus enter society. They want to be like other people. The Mexicans have suffered a less violent rejection, but instead of attempting a problematical adjustment to society, the *pachuco* actually flaunts his differences. The purpose of his grotesque dandyism and anarchic behavior is not so much to point out the injustice and incapacity of a society that has failed to assimilate him as it is to demonstrate his personal will to remain different.

It is not important to examine the causes of this conflict, and even less so to ask whether or not it has a solution. There are minorities in many parts of the world who do not enjoy the same opportunities as the rest of the population. The important thing is this stubborn desire to be different, this anguished tension with which the lone Mexican—an orphan lacking both protectors and positive values—displays his differences. The *pachuco* has lost his whole inheritance: language, religion, customs, beliefs. He is left with only a body and a soul with which to confront the elements, defenseless against the stares of everyone. His disguise is a protection, but it also differentiates and isolates him: it both hides him and points him out.

II. THE OTHER MEXICO

These pages are both a postscript to a book I wrote some twenty years ago and, equally, a preface to another, unwritten book. I have alluded in two of my works, *The Labyrinth of Solitude* and *Corriente alterna* [*Alternating Current*], to that unwritten book: the theme of Mexico leads to a reflection upon the fate of Latin America. Mexico is a fragment, a part, of a vaster history. I know that that reflection should be a recovery of our true history, from the time of Spanish domination and the failure of our revolution of independence—a failure that corresponds to those of Spain in the nineteenth and twentieth centuries—to our own day. I also know that the book should deal with the problem of development, taking it as its central theme. . . .

. . . the models of development that the West and East offer us today are compendiums of horrors. Can we devise more humane models that correspond to what we are? As people on the fringes, inhabitants of the suburbs of history, we Latin Americans are uninvited guests who have sneaked in through the West's back door, intruders who have arrived at the feast of modernity as the lights are about to be put out. We arrive late everywhere, we were born when it was already late in history, we have no past or, if we have one, we spit on its remains, our peoples lay down and slept for a century, and while asleep they were robbed and now they go about in rags, we have not been able to save even what the Spaniards left us when they departed, we have stabbed one another . . . Despite all this, and despite the fact that our countries are inimical to thought, poets and prose writers and painters who equal the best in the other parts of the world have sprung up here and there, separately but without interruption. Will we now, at last, be capable of thinking for ourselves? Can we plan a society that is not based on the domination of others and that will not end up like the chilling police paradises of the East or with the explosions of disgust and hatred that disrupt the banquet of the West?

36

Underemployment, The Social Crisis of Latin America in the Twentieth Century

Latin America is presently undergoing a monumental crisis. Population growth is outstripping the pace of job creation so that increasing numbers of people, particularly in cities, are just barely surviving. Economists describe the situation with the term *underemployment,* a seemingly innocuous word that hides an ugly reality. Most of the urban poor pick up odd jobs day by day. When no work is available, they sponge off their relatives or beg. They have no security. They live a marginal existence, often preying on other poor people to survive. Population statistics describe the magnitude of the problem but not its intensity. Latin America's population increased from 63 million in 1900 to 220 million in 1960 to 379 million by 1979. The comparatively few jobs created by capital-intensive industrialization could not accommodate these people. New manufacturing plants located in cities attracted the rural poor and increased their expectations of finding a better life, but when they reached the city they met disappointment. The following short biographical accounts describe the lives of marginal people in Lima, Peru. Considering their lifestyle and political attitudes, do these people constitute a revolutionary threat to the established order?

Chorrillos 1967

Jacinta Vegas "I come from the district of Piura in northern Peru, and I have lived in Lima for sixteen years, almost half my life. It is difficult living here, but I have got

From Sven Lindqvist, *The Shadow: Latin America Faces the Seventies,* translated by Keith Bradfield (Harmondsworth, England: Penguin, 1972), pp. 19–22. Copyright © Sven Lindqvist, 1969. First published by Albert Bonniers Förlag AB, Stockholm.

used to it and my children, after all, were born here. I have no money in Lima, but then I wouldn't have any money in Piura either.

"The father of my eldest boy was a good-for-nothing, he denied paternity. But the boy bears my present man's name. We aren't married. We met here in Lima, but he is also from Piura.

"My eldest boy wants to be an engineer or doctor. He'll go to night school, he says. He is twelve years old now, and in the fifth grade. The eldest girl is five, and she goes to kindergarten for a dollar 20 cents a month. She gets food there and they look after her while I work. The two youngest I take with me.

"I work at the Regatta Club down by the beach. It's a very exclusive club. I clean the toilets and work as a cloakroom attendant, looking after people's cases and clothes while they bathe. I work for two days a week, and make two dollars a day. For three months during the summer I have work every day, and on top of that I get an annual bonus of twelve dollars. That's when I buy school things for the boy, he gets a big writing book with over 100 pages.

"We moved to this shed four years ago, and we own the site, it's a good shed, very solid, fresh bamboo mats in the walls. And two rooms! Everything looked fine, but two years ago I got a sore on my foot, and had to stay in bed for a month. Then my man fell sick, and was in bed for six months. And then the boy got appendicitis. The operation cost 120 dollars. We took the money we had saved to build a proper house, and borrowed the rest.

"Three months ago it happened. My man is a driver, he got mixed up in a traffic accident, hit someone in the dark and the police took his papers away. He was supposed to pay 200 dollars in damages, so he had to go underground. He ran away, and I haven't heard from him since. I have to manage on my own. We spend about twenty or forty cents a day. We eat porridge made from pea-meal or oatmeal. On Sundays, we eat porridge made with flour. Sometimes we manage rice and stewed vegetables. Never meat.

"I've never voted. I don't have a birth certificate. I went to the authorities, and asked for dispensation. It cost twelve dollars, I took my annual bonus and paid. But I got a paper that was no good, the signature was wrong and the stamp. My employer went back with me, and the man was sent to prison. But I never got my money back, and I still have no birth certificate. So I've never voted."

Rinaldo Rivas Loude   "I work for Manufactura de Calzado [shoe factory] Glenny, España 211, Chorrillos. I'm the one who sews on the uppers. I get a dollar 30 per dozen, and I do a dozen to a dozen and a half a day. I don't get more work than that until Christmas, then I get as much as I want and can work all round the clock.

"I support a wife and four children, and my two brothers, aged fifteen and eight, all with this machine. I had a bit of luck when I picked it up second-hand eight years ago. Then it cost 72 dollars. Today a new one would cost 480 dollars. I also work as guard for the Leasehold Association, which means that I can live in this house for two dollars a month. Of course, this means that one of us—my wife or I—must always be at home. But I sit here all day in any case, at the machine.

"There are fifteen guards here altogether. We have to sound the alarm if there is an invasion. Yes, you see, those who have leases here don't want other people to come and settle and build huts. Four years ago, this was one great rubbish heap. The Association, they say, paid 4,000 dollars to get the rubbish away, and in the end the members had to come and move it out themselves. Now everything has been cleaned up, and they don't want anyone else moving in.

"I was born in Lima, just near here in Barranco, in 1933. My parents rented a room in a *barriada* [slum town]. I started early as an apprentice, and I have worked for six years since my training ended.

"Better pay? Well, I could take an extra job. Or look for some other job. More than a dollar 30 per dozen? I never thought of it. No, I'm not a union member. It's just not worth it. The factory is owned by Juan García and Víctor Glenny. They decide. There are ten of us working for them. The factory provides the leather, I buy my own thread, needles, whetstone and other bits and pieces. It makes a bit of a change to go into Lima on business.

"My eldest brother is in the *primaria,* in fifth grade. I think he can go on to the first or second year of the *secundaria.* I can't support him any longer than that, the secondary school is more expensive. Then he can start in the police school or join the army if he wants to go on studying. But my brothers are not big enough yet to understand what a burden they are to me.

"When did I last eat meat? On Sunday. We have meat on Sundays. Otherwise we have soups and porridge. The worst thing is that the children never get milk. The cinema? I get round to it every other week, I suppose. And every other week some friends come over, and we have a few drinks. Otherwise, I have the transistor here on the machine.

"Yes, I've voted. I voted for the present mayor. I believed in him, he grew up in a *barriada* himself. He has promised water, street lights, sewerage, pavements, everything. So far there's only lighting on the main road over there, it's still a long way to us. But he's got two years to do the job.

"Fidel? I've read the newspapers. He's done some good things. But here in Peru, well, we have Hugo Blanco [Peruvian revolutionary], of course, but I don't think he's the sort of man who could fight a guerrilla war in the hills, like they're doing in Bolivia.

"What I fear most is eviction. What I want most of all is a safe site, where no one can put us out, and a house of sun-dried brick. Also, of course, I can fall sick. I have no insurance, and the factory doesn't do anything for you if you are ill. It should, of course. I must try to find out a bit more about it."

The whole time we are talking, I can hear a whining sound as if from a dog that has been shut in. It comes from a little cubicle by the door. A small boy is lying there, in the rags of the family bed. Lying absolutely silent in the darkness, perfectly still, with fright in his eyes. The new baby is on the earthen floor, smeared with faeces. Flies are crawling round his eyes. The whining is from him.

37

African Nationalism

Nationalism was one of the crucial, though unintended, products of European imperialism. Local leaders — particularly aspiring newcomers often exposed to European education — saw the importance of nationalism in Western society and used it as a vehicle for protesting colonial controls and demanding independence. Nationalism could also be used to elicit loyalty to a newly free state, especially when appeals to tradition could not suffice because the nation combined different cultural groups. Thus nationalism had the merit of appealing both to past values and to the idea of progress, though the combination could sometimes be uncomfortable.

Nationalism began to blossom in Africa between the world wars. It had several facets, as indicated in the passages that follow. One nationalist source stemmed from Black leaders in the United States and West Indies sincerely concerned about Africa but also eager for the liberation of their own people. Marcus Garvey's Black nationalist movement won loyalties on both sides of the Atlantic in the 1920s and helped define a positive, African spirit. Jomo Kenyatta, a British-educated Kenyan — ultimately the first president of Kenya after many jail terms as a nationalist agitator under the colonial government — represents African nationalism directly. Writing in 1938, Kenyatta used traditional kinds of allegory

Selection I from Marcus Garvey, "Redeeming the African Motherland," in *Philosophy and Opinions of Marcus Garvey,* Vol. I, Amy Jacques Garvey, ed. (New York: University Publishing House, 1923), pp. 71–74. Selection II from Jomo Kenyatta, *Facing Mt. Kenya* (New York: Random House, Inc., 1962). Copyright © 1962 by Random House, Inc. Reprinted by permission. Selection III from Kwame Nkrumah, *Revolutionary Path* (London: Panaf Books Limited, 1973). Copyright © 1973 Panaf Books Limited. Reprinted by permission.

to blast European greed and also defined a special African agenda of combining tradition with change plus very selective borrowing from the West.

The final selection is postcolonial and invites comparison with the earlier nationalist expression: How was nationalism maintained once independence had been achieved, and what changes resulted in tone and purpose? Written by Kwame Nkrumah, an American-educated leader and first president of Ghana, this nationalist statement reflects a turn away from Africa-in-general to a specific new nation. It also shows some shifts in goals. Once independence was achieved, what targets did African nationalists have? Nkrumah's own career illustrates some of the nationalist dilemma. A brilliant agitator, he proved less successful in running an independent Ghana. The economic problems he defined as next on the nationalist agenda proved more elusive than earlier goals of independence. Yet nationalism remained a factor in Africa, a guide to policy and popular rallying point in the new nations. These three selections, from different decades as well as different inspirations, give a flavor of African nationalism and some indication of its power. They also permit comparison of African with Indian or Arab nationalism. Is nationalism always the same movement?

I. MARCUS GARVEY PREACHES AFRICAN REVOLUTION

George Washington was not God Almighty. He was a man like any Negro in this building, and if he and his associates were able to make a free America, we too can make a free Africa. Hampden, Gladstone, Pitt and Disraeli were not the representatives of God in the person of Jesus Christ. They were but men, but in their time they worked for the expansion of the British Empire, and today they boast of a British Empire upon which "the sun never sets." As Pitt and Gladstone were able to work for the expansion of the British Empire, so you and I can work for the expansion of a great African Empire. Voltaire and Mirabeau were not Jesus Christs, they were but men like ourselves. They worked and overturned the French Monarchy. They worked for the Democracy which France now enjoys, and if they were able to do that, we are able to work for a democracy in Africa. Lenin and Trotsky were not Jesus Christs, but they were able to overthrow the despotism of Russia, and today they have given to the world a Social Republic, the first of its kind. If Lenin and Trotsky were able to do that for Russia, you and I can do that for Africa. Therefore, let no man, let no power on earth, turn you from this sacred cause of liberty. I prefer to die at this moment rather than not to work for the freedom of Africa. If liberty is good for certain sets of humanity it is good for all. Black men, Colored men, Negroes have as much right to be free as any other race that God Almighty ever created, and we desire freedom that is unfettered, freedom that is unlimited, freedom that will give us a chance and opportunity to rise to the fullest of our ambition and that we cannot get in countries where other men rule and dominate.

We have reached the time when every minute, every second must count for something done, something achieved in the cause of Africa. We need the freedom of Africa now, therefore, we desire the kind of leadership that will give it to us as quickly as possible. You will realize that not only individuals, but governments are using their influence against us. But what do we care about the unrighteous influence of any government? Our cause is based upon righteousness. And anything that is not righteous we have no respect for, because God Almighty is our leader and Jesus Christ our standard bearer. We rely on them for that kind of leadership that will make us free, for it is the same God who inspired the Psalmist to write "Princes shall come out of Egypt and Ethiopia shall stretch out her hands unto God." At this moment methinks I see Ethiopia stretching forth her hands unto God and methinks I see the Angel of God taking up the standard of the Red, the Black and the Green, and saying "Men of the Negro Race, Men of Ethiopia, follow me." Tonight we are following. We are following 400,000,000 strong. We are following with a determination that we must be free before the wreck of matter, before the crash of worlds.

It falls to our lot to tear off the shackles that bind Mother Africa. Can you do it? You did it in the Revolutionary War. You did it in the Civil War; You did it at the Battles of the Marne and Verdun; You did it in Mesopotamia. You can do it marching up the battle heights of Africa. Let the world know that 400,000,000 Negroes are prepared to die or live as free men. Despise us as much as you care. Ignore us as much as you care. We are coming 400,000,000 strong. We are coming with our woes behind us, with the memory of suffering behind us—woes and suffering of three hundred years—they shall be our inspiration. My bulwark of strength in the conflict of freedom in Africa, will be the three hundred years of persecution and hardship left behind in this Western Hemisphere. The more I remember the suffering of my fore-fathers, the more I remember the lynchings and burnings in the Southern States of America, the more I will fight on even though the battle seems doubtful. Tell me that I must turn back, and I laugh you to scorn. Go on! Go on! Climb ye the heights of liberty and cease not in well doing until you have planted the banner of the Red, the Black and the Green on the hilltops of Africa.

II. JOMO KENYATTA DEFINES AFRICAN NATIONALISM

Once upon a time an elephant made a friendship with a man. One day a heavy thunderstorm broke out, the elephant went to his friend, who had a little hut at the edge of the forest, and said to him: "My dear good man, will you please let me put my trunk inside your hut to keep it out of this torrential rain?" The man, seeing what situation his friend was in, replied: "My dear good elephant, my hut is very small, but there is room for your trunk and myself. Please put your trunk in gently." The elephant thanked his friend, saying: "You have done me a good deed and one day I shall return your kindness." But what followed? As soon as the elephant put his trunk inside the hut, slowly he pushed his head inside, and finally flung the man out in the rain, and then lay down comfortably inside his friend's hut, saying: "My dear good friend, your skin is harder than mine, and as there is not enough room for both of us, you can afford to remain in the rain while I am protecting my delicate skin from the hailstorm."

The man, seeing what his friend had done to him, started to grumble; the animals in the nearby forest heard the noise and came to see what was the matter. All stood around listening to the heated argument between the man and his friend the elephant. In this turmoil the lion came along roaring, and said in a loud voice: "Don't you know that I am the King of the Jungle! How dare anyone disturb the peace of my kingdom?" On hearing this the elephant, who was one of the high ministers in the jungle kingdom, replied in a soothing voice, and said: "My Lord, there is no disturbance of the peace in your kingdom. I have only been having a little discussion with my friend here as to the possession of this little hut which your lordship sees me occupying." The lion, who wanted to have "peace and tranquillity" in his kingdom, replied in a noble voice, saying: "I command my ministers to appoint a Commission of Enquiry to go thoroughly into this matter and report accordingly." He then turned to the man and said: "You have done well by establishing friendship with my people, especially with the elephant who is one of my honourable ministers of state. Do not grumble any more, your hut is not lost to you. Wait until the sitting of my Imperial Commission, and there you will be given plenty of opportunity to state your case. I am sure that you will be pleased with the findings of the Commission." The man was very pleased by these sweet words from the King of the Jungle, and innocently waited for his opportunity, in the belief that naturally the hut would be returned to him.

The elephant, obeying the command of his master got busy with other ministers to appoint the Commission of Enquiry. The following elders of the jungle were appointed to sit in the Commission: (1) Mr. Rhinoceros; (2) Mr. Buffalo; (3) Mr. Alligator; (4) The Rt. Hon. Mr. Fox to act as chairman; and (5) Mr. Leopard to act as Secretary to the Commission. On seeing the personnel, the man protested and asked if it was not necessary to include in this Commission a member from his side. But he was told that it was impossible, since no one from his side was well enough educated to understand the intricacy of jungle law. Further, that there was nothing to fear, for the members of the Commission were all men of repute for their impartiality in justice, and as they were gentlemen chosen by God to look after the interest of races less adequately endowed with teeth and claws, he might rest assured that they would investigate the matter with the greatest care and report impartially. . . .

Then the man decided that he must adopt an effective method of protection, since Commissions of Enquiry did not seem to be of any use to him. He sat down and said: "Ng'enda thi ndeagaga motegi," which literally means, "there is nothing that treads on the earth that cannot be trapped," or in other words, you can fool people for a time, but not forever.

Early one morning, when the huts already occupied by the jungle lords were all beginning to decay and fall to pieces, he went out and built a bigger and better hut a little distance away. No sooner had Mr. Rhinoceros seen it than he came rushing in, only to find that Mr. Elephant was already inside, sound asleep. Mr. Leopard next came in at the window, Mr. Lion, Mr. Fox, and Mr. Buffalo entered the doors, while Mr. Hyena howled for a place in the shade and Mr. Alligator basked on the roof. Presently they all began disputing about their rights of penetration, and from disputing they came to fighting, and while they were embroiled together the man set the hut on fire and burnt it to the ground, jungle lords and all. Then he went home, saying "Peace is costly, but it's worth the expense," and lived happily ever after. . . .

There certainly are some progressive ideas among the Europeans. They include the ideas of material prosperity, of medicine, and hygiene, and literacy which enables people to take part in world culture. But so far the Europeans who visit Africa have not been conspicuously zealous in imparting these parts of their inheritance to the Africans, and seem to think that the only way to do it is by police discipline and armed force. They speak as if it was somehow beneficial to an African to work for them instead of for himself, and to make sure that he will receive this benefit they do their best to take away his land and leave him with no alternative. Along with his land they rob him of his government, condemn his religious ideas, and ignore his fundamental conceptions of justice and morals, all in the name of civilisation and progress.

If Africans were left in peace on their own lands. Europeans would have to offer them the benefits of white civilisation in real earnest before they could obtain the African labour which they want so much. They would have to offer the African a way of life which was really superior to the one his fathers lived before him, and a share in the prosperity given them by their command of science. They would have to let the African choose what parts of European culture could be beneficially transplanted, and how they could be adapted. He would probably not choose the gas bomb or the armed police force, but he might ask for some other things of which he does not get so much to-day. As it is, by driving him off his ancestral lands, the Europeans have robbed him of the material foundations of his culture, and reduced him to a state of serfdom incompatible with human happiness. The African is conditioned, by the cultural and social institutions of centuries, to a freedom of which Europe has little conception, and it is not in his nature to accept serfdom for ever. He realises that he must fight unceasingly for his own complete emancipation; for without this he is doomed to remain the prey of rival imperialisms, which in every successive year will drive their fangs more deeply into his vitality and strength.

III. ECONOMIC NATIONALISM: KWAME NKRUMAH

Organization presupposes planning, and planning demands a programme for its basis. The Government proposes to launch a Seven-Year Development Plan in January, 1963. The Party, therefore, has a pressing obligation to provide a programme upon which this plan could be formulated.

We must develop Ghana economically, socially, culturally, spiritually, educationally, technologically and otherwise, and produce it as a finished product of a fully integrated life, both exemplary and inspiring.

This programme, which we call a programme for "Work and Happiness," has been drawn up in regard to all our circumstances and conditions, our hopes and aspirations, our advantages and disadvantages and our opportunities or lack of them. Indeed, the programme is drawn up with an eye on reality and provides the building ground for our immediate scientific, technical and industrial progress.

We have embarked upon an intensive socialist reconstruction of our country. Ghana inherited a colonial economy and similar disabilities in most other directions. We cannot rest content until we have demolished this miserable structure and raised in its place an edifice of economic stability, thus creating for ourselves a veritable paradise of abundance and satisfaction. Despite the ideological bankruptcy and moral collapse of a civilization in despair, we must go forward with our preparations for planned economic growth to supplant the poverty, ignorance, disease, illiteracy and degradation left in their wake by discredited colonialism and decaying imperialism.

In the programme which I am today introducing to the country through this broadcast, the Party has put forward many proposals. I want all of you to get copies of this programme, to read and discuss it and to send us any observations or suggestions you may have about it.

Tomorrow, the National Executive Committee of the Party will meet to discuss the Party programme and officially present it to the nation. I feel sure that it will decide in favour of an immediate release of this programme to the people. The Party, however, will take no action on the programme until the masses of the people have had the fullest opportunity of reviewing it.

This programme for "Work and Happiness" is an expression of the evidence of the nation's creative ability, the certainty of the correctness of our Party line and action and the greatest single piece of testimony [to] our national confidence in the future.

Ghana is our country which we must all help to build. This programme gives us the opportunity to make our contribution towards the fulfillment of our national purposes.

As I look at the content of the programme and the matters it covers, such as Tax Reform, Animal Husbandry and Poultry Production, Forest Husbandry, Industrialization, Handicrafts, Banking and Insurance, Foreign Enterprise, Culture and Leisure, I am convinced beyond all doubt that Ghana and Ghanaians will travel full steam ahead, conscious of their great responsibilities and fully aware that the materialization of this bright picture of the future is entirely dependent on their active and energetic industry. Remember that it is at the moment merely a draft programme and only your approval will finalize it.

At this present moment, all over Africa, dark clouds of neocolonialism are fast gathering. African States are becoming debtor-nations and client States day in and day out, owing to their adoption of unreal attitudes to world problems, saying "no" when they should have said "yes," and "yes" when they should have said "no." They are seeking economic shelter under colonialist wings, instead of accepting the truth—that their survival lies in the political unification of Africa.

Countrymen, we must draw up a programme of action and later plan details of this programme for the benefit of the whole people. Such a programme is the one that the Party now brings to you, the people of Ghana, in the hope that you will approve it critically and help to make it a success.

We have a rich heritage. Our natural resources are abundant and varied. We have mineral and agricultural wealth and, above all, we have the will to find the means whereby these possessions can be put to the greatest use and advantage. The Party's programme for work and happiness is a pointer to the way ahead, the way leading to a healthier, happier and more prosperous life for us all. When you have examined and accepted this programme, the Government and the people will base on it and initiate our Seven-Year Development Plan, which will guide our action to prosperity.

38

Changes in African Society

New forces continued to impact on the traditional culture of sub-Saharan Africa in the later twentieth century. Conversions both to Islam and Christianity gained ground, though an animist minority remained. Conversion brought more than new beliefs about the deity; it also attacked family traditions (such as polygamy, for Christians) and traditional ideas of harmony with nature. Some African conservatives blamed the new religions for Africans' willingness to attack animals and forests with a new vigor that threatened ecological balance, for the monotheistic religions held man to be above nature. Education spread, and with it not only literacy but, often, knowledge of a European language—another force for change.

The selections that follow deal with urbanization and changes in family roles as sources of change and tension in twentieth-century African society. African cities, once small, grew rapidly both under colonial administration and with independence. About a quarter of all sub-Saharan Africans lived in cities by the 1970s, and the rate increases steadily. Urban Africans, though often poor, were more often educated than their rural counterparts, and they enjoyed excitements in city life. But they were also confusingly torn from traditional community customs. In the first selection Chinua Achebe, the Nigerian novelist, describes a mid-twentieth-century scene after World War II but before independence, using characters from the Ibo village we have seen described in earlier selections, and from a later generation of the Okonkwo family (see Volume I, selection 33, and selection 19 in this volume). Obi Okonkwo is the first village member to receive higher education in British-run schools. He goes to Lagos, the growing Nigerian capital, to take a civil-service job. He finds the glitter of city life there, but also a consumerist culture and a pleasure-seeking sexual ethic both influenced by Western standards. These at first shock and then beguile him so that he cannot respond as village customs expect to tragedies such as his mother's death. The combination of stimulation and confusion gives this Achebe novel its title, *No Longer At Ease*.

The second selection focuses less on confusion, more on new aspirations and opportunities. Many African women found new roles as they moved to cities and gained education. Even rural women had new power when their men left to take urban jobs; willy-nilly, they had to run their families and often support themselves. Thus African family bonds, which once gave women security while holding them subordinate, loosened rapidly. The passages come from a series of interviews with women in Kenya, including one group organized in a cooperative to try to compensate for new uncertainties about family ties and support from men.

Cultural change, including some expressions striking for their resemblance to modern Western movements such as feminism, is clearly a double-edged sword in contemporary Africa. The change expresses new influences, but also new uncertainties as older institutions unravel; as in the West in previous periods, greater individualism can be both exhilarating and frightening. Africans themselves disagree over whether new opportunity or the erosion of vital traditions should receive the main emphasis. Not surprisingly, some traditional emphases, such as on family solidarity, persist as well.

I. NO LONGER AT EASE

As a boy in the village of Umuofia he had heard his first stories about Lagos from a soldier home on leave from the war. Those soldiers were heroes who had seen the great world. They spoke of Abyssinia, Egypt, Palestine, Burma and so on. Some of them had been village ne'er-do-wells, but now they were heroes. They had bags and bags of money, and the villagers sat at their feet to listen to their stories. One of them went regularly to a market in the neighboring village and helped himself to whatever he liked. He went in full uniform, breaking the earth with his boots, and no one dared touch him. It was said that if you touched a soldier, Government would deal with you. Besides, soldiers were as strong as lions because of the injections they were given in the army. It was from one of these soldiers that Obi had his first picture of Lagos.

"There is no darkness there," he told his admiring listeners, "because at night the electric shines like the sun, and people are always walking about, that is, those who want to walk. If you don't want to walk you only have to wave your hand and a pleasure car stops for you." His audience made sounds of wonderment. Then by way of digression he said: "If you see a white man, take off your hat for him. The only thing he cannot do is mold a human being."

For many years afterwards, Lagos was always associated with electric lights and motorcars in Obi's mind. Even after he had at last visited the city and spent a few days there before flying to the United Kingdom his views did not change very much. Of course, he did not really see much of Lagos then. His mind was, as it were, on higher things. He spent the few days with his "countryman," Joseph Okeke, a clerk in the Survey Department. Obi and Joseph had been classmates at the Umuofia C.M.S. Central School. But Joseph had not gone on to a secondary school because he was too old and his parents were poor. He had joined the Education Corps of the 82nd Division and, when the war ended, the clerical service of the Nigerian Government.

Joseph was at Lagos Motor Park to meet his lucky friend who was passing through Lagos to the United Kingdom. He took him to his lodgings in Obalende. It was only one room. A curtain of light-blue cloth ran the full breadth of the room separating the Holy of Holies (as he called his double spring bed) from the sitting area. His cooking utensils, boxes, and other personal effects were hidden away under the Holy of Holies. The sitting area was taken up with two armchairs, a settee (otherwise called "me and my girl"), and a round table on which he displayed his photo album. At night, his houseboy moved away the round table and spread his mat on the floor.

Joseph had so much to tell Obi on his first night in Lagos that it was past three when they slept. He told him about the cinema and the dance halls and about political meetings.

"Dancing is very important nowadays. No girl will look at you if you can't dance. I first met Joy at the dancing school." "Who is Joy?" asked Obi, who was fascinated by what he was learning of this strange and sinful new world. "She was my girl friend for—let's see. . ."—he counted off his fingers—". . . March, April, May, June, July—for five months. She made these pillowcases for me."

Obi raised himself instinctively to look at the pillow he was lying on. He had taken particular notice of it earlier in the day. It had the strange word *osculate* sewn on it, each letter in a different color.

"She was a nice girl but sometimes very foolish. Sometimes, though, I wish we hadn't broken up. She was simply mad about me; and she was a virgin when I met her, which is very rare here."

Joseph talked and talked and finally became less and less coherent. Then without any pause at all his talk was transformed into a deep snore, which continued until the morning.

The very next day Obi found himself taking a compulsory walk down Lewis Street. Joseph had brought a woman home and it was quite clear that Obi's presence in the room was not desirable; so he went out to have a look round. The girl was one of Joseph's new finds, as he told him later. She was dark and tall with an enormous pneumatic bosom under a tight-fitting red and yellow dress. Her lips and long fingernails were a brilliant red, and her eyebrows were fine black lines. She looked not unlike those wooden masks made in Ikot Ekpene. Altogether she left a nasty taste in Obi's mouth, like the multicolored word *osculate* on the pillowcase. . . .

On top of it all came his mother's death. He sent all he could find for her funeral, but it was already being said to his eternal shame that a woman who had borne so many children, one of whom was in a European post, deserved a better funeral than she got. One Umuofia man who had been on leave at home when she died brought the news to Lagos to the meeting of the Umuofia Progressive Union.

"It was a thing of shame," he said. Someone else wanted to know, by the way, why that beast (meaning Obi) had not obtained permission to go home. "That is what

Lagos can do to a young man. He runs after sweet things, dances breast to breast with women and forgets his home and his people. Do you know what medicine that *osu* woman may have put into his soup to turn his eyes and ears away from his people?" . . .

"Everything you have said is true. But there is one thing I want you to learn. Whatever happens in this world has a meaning. As our people say: 'Wherever something stands, another thing stands beside it.' You see this thing called blood. There is nothing like it. That is why when you plant a yam it produces another yam, and if you plant an orange it bears oranges. I have seen many things in my life, but I have never yet seen a banana tree yield a coco yam. Why do I say this? You young men here, I want you to listen because it is from listening to old men that you learn wisdom. I know that when I return to Umuofia I cannot claim to be an old man. But here in this Lagos I am an old man to the rest of you." He paused for effect. "This boy that we are all talking about, what has he done? He was told that his mother died and he did not care. It is a strange and surprising thing."

II. KENYAN WOMEN SPEAK OUT

What we need in this village is teachers to teach women handicrafts and sewing and agricultural skills. We have organized a women's group. I am one of the leaders. We are saving up for a building to meet in. All women are trying to earn money, and we want to have a building for our meetings. It will be called the "adult education building"—with rooms for handicrafts, literacy, and other things.

We also want our children to be educated—so we can have good leaders to keep our country good. I think now it is best to have only four children—so you can take care of them.

It is better to educate a girl than a boy, although one should educate both. Girls are better. They help a lot. See this house? My daughters built it for me. If you don't have any daughters, who will build for you? The boys will marry and take care of their wives—that's all. They don't care about mothers. For example, if my son gets married, the daughter-in-law will say, "Let's take our mothers to live with us." The son will say, "No, we will just have our own family and do our own things." So you are left alone. What do you do? . . .

My mother has eleven children. She is my father's only wife. She works in the fields and grows the food we eat. She plants cabbage, spinach, and corn. She works very hard, but with so many children it is difficult to get enough food or money. All of my sisters and brothers go to school. One is already a teacher, and that is why I am trying to learn a profession. If I can get enough schooling, I can serve the country and my own family. I can also manage to have a life for myself. That is why I came to this school. We have a big family, and I have to help.

My life is very different from my mother's. She just stayed in the family until she married. Life is much more difficult now because everybody is dependent on money. Long ago, money was unheard of. No one needed money. But now you can't even get food without cash. Times are very difficult. That is why the towns are creating day-care centers—so women can work and have their own lives. I have to work, for without it I will not have enough money for today's life.

These are the problems I face and try to think about. How shall I manage to pick up this life so that I can live a better one? You know, we people of Kenya like to serve our parents when they are still alive—to help the family. But first, women have to get an education. Then if you get a large family and don't know how to feed it—if you don't have enough money for food—you can find work and get some cash. That's what I will teach my children: "Get an education first."

If I had a chance to go to the university, I would learn more about health education. I could help women that way. If I were in a position of authority, I would really try to educate women. Right now, girls are left behind in education. It costs money, and parents think it is more important to educate boys. But I think that if people are intelligent, there is no difference. Girls and boys should be educated the same. I would make rules and teach women who are not educated and who have never been to school. They, too, must understand what today's problems are. If I have any spare time, I want to learn new things. I would like to learn how to manage my life, my future life, and have enough say in things so that my husband and I could understand each other and share life with our family. And I would change the laws so that men would understand women and their needs and not beat them as they do.

I only hope that I will have a mature husband who will understand and discuss things with me. . . .

Most women don't rely on their husbands now. If they get some money, well and good; and if they don't, they just try to get money for themselves—selling vegetables or making and selling handicrafts.

Life is very difficult these days, and men are paying less attention to their wives. You see, men have wrongly just taken advantage of having more money. Instead of using money properly, to improve the lives of their families, they spend it on all the "facilities" available at hotels. Instead of spending nights in their own homes, they fight at home and seek women outside—in the hotels. Many men cheat on their wives now because they are employed and have money. A husband can say, "I have been sent as a driver to Nairobi" (or elsewhere), when he actually spends the money on girls.

So women are fed up. They think now that relying on a man can be a problem. They say, "We should try to do something ourselves. Then, whether we get something from our men or not, we still we be able to raise our children properly." The problem that many women face is that they msut become self-supporting. They either have no support from their husbands at all, or very little. And there is no law to protect them.

But women *are* trying to do something for themselves, and if they had the capital they could establish businesses to help them make money. The main problem here is the money problem. Many women are alone. They need to earn for their families.

Women feel very hurt because they think their men don't recognize them as human beings. They are unhappy because of this inequality. I am lucky; my husband is good. He never took another wife. We are still together. . . . My wish would be that men and women could live as two equal people.